For my dearest
Roy —
Thanks for making
a Phillies fan
Mom

D0442813

For
Phillies
Fans
Only!

by
Rich Wolfe

Layout: The Printed Page, Phoenix, AZ
Author's agent: T. Roy Gaul

Rich Wolfe can be reached at 602-738-5889

ISBN: 978-0-9800978-8-7

DEDICATION

To

Ed and Marge Butler
of Erdenheim, PA

and

Adrian King
Notre Dame '64

In Memoriam

Robin Roberts, 1926-2010

ACKNOWLEDGMENTS

Wonderful people helped make this book a reality, starting with Ellen Brewer in Edmond, Oklahoma and Lisa Liddy at The Printed Page in Phoenix—wonder women who have been indispensible sidekicks for many years. Ditto for Barbara Jane Bookman in Falmouth, Massachusetts. A big thanks to Mary Kellenberger in Moline, Illinois, Terry Daily in Los Gatos, California, Mike Kinsella in Newtown Square, Pennsylvania, and the good guys over at Wolfegang Marketing Systems, Ltd.—But Not Very.

We certainly can't forget Pat Hughes the play-by-play announcer for the Chicago Cubs who produced the wonderful Harry Kalas sampler CD that is part of this book. Certainly, Andy Jasner was vital in the production of the stories for this book (and a real pleasure to work with) as well as Tucker Wolfe out in Phoenix, Arizona and the incomparable Jonathan Fraser Light....and there's only one Mark Carfagno.

The chapter opening photographs are courtesy of Don P. Marquess. His work can be purchased from Marquess Gallery at www.baseballfineart.com.

The biggest thank you must go to Joe Queenan, the multi-talented author who might be Philadelphia's greatest sports fan, even though he lives in Westchester County, New York. Our favorite book of Joe's is *True Believers*, which is a compilation of his Philadelphia sports memories and is an exceptional book. It was published by the Henry Holt Company.

It was great "Livin' the Dream" with Brian Adams at Wawa.

A tip of the hat to all those interviewed who missed the final cut—we just flat ran out of time. Three chapters were cut indiscriminately due to space limitations. It was close, and we're going to do it again next year.

Thanks everybody.

CHAT ROOMS

PREFACE

For some of us, baseball recalls broken windows, broken bats, and broken dreams of a simpler, more innocent time.

For many of us, baseball defined our youth, still overly impacts our adulthood, and is one of the few things that can make us feel young and old at the same time.

For all of us, it is—most of all—a game of memories: the transistor under the pillow at nighttime, sitting outside a small mom-and-pop store feverishly opening packs of newly purchased baseball cards, our first baseball uniform, learning to keep score for the first time, the dew and the mosquitoes at the park during our first night games, the sounds of our first big-league game. Little did many of us know that baseball would be the best math and geography teacher we would ever have...and none of us knew that the vibrant green of the field during our first major league game would be the most verdant, lush, and unforgettable green we would ever see in our entire lifetime.

Our favorite baseball team is usually the one nearest to where we were raised. In my case, that was baseball's St. Louis Cardinals. Growing up on a farm near the town of Lost Nation, Iowa, every summer night, we tuned in to KMOX in St. Louis to listen to Harry Caray and Jack Buck describe the Cardinal action for us.

Lost Nation, Iowa, was just under a thousand miles from Philadelphia. But it might as well have been a million. Nevertheless, I met four Phillies icons long before anyone in Philly: Harry Kalas, Dallas Green, Tug McGraw, and Tim McCarver. I sat next to Harry Kalas at an Iowa Hawkeyes basketball game when Harry was a senior at Iowa, got Dallas Green's autograph when he pitched for the Mattoon (Illinois) Phillies in the Mississippi–Ohio Valley League (and his catcher

Jim Coker's autograph the same night). I was introduced to Tug McGraw through his brother Hank, who roomed with my Notre Dame baseball teammate Shaun Fitzmaurice in 1965 at Williamsport in the Eastern League (Hank and Shaun were big-time Mets bonus babies). Finally, I met Tim and Ann McCarver in Acapulco in 1967 and spent a fun-filled week with them.

Ironically, my cousin and contemporary from that small town, Jim McAndrew, was the winning pitcher in Robin Roberts' last professional start. McAndrew pitched for the Williamsport Mets in the mid-sixties when Roberts made his final start for the Reading Phillies. Also in that small town, where most people were either Cubs or Cardinal fans, was a good friend named Gene Rasmussen. For whatever reason, he was an incredible Philadelphia Phillies fan, always talking about the Phillies...always idolizing Robin Roberts.

There are many stories in this book about the heartbreak of the 1964 Philadelphia Phillies season. They are scattered throughout so as not to hit Phillies fans over the head with all the heartbreak at once. My story about that '64 season concerns a Labor Day doubleheader in St. Louis where the Cardinals beat the Reds 3–2 in both games, with Tim McCarver driving in the winning run in each game. Driving back to Iowa that evening with my future father-in-law, who was the greatest Cardinals fan I've ever seen. I was paging through *Baseball Digest*. At the tail end of the magazine, during the baseball season, are the remaining schedules for each major league team. I was studying the schedules, turned to my future father-in-law, and said, "Hey, the Cardinals could win the pennant." He looked at me and laughed, even though he was a die-hard Cardinals fan. I said, "No, really, the Cardinals have a pretty easy schedule from here on out, and the Phillies have a brutal schedule the rest of the year." Well...you don't have to be told what happened.

One thing I've learned from doing two dozen books on sports fans is that the most passionate, knowledgeable fans are on the East Coast. Cardinal fans delight in being told we are the best baseball fans in the country. What Cardinal fans really are are the *nicest* baseball fans in the country. But for sheer knowledge of the game, pure passion for the game, you can't beat the Phillies, Mets, Yankees, and Red Sox fans.

This Phillies book contains something that none of my previous 38 books have had: a CD. Thanks to Pat Hughes, the play-by-play announcer for the Chicago Cubs, we have included in this book a half-hour sampler of the best of Harry Kalas' calls.

Also, for the second time in a year, the exclusive outlet for my book, at least initially, will be the Wawa stores as it was for my 2009 book entitled *Remembering Harry Kalas*. Wawa was the exclusive outlet for that book for the first six months, even though they had never sold a book in the entire history of their chain. Furthermore, in order to give their customers a great deal, Wawa sold the $24.95 book for $9.99. Wawa earned the goodwill of their customers by offering them an unbeatable deal. It was a win-win situation for everybody. Of all the retailers in all my years in the book business, no one was more concerned about their customers' well-being and no one was easier to work with than Wawa. They were absolutely terrific.

Regarding the Phillies, I must mention the wonderful cooperation of a gentleman named Larry Shenk. I have found over the years that the public relations/media relations director at most college and pro teams is actually a hindrance to getting your job done, rather than one who facilitates the process. Larry Shenk is the opposite; he's the prototype of what a media relations person should be.

Since the age of 10, I've been a serious collector of sports books. During that time—for the sake of argument, let's call it 50 years; no, wait, make it 20—my favorite book style is the eavesdropping type where the subject offers straight talk in his or her own words—without the "then, he said" or "the air was so thick you could cut it with a butter knife" waste of verbiage that makes it so hard to get to the meat of the matter. Books such as Lawrence Ritter's *Glory of Their Times* and Donald Honig's *Baseball When the Grass was Real* are worth emulating. Thus, I adopted that style when I started compiling oral histories of the Vin Scullys and the Harry Kalas's of the world. I'm a sports fan first and foremost—I don't even pretend to be an author. This book is designed solely for other sports fans. I really don't care what the publisher, editors, or critics think. I'm only interested in Phillies fans having an enjoyable read and getting their money's worth. Sometimes a person being interviewed will drift off the subject, but if I think Phillies fans will enjoy the digression, it stays in the book.

I'm the least likely person in the country to write a book. I can't type, have never turned on a computer, and have never seen the Internet. I refuse to sit in press boxes and corporate suites. To me, the cheaper the seat, the better the fan.

In an effort to get more material into the book, the editor decided to merge some paragraphs and omit some of the commas, which will allow for the reader to receive an additional 20,000 words, the equivalent of 50 pages. More bang for your buck...more fodder for English teachers...fewer dead trees.

As stated on the dust jacket, there have been dozens of books written about the Phillies, but not a single one about Phillies fans—until now. From one baseball fan to another, my sincere wish is that you enjoy this unique format.

Go now.

Rich Wolfe
Scottsdale, Arizona

Chapter 1

GROWIN' UP A PHILLIE

12 Years Old Forever

MAYBE THAT WAS JUST COUSIN LILLIAN'S WAY OF SAYING "HELLO"

Doug Verb

Doug Verb is a Temple University graduate who began his professional career as a sports writer and editor for the Philadelphia Inquirer, Philadelphia Daily News, and Washington Post News Service. Today, as founder and president of ACTION Sports America, he is one of the country's most successful executives for new program "start-ups", partnering with major pro leagues and college conferences to market international promotions.

One of a handful of people who have developed two professional sports leagues, Verb was one of the founders of the Major Indoor Soccer League (MISL) and the Arena Football League. He moved to Las Vegas from Philly in 2004 to launch and promote various projects, including the Las Vegas International Cycling Championship, The Ultimate 3-on-3 Challenge, and World Series of Golf.

I was six when I first realized the third section of the Bulletin was always the sports, so I could jump right there to find the details of what the Phils did the night before. It was 1956, hardly ever a game on TV. *I know this is kind of a weird memory, but the vision of this 'ah-ha' moment scene is plastered in my mind.*

Here's without a doubt my best weekend as a kid: I have a girl cousin who is about 13 years older. Crazy Cousin Lillian—and she took to me to all kinds of places, especially sports since neither of my parents had much interest. We had moved way up to the far, far Northeast, but she drove all the way from Overbrook Park, picked me up and took me to Connie Mack for a twilight night doubleheader: Phils vs. the Milwaukee Braves. It was

1961 and I was 11. It was another banner season for the Phils [47-107; won 14 fewer games than any other team in baseball].

I knew we wouldn't miss a thing: She got us there for batting practice. There was a rain delay in each game and the usual time between games. It was a long night BUT I loved every minute of it. I'm sure it was after 1A.M. when the second game ended. Then she said the magical words: "You do want to wait around for autographs, right!?" The family all called her crazy, but I know she was just misunderstood.

The visitor's bus was parked on Lehigh, the Phillies' cars parked on the tiny lot across 21st. (some players lived in the neighborhood and actually walked home). Remember the single door on the 21st side of the famous corner? That's where the players came through and that's where the throng of baseball brats waited for autographs. Well at 1 A.M. in the morning after a pair of long games, there was no one there...no competition. For sure, this was heaven.

Cousin Lillian went to fetch the car while I waited by the door. All I had was the 15-cent program and the little red pencil, but that's what they all signed. **CLAY DALRYMPLE***, Pancho, Bobby Malkmus, Joe Koppe, Baldschun, Short, Mahaffey (to name a few). I met Joe Adcock at the Braves' bus and he took my program in and passed it around. Burdette, Joe Torre, Gino Cimoli, Crandall, Roy McMillan, and Eddie Matthews (who I liked because we shared a birthday).

So when it trickled down to a few players, I looked for Lillian. She had parked by the door. As I approached I noticed people in the back seat. I hopped in and Lillian said in her usual commanding tone: "This my little cousin Dougie, introduce yourself, guys." Bob Boyd said hi and the other guy stuck out the biggest

*On July 19, 1960, Giants pitcher Juan Marichal, threw a one-hit, 2-0 shutout against the Phillies at Candlestick Park in his major league debut. The only hit was an eighth inning single by CLAY DALRYMPLE.

paw I had ever seen. "Hi, I'm Hank Aaron," he said. "Your gorgeous cousin is taking us back to the hotel." I was dumbfounded.

This was 35 years before cell phones. Lillian decided my parents might be wondering about my whereabouts. So she told 'the guys' we'd take me home first. She also decided we all would go inside to take the heat off of her (from my Mother). Wooooooooo. Now Hank Aaron and the other guy was standing in my kitchen... and it was in the middle of the night. I was not dreaming.

They asked if I wanted to come to the game the next night. I looked at Lillian. My mother said, "Haven't you had enough baseball?" and then realized it was a stupid question. Tickets would be left.

It rained all day Saturday and the game was rained out. So on Sunday, Lillian called and picked me up. Hank left tickets. More rain delays. Much more baseball...Phils lose 11-10 in 12 innings (4 hours, 20 minutes) and then win the nightcap when Mahaffey pitched a six-hit shutout. We met after the game. There was no player whose autograph I didn't get on Friday, but remarkably I never asked Aaron or Boyd.

Hank asked if we wanted to come to Monday night's game— for some reason it was a 5-game series. Lillian couldn't make it and of course I was not old enough to ride the 59B bus—to the El—to the bus—to Connie Mack—over 90 minutes—by myself. He asked if there was anything else he could do...anything to make me into a Braves fan. I said a ball *might* do the trick (knowing I had my fingers crossed behind my back).

That was late August. In the middle of the winter, a box arrived in the mail. It was from Charlie Dressen, the manager, with an official National League ball and a note saying Hank asked him to send it to me. He never mentioned the commitment to becoming a Braves fan. Hopefully, he realized it was a hopeless cause. I was a Phillies fan (a diehard following a different kind of hopeless cause).

The next season I took the ball to every game I attended, but only had 'special' players sign it. Went to a Braves game, got down to the dugout, called over to Hank. Reminded him of Lillian and he signed the ball. Warren Spahn, who, as a lefty was a hero of mine, looked at the ball, said it 'looked nice', but wouldn't sign.

The following year, while standing near the visitor's bus, a neighborhood kid swiped the ball out of my hand and ran down Lehigh Ave. Back in the day I was fast. I chased him for 2-3 blocks. He suddenly turned down an alley, and I suddenly learned the lesson: discretion was the better part of valor. I would live to get another ball but just not the one Hank Aaron sent me. I was heartbroken.

Early in the magical/tragic season of '64, I was playing step ball out front when my Mother called out that some radio guy was on the phone. I had sent in a postcard to enter the quiz contest on the Phillies pre-game radio show. The question was: "Is it possible to pitch a no-hitter and lose the game?"

Not having time to be nervous, and at 14, I knew everything there was to know about baseball: So "yes," I said. "In fact, last night Ken Johnson of the **HOUSTON COLT .45**s* lost to the Reds, 1-0, when Pete Rose scored in the top of the ninth inning on an error, groundout, and another error."

"A simple yes or no was good enough," the announcer said. "You certainly know your baseball." That compliment was as good as the prize: sunglasses, Phillies' hat, and pair of tickets. *(I wonder if the announcer was Benny Bengough, the old Phillies coach who did a pre-game TV show from up in the corner in Connie Mack?)*

---

*The public address announcer for the **HOUSTON COLT '45**s (later the Astros) in their 1962 inaugural season was Dan Rather... the P.A. announcer for the Brooklyn Dodgers in 1936 and 1937 was John Forsythe, later a TV and movie star.

So Say You One, So Say You All

We moved from Brooklyn to Philadelphia and I just fell in love with **SHIBE*** Park and Connie Mack Stadium. It was the Phillies fans and how they banded together which struck me.

Shibe Park was majestic. It even had real grass across the broad expansive playing area, with a shot of 446 feet to straight-away centerfield. Of course, even after expanding the seating capacity, only 33,166 fans constituted a sellout crowd there.

I remember my mother putting me on the trolley car at our corner and giving me a dollar to go to the ball games. One dollar!!! Most times, especially when the team was playing, kids my age—maybe six or seven—were sometimes let in free by the friendly ticket takers. I remember going to the top of the upper deck stands and sitting with an old man in a straw hat. I didn't know him, but occasionally he would buy me a hot dog. I learned later the man in that top row seat was none other than Connie Mack himself. That never meant much to me until I was grown up and realized just who and what Mr. Mack was. Do you believe that? Connie Mack!!!!!! I don't know if I believe it, but it happened to me!

The stadiums were incredible for watching baseball games back then. The stands started close to the field. The variations of the walls made a ball hit off the wall an experience. Outfielders had to learn to play the nooks and juts of every wall. It was kind of like a modern day Fenway Park. The infielders had to learn to

*Benjamin **SHIBE** was a manufacturer of whips and other leather products who got into the baseball glove business with Alfred J. Reach. Reach was also a sporting goods manufacturer in Philadelphia and was the one who bought the Worcester team and moved it to Philadelphia and called it the Phillies. The classic old Philadelphia name, the Athletics, had already been taken by the American Association team so Reach called his team 'the Philadelphias,' and eventually that name was shortened to Phillies.

field a ball on the grass and on the dirt, not on a plastic carpet with seams and spots of dirt. I mean, what was Astroturf?????

Baseball was different back then. The players were different and the fans were different. The talent in the major leagues had not been watered down by vast expansion and the players were proud to be major leaguers. What was free agency???? What was a fringe player? Everyone could play and the rosters were smaller.

I know I'm a little all over the place here, but I grew to love the Phillies, especially Robin Roberts. I was a pitcher myself and I tried to mimic his pitching style when I played. He was a player with no excuses. He went out and busted his butt every night. He didn't care if he was being asked to pitch for 10 outs or 20 innings. Whatever the manager needed, he would give them. And he would never complain. Well, there was one night when I desperately wanted his autograph. I was near the dugout and called for him. He said to send down my program and he'd sign it. I didn't have a pen!!! Can you believe that??? Someone else did and I fished down the program to him. He signed it and then told me, "Son, never give up on your hopes and dreams." He wrote that in the program, too, which I still have framed. I think that one moment helped to change my life. It may sound a little corny but I believe that. I was just a skinny kid looking for an autograph. To this day, when someone needs help, if I can help them, I try to do it. This is all from a minute's lesson from that day at Connie Mack Stadium with Robin Roberts. It's amazing what sticks with you through the years."
—**Ronnie Batser**, 69, Retired...war veteran

I remember my parents promised me that if I behaved in school my dad would take me to a Phillies gme. I was in the third grade and was not the best behaved kid, but I really did want to go see the Phillies play. I loved Johnny Callison, **RICHIE ALLEN***, Jim Bunning, Chris Short, etc., even when I was that young.

> ***RICHIE ALLEN** was one of the earliest players to regularly wear his protective helmet while playing defense...to protect against objects thrown by fans.

In June when I got my last report card, they weren't the greatest grades. Lots of 'Cs.' My parents made a deal with me that if I went to my Phillies game, would I study that much harder the following school year. If my grades improved, they would take me more. If they dipped, they wouldn't take me. Seemed fair enough.

That first day, we piled in the station wagon and off we went to Lehigh Avenue to beautiful Connie Mack Stadium. My dad kept calling it Shibe Park because that's what it was before changing names. I remember when we parked, this man asked if he could watch the car while we were in the stadium. My dad gave him 25 cents. Lo and behold, when we came out, the car was fine and the man shook my dad's hand. It's funny that I've remembered that my whole life.

Anyway, I remember walking up to the stadium and being in awe. It was beautiful. Dad got a Ballentine Beer. That was a team sponsor at the time. I had a soda and some popcorn. Food has always tasted better at the ballpark since that very first day. Dad pointed out the green grass to me and it was just something. Beautiful. Dad taught me how to keep score. That's how I learned.

You know what? I got good grades the rest of my school years. The better my grades, the more games my dad took me to. I realized that if you did things the right way, you'd be rewarded. I used that logic for my kids. It works. It teaches you that if you work hard, good things happen. And all this happened because of a trip to the ballpark for the Phillies. I think it's pretty amazing.

—**Lou McGovern**, Key West, FL

I remember being chided by my friends for telling them the Phillies have not wrapped up anything in 1964—I was the only one worried before the collapse. When they collapsed no one gave me "credit" for foreseeing some of their problems, and I was too distraught to say "I told you so."

Of course, going to Connie Mack was always interesting. My father was not a fan, so often his friend Manny Solomon would take me, starting in 1960 or so when I was 10. We would find a parking spot and, as usual, have to pay the locals to "watch" the car else we get a flat tire on the return. The first time I saw the field I thought, "Wow—all that grass so green inside an enclosed park!"

On April 23, 1961, Manny took me to a Phillies game. The MLB record for strikeouts in a nine-inning game was 18 by Bob Feller, known to me even then. Young Art Mahaffey was facing the Cubs and his fastball was working great. The Ks started to pile up, to the point that even when the Cubs hit a foul ball the place was going crazy—as it was on every strike. It was the most exciting thing I had ever seen. At the start of the ninth, Mahaffey got it to 16 strikeouts after eight innings when... Manny announced to me that we had to leave so he can get to his car and beat the crowd! I protested, but to no avail. As we were leaving the stadium we heard roars, but it was tough to tell if it was a strikeout or just a foul ball. Mahaffey struck out his 17th in the ninth but failed to tie or break Feller's 18. I don't mind leaving games early, but this was one time I would have given a lot to stay...

—**Dan Heisman**, 59, Wynnewood, PA

The bigger connection being here in Reading is that we've had a long relationship with the Reading Phillies in the Eastern League. We'd go out on a Friday night and there probably weren't even a thousand people there. They had concession stands, but you could bring in your own food and picnic in the stands. Municipal Stadium in Reading has been renovated and it's very nice. But it was built in 1950. Some of the players gripe that the clubhouse and dugout are separate. They have to walk across the concourse to get to the dugout. And walking across the concourse gives the fans a chance to see players and get their pictures taken with them, which is still pretty neat. The prima donnas complain, but some of the players embrace it.

I take my eight-year-old daughter and she likes to see the players. She knows some Spanish because my wife teaches ESL. She talks to some of the Spanish players in their language and they like that. I have attended hundreds of games out there. The first time my dad took me was in '68 when I was eight. Larry Bowa was playing for them then. I was very fortunate to see Bowa play there and Luzinski and Boone. Schmidt was a shortstop there. It was real interesting to see those Phillies of the early 70s come up through Reading. My dad lured me out to the ballpark on a day they were raffling off a pony. The main reason I wanted to go was to see if I could win that pony. There was a fence and a big grass berm around the outfield and a brick wall behind that. The whole game they paraded this pony along that berm, and I was convinced I was going to win it. Of course, when they read the numbers off those little raffle tickets, I hadn't won the pony. I was heartbroken. My dad thought it was so funny that I was sure I was going to win that pony.

Dad had a jewelry store in Reading and a lot of the ballplayers used to come in and talk to my dad because it was next to a really good diner. On the other side was the barbershop. Frank **LUCCHESI*** was managing the Reading Phillies at that time, and he and my dad were acquaintances. Dad told him about how sad I was that I didn't win the pony, so he brought in an autographed ball for my dad to give to me. That turned me on to baseball. We were probably playing with the ball already the next day, though. Dad also sold transistor radios in his store. He'd always have the game on in the store, partly as a sales pitch to sell radios. Even on the Thursday nights when he was always open, if there was a game, he'd have it on the radio

*In 1974 Billy Martin was managing the Texas Rangers and Frank **LUCCHESI** was his third base coach. Martin tried using a transistor hook-up to his coaches to relay signals. One game the system was broken, but Martin kept yelling instructions for a suicide squeeze into the microphone. Red Sox pitcher Luis Tiant finally stepped off the mound and yelled: "Frank, Billy said he wanted the suicide squeeze."

in the store. Over the years we listened to thousands of games together. Dad explained the strategies to me. I remember how Lou Brock just befuddled the Phillies with his base running and how that took over the game. Dad explained that to me, too.

I wouldn't trade those memories for all the money in the world.

People ridiculed the Vet and called it a dump, but if that's your memories, that's what's important. That's what memories are made of. I thought that maybe it's a dump, but it's *our* dump.

—**Peter Chiarelli**, 50, Reading, PA

One of the main reasons for my baseball passion was my mother's father. My grandpa Lou was a great man. He was a massive Cubs fan and loved attending baseball games. When I was young, he worked for Sears and Roebuck and would often get tickets for my family. These were times that I loved as a kid. Walking into Dodger Stadium with my grandparents and watching the Dodgers play. The seats were usually down in the field boxes right behind the visitor dugout. I would often autograph hunt with envelopes, programs, cards, or balls.

On one of these occasions, in 1980, we got to the park early to watch batting practice and the surging Phillies were in town. I loved catchers. I collected their cards because I loved the gear. As a kid I always thought of it as armor. One of my favorites of the time was Bob Boone. He grew up in Southern California, his dad played ball, and he was tough! I remember that I wanted his autograph that day. Badly!

I asked my grandmother for a pen and took the ball I had brought with me down the third-base line and tried to get an autograph as Boone warmed up pitchers. I was a nine-year-old dynamo! I was yelling his name, pleading, screaming, begging, and generally being a pain...nothing seemed to work. I don't think he ever turned around or glanced my way.

I was still calling his name as the team started to walk off the field. As one of the last players walked toward the dugout, he grabbed my ball and pen and went into the dugout. I was shocked and then near tears as I realized that the Phillie player just stole my ball! I turned back around to my grandparents, who gave that look only grandparents can give saying, "Oh well, guess you should have been a little quieter, but we love you anyway!"

As the tears neared and the frustration mounted, the player came back out, handed me the ball, and said, "I hope this keeps you quiet now!" My mouth dropped as I took the ball back. It was signed by three Phillies players—Boone, Schmidt, and the player who grabbed the ball, Steve Carlton! I was stunned. I thanked him and ran to my grandfather to show him. He was amazed. I was an instant Phillies fan and Steve Carlton fan from that point forward. I collected every baseball card he ever had— my Steve Carlton and Bob Boone collections are rather large.

As we were leaving the park, I added one more signature to that ball...Tug McGraw, who stopped on the way to their bus to sign for me. It was still not for many years that I learned that Carlton could be downright surly to fans and the media. It did not matter to me though. I still own the ball and although my grandfather has been gone for a few years now, that ball always reminds me that my love for the Phillies is only slightly less than my love for my family.

—**Joshua Levine**, 39, Southern California

One Sunday in May 1946, my uncle and I went to a Sunday doubleheader between the Phillies and Pirates. My uncle believed in good seats and getting to the park as earlier as possible. This Sunday it was rainy and overcast so seats were not a problem. We had seats in the first row down the third-base line. We read the Sunday paper, watched batting practice, and, in general, relaxed.

Shortly before the game began my uncle looked up and asked if I recognized the player coming down from the left-field area. I looked up and saw an old man in a Pirates uniform wearing rubbers not baseball spikes. I told my uncle, "That's Honus Wagner." Wagner walked down to the dugout not on the grass but on the area right beside the fence. As he approached us my uncle said, "Honus, say hello to the kid." Without breaking stride, he reached over the fence, shook my hand, but never said a word and kept on going. I still remember those incredibly bowed legs and his hand, which seemed as big as a baseball glove to me.

I tell the students in my Baseball and American Culture class that that handshake encompasses almost the entire history of baseball. Wagner started playing the 1890s, and I am still a fan at the end of the first decade of the 21st century.

—**John Rossi**, 74, author, *Baseball and American Culture*

My earliest Phillies memory was jumping on a black leather couch as a five-year-old, imitating my 32-year-old father as Manny Trillo lined a triple down the left field foul line. I had never witnessed Dad jumping on furniture before, so the Phillies were alright in my book. I didn't know the players' names, or why we were jumping on couches, but it seemed fun at the time. I only have short visual memories of this event, but both the Phillies and my father were involved. Shortly thereafter I began playing tee-ball. Baseball became my favorite sport. I have a very vivid memory of the time my Dad took me to my first Phillies game. I actually looked up the box score on Baseball Almanac.com. I was able to find it because my Dad took several great photos of that day, including shots of Nolan Ryan pitching against Mike Schmidt, Pete Rose standing on second base at the end of an inning placing his batting gloves into his batting helmet. The **PHILLIE PHANATIC*** came to our row, and played around with my bowl haircut. That was the day when I fell in love with the game. Dad was sitting next to me explaining things like pitching changes, hit and runs and other nuances of the game that don't come readily to seven-year-olds. It was a great day.

Unfortunately, I suffered though the mid to late '80s as a Phillies fan. They were terrible from the top down. Mike Schmidt, my favorite player, was the only real reason to watch

*The **PHILLIE PHANATIC** debuted on April 25, 1978. The Phanatic's costume was added to the National Baseball Hall of Fame's collection on July 27, 2002.

the team. However, we didn't get to watch too many games, as we didn't have Prism. So Harry Kalas and Richie Ashburn told us how the games played out. The Internet age erased the concept of radio broadcast games as the sole source of Phillies information from this thirty-something's memory banks. I remember listening to Harry and Whitey grouse about guys like Al Oliver, Tommy Herr, George Hendrick, Dave Parker and John Tudor beating the Phillies. Good players seemed like mega-stars every time they faced the Fightin's. I remember Whitey schilling for Lebanon Bologna. I listened to twice as many games as I watched in the '80s, almost every night while doing homework, or while falling asleep during West Coast trips. My most memorable game that I ever listened to was the 26-7 beatdown we put on those '85 Mets. I remember being so happy that we finished second to them in '86, by 26 games.

Every year my Dad would focus on one Phillie as his new favorite, Glenn Wilson (gamer); Juan Samuel (loved his glove bat and speed), Bruce Ruffin/Don Carman/Pat Combs/insert "up and coming pitcher here". Most of these guys were middling players who looked much better than they were because they played on terrible teams.

By 1993, the Phils had become almost an afterthought for both my Dad and me. I was a senior in high school getting ready for college tennis, and Dad worked a lot. We had other things to discuss other than baseball, and the Phils weren't really that much fun to talk about anyway. My 1993 memories revolved around my friends: I was studying for my physics midterm with my friend Steve when Mitch struck out the Braves and did his Van Halen impersonation. I remember sitting front and center on the basement floor of a high school homecoming party when Joe Carter went yard. I still turn the channel every time I see that pitch on TV.

The Phillies generously became irrelevant for my college and law school years as I could focus on other endeavors, such as class. The Larry Bowa years were almost more depressing then the previous years of below mediocrity. The Bowa teams had talent, likeable players (especially Thome) and always competed but never contended. I figured that was the best I was ever going to get with this team. But, a funny thing happened with those teams, Dad and I started talking baseball again. Dad started following the team again, even went to his first Phillies game in ten years during that run. He began talking about players who really turned out to be players ("I love this kid Utley." ..."Have you heard about this kid Howard?"). The days of propping up Glenn Wilson were over, we had legitimate players to root for.

I'll admit it. I wanted **JIM LEYLAND***. Dad wanted Charlie Manuel. Phone discussions always went from a general discussion about life to a specific discussion about the direction of the Phils. Dad even sprung for a 20-game package. Nights at the ballpark served as a meeting place for a Dad and his son to catch up, drink a beer or two and watch some baseball. As we both get older, time together becomes more of a premium. Phils games were the perfect outlet. Anytime we had nothing to talk about regarding life in general, we'd always revert back to a discussion about the present game.

October 26, 2008 will go down as one of the highlights of my life. That was the night that my Dad and I attended our first World Series game together. Joe Blanton hit a home run. The game was never in doubt.

—**John F. Kennedy**, Attorney, Philadelphia

I was born and raised in Jersey City. It was 1964. My dad was a very loyal Yankee fan. However, my mom was born in Philadelphia and her dad—my grandfather—brainwashed my brothers and me. We became Phillies fans. My friends knew this, and it made for some very lopsided baseball card trades. They would seek me out anytime they got a Phillie in a pack. My best friend, Bobby Cole, and I made this blockbuster trade. He got Mickey

---

*Tigers manager **JIM LEYLAND** was once a second-string catcher for Perrysburg High School, in the Toledo area. The starting catcher was Jerry Glanville, later a head coach in the NFL.

Mantle, Roger Maris, Yogi Berra, and Johnny Blanchard. I got Choo-Choo Coleman, Harry "The Horse" Anderson, and Jack Meyer. Boy, what a dope!

We used to play a game called Colors. We held the cards stat side up and then put them down with the picture side up. We made one big pile with the cards. If you matched the color of the border with the card put down just before it, you got the entire pile. I got into too many fights any time the 1959 **CHICO FERNANDEZ*** came up. It was the only card with a pink border. They would tease me that only a Phillie would have a pink border. I defended Chico's honor many times.

As the summer came to an end and we went back to school, it looked like the Phillies were a sure thing. My Yankee fan friends were very worried about the White Sox. But they were sure the Yanks would make it and we made many bets. All we had to do was wait for the World Series. I couldn't stay up to watch the 11 o'clock news. I am not sure I knew it existed back then. So, on the way home from school, I would stop at Gold-stein's Candy Store and buy a *New York Daily News* to check out the box scores. As the slump got deeper, the Phillies became a back-page headline. The final weekend I got to watch the Mets-Cardinals games on WOR Channel 9. The Mets won the first two games. The cartoon on the sports page had a Phillie, a Red, and a Cardinal singing to a Met sitting on a throne—"I can be a beggar, I can be a king. It all depends on you."

The Phillies won their last game, which ended before the Mets game. I watched, hoping that the Mets could pull off just one more. They didn't. Tim McCarver caught a foul pop to end the game. The Cardinals started to celebrate. I started to cry. I was watching the game with my Uncle Sal—my dad had passed away a few years before. I told him, "Uncle Sal, you like

*In the late 1960s, **CHICO FERNANDEZ** was beaned and almost killed. He was in a coma for 11 days and took 18 months before he was able to speak again.

the Yankees. You don't understand. It's not a ballgame. It's the World Series." I went upstairs and cried myself to sleep.

—**Rob Mattaliano**, 57, Royersford, PA

In June, of 1970, I made my first and only trip to Connie Mack Stadium to see an exhibition game between the Phillies and the Baltimore Orioles. Up until that point, all of the images of the Phils came through on a black and white TV. So when I got inside the ballpark, I was blown away by the colors that seemed to jump out at me. The green grass, the billboards, the pinstripes on the Phillies new uniforms—they were supposed to have moved to the Vet sometime during the season hence—the new look uniforms—even the Orioles gray jerseys looked good. The other memory was seeing Clay Dalrymple, who was traded to the O's the previous season, come to bat late in the game. As he was given a standing ovation by the crowd, he took his hat off. I remember reacting in horror when I found out one of my favorite Phils was bald.

—**Michael Luongo**, radio contributor for various media outlets since 1987

I do not recall the specifics of the first baseball game I ever attended, but I do remember that it was part of a Cub Scouts outing in August 1958 at Connie Mack Stadium, that my father chaperoned, and that the Phillies lost. The Chicago Cubs were 138 games out of first place that year, as they always were, and the Phillies were either 438 or 439 games behind them. The great **ERNIE BANKS*** probably played that day, though I cannot say for sure; Robin Roberts may well have pitched for the Phillies, though more likely it was some stiff like Dennis Bennett or Seth Morehead. It was boiling hot; we were tethered to splintering planks in a Bedouin sun field in the left-field bleachers; the whole experience lacked drama, pathos, or charm. We'd been given free tickets to a meaningless late-season game

***ERNIE BANKS** and O. J. Simpson are cousins. Their grandfathers were twin brothers.

between two putrid teams that nobody actually liked, and we certainly didn't have any fun.

Perhaps now that I look back on it, this was all part of my father's master plan. Perhaps my father—trading on his extensive connections in the Philadelphia gaming community—had actually been given tickets to seats directly behind home plate but had reluctantly decided that he would be sending me the wrong message by introducing me to such sybaritic splendor at the impressionable age of eight. Instead, at the very first sporting event I attended in my entire life, he decided that it was important that I be given a private screening of the hell that awaited me. Defeat. Despair. Crummy food. Rotten seats. Intolerable heat. A disintegrating stadium in a terrible neighborhood. But mostly defeat. Thus, at no point did it cross my mind to say, "Dad, these are the best seats in the whole place, and I am having so much fun!" He would have hit me with a two-by-four.

I doubt if my son can recall the first game of his life. But I know he can recall one fairly early on. By the time **BARRY BONDS***—a latter-day Beelzebub—had finished setting off not one but two rhubarbs after stealing second with a 9-1 lead at the Vet in 1998, my son had consumed three Cokes, two hot dogs, a pretzel, some Cracker Jacks, and a gargantuan black-and-white cookie. Having never before witnessed the sight of seventy players, managers, bat boys and trainers slugging it out on the pitcher's mound, he briefly lost his composure and asked if he could have some blue cotton candy. I warned him that the blue cotton candy could be his personal Gotterdammerung, but he ignored me. Later that day, back at a friend's house, I issued a second warning to avoid the rancho-flavored Doritos chips after having eaten a pepperoni pizza, cheese whizzies and onion-and-vinegar potato chips on top of the dreaded blue cotton candy. Later that night, he said, "I really like going to baseball games

*Dusty Baker's dad was Bobby **BONDS'** Little League coach in Riverside, CA.

with you, Dad." I asked him why this was so. He replied, "Because you're not like Mom. She wouldn't let me eat all this stuff."

"True, but when you're puking your guts out at three o'clock in the morning, I'm not going to be like Mom and come in and console you," I responded. "He who eats the blue cotton candy pukes alone."

This was my son's first true rite of passage, and he profited from it. He had seen his first brawl. He had seen the quintessential modern baseball player at the height of his arrogance and self-absorption. And he had learned, to his great sorrow to never eat the blue cotton candy in August, no matter how good it looks from a distance.

—**Joe Queenan**, Author, *True Believers*

It was 1961 and I was an 11-year-old kid at the game. I was with my friend Doug Verb. It's hard to think now that we'd take the bus and the El from far northeast to 21st and Lehigh. Can you imagine 11-year-olds doing this today? Anyway, we'd always wait outside the player's entrance after the game for autographs. So I spot Jim Owens, a less than stellar pitcher who had a reputation for liking the booze, standing on Lehigh Avenue at a bus stop. I guess he didn't make enough to buy a car (I think new cars back then were probably around 2-3K). I think he even had a brown paper bag in his hand so he probably brought his lunch, too. So I run across the street with my pencil and program in hand and ask for an autograph. I'm the only one there. He belches from his big beer gut and totally ignores me. I couldn't believe a bum like that treated me that way. About a year later the Phils fleeced the Reds badly by trading him for Cookie Rojas, which made me very happy. What a steal that turned out to be.

—**Ken Rosenberg**, 61, born and raised in NE Philly

Friends took my brother and me to a game at Connie Mack. Late, late in the game, Robin Roberts was pitching and Gil Hodges hit a foul ball, which hit the façade and dropped straight down. It was late at night, and I was half asleep—the ball hit me in the back of the head and lodged between my back and the seat. I grabbed the ball. There were a bunch of old guys behind me trying to grab the ball from me. A lady behind me beat them off, telling them to let the kid have it. I ended up with ball.

I wrote to Robin Roberts asking him if he would sign the ball. He wrote me back telling me to come to the park the next Saturday game, and he would sign it for me. I thought this was really cool. We went back to the park on that day. He took forever to come out because they lost the game to the Pirates. I had been told that whenever he lost a game, he stayed back in the clubhouse and takes forever to come out. I don't know if he was sulking or what. I waited over an hour after the game was over for Robin to come out. The other players had long gone. He came out and apologized profusely and signed for me.

Later on, as a member of SABR, I got familiar with *Retrosheet*, and found I was able to go back and search for the game which Roberts lost 4-3 and then go back to the last game against the Dodgers to find out what game that was. I found out it was ten days earlier than when I got the autograph. I learned that Gil Hodges had come up to bat as a pinch hitter in the eighth inning, and he fouled off one ball. So, I knew that I had caught the fourth ball pitched to Gil Hodges in his one at-bat in the game against Robin Roberts. Another interesting thing I found out was that was a game when Frank Howard, who had just been called up by the Dodgers from the minors that day, hit his first major league home run.

Then, fast forward to January, 2009, when I went to the Potomac Nationals banquet, and Frank Howard is the featured speaker. He's sitting there signing autographs, and I took a copy of the LA Times clipping of the game for him to sign. He signed it for me, and he tells me the story that the next day he was warming up, and Robin Roberts came over to him. He said, "Hey, Hondo, how'd you like that little soft ball I served up to you last night? I just didn't want you to get sent back down too soon." Frank told me he thought Roberts was the greatest guy—that "he was careful to treat me right as a rookie even though I was on the opposing team, and he didn't want me sent back down on the same day I had just been called up. He gave me something easy to hit, and I was able to hit a home run off of it. Robin Roberts is a class act." I thought it was a great story, and it speaks well of Robby, of course.

It's fun being a Phillies fan...frustrating, of course. My dad was always one who hated the beach, but one summer, after much begging, he finally consented to take us. We got a little cottage and went down. We didn't have a TV and I don't remember that we had a radio. I got up on that Monday morning and get the newspaper and find out that Jim Bunning has pitched a **PERFECT GAME***...and because we were at the beach we didn't get to see it. That was awful—any other game, I'd have been glued to the set on a Sunday afternoon at home.

—**Wayne Voltz**, 60, Stafford, VA, SABR member since 1996

My first memories of the Phillies are watching them at my grandparents' house on Sunday afternoons. I can remember vaguely watching them at Connie Mack in 1970, back when Channel 6 carried the games.

I can remember watching the opening of Veterans Stadium and seeing Mike Ryan catch the first pitch from a helicopter. I got to my first Phils' game later that season and thought the Vet was unlike anything I'd ever imagined.

Back then, Astroturf was cool, as was having different colored seats in every level. Then there were the huge scoreboards and the "dancing fountains" that made the stadium a lot more interesting than the team that season.

Starting in '72, my family would usually get to a couple of games a year, with a lot of Sunday games—back when double-headers were commonplace; not avoided at all costs by owners

---

*In the Yankee locker room, on the day of Don Larsen's **PERFECT GAME**, Larsen was served divorce papers....Years later Don Larsen threw out the first pitch the same day David Cone threw his perfect Yankee game....Larsen and David Wells, another Yankee with a perfect game, graduated from the same high school in San Diego, Point Loma.

looking to maximize ticket sales. The Flying Wallendas are the most memorable part of those doubleheaders.

But my most endearing memory comes from my eighth birthday, when the Cardinals were at the Vet. We were sitting down the third-base line in the 200 level when Lou Brock scorched a foul ball that slammed off the hands of the woman a row behind us.

The ball then went off my mom's leg—leaving quite the bruise—and pretty much wound up in my lap. The next thing I know, I'm being handed a "contract" for "catching" a foul ball. Meanwhile, my younger brother was quite unhappy he didn't have a ball of his own, but at a later game my dad was able to purchase a ball used briefly and taken out of play due to rain. That solved that.

In high school, I took part in a program the Phils sponsored for would-be journalists and eventually spent years in the press box covering the team for the Daily Local News in West Chester. That started a stretch where I didn't care whether they won or lost; just as long as something interesting happened to write about.

—**Mark Ashenfelter**, native of Coatesville, PA

My introduction to the Phillies came in September 1963. On two consecutive Sundays, my dad took me down to Connie Mack Stadium to catch the Phillies in an unexpected pennant race. A team at the bottom of the league just two years earlier was actually alive in the pennant hunt in September!

Realists in town did not really expect them to come through, however. The Phillies had a serious weakness—they could not hit left-handers. Manager Gene Mauch had to platoon to get the most out of his ballplayers, and he had no right-handed bats at a couple of positions, which severely hampered his lineup. It was not unusual for opposing teams to stockpile their southpaws until they came to the Quaker City, and sometimes they would make quick call-ups from their minor leagues for somebody—anybody—who could throw strikes from the port side.

On Sunday, the first day of September, the Cardinals came to town. And so did my dad and me. At the tender age of eight, it was a real thrill to ride down North Broad Street for the first time, seeing for real the advertisers I had only seen pictured on television (like Earl Scheib Auto Painting and the Pep Boys). We parked at the car lot at 21st and Lehigh the old-fashioned way—lined up directly behind the car in front. After the game, we could not leave until that car left. It made for a controlled outflow of traffic—and many upset suburban drivers like my dad. We got two tickets in the grandstands and my 25-cent souvenir program with free pencil. My dad taught me how to score a game that day.

The Cardinals certainly had stockpiled the lefties. Ray Sadecki and Bobby Shantz had taken care of the locals the previous two games, and now it was Curt Simmons taking a turn on the mound. Chris Short tried to pitch that day for the locals, but he didn't have his usual stuff, and it was more like batting practice for the Cardinals. They won 7–3.

But the big deal to me was seeing The Man. It was an open secret that **STAN MUSIAL*** was making his farewell tour throughout the league and was expected to retire after the season ended. He was a legend even to a little kid like me in another part of the country. He poked a couple of long balls during batting practice, though all I recall of him in the game was a couple of walks as Short pitched around him. But he was awesome to see live.

I told my dad I had so much fun, so imagine my surprise the next Sunday when my dad said we were going back! Same drive, same parking lot, same pencil. This time Milwaukee came to town. Following the same pattern of exploiting the Phillies' weakness to the southpaw, out to the mound came Warren Spahn, the greatest left-hander of the past 30 years. This was Spahn's last great season, winning 21 games. Of

*Dodger relief pitcher Clem Labine once retired **STAN MUSIAL** 49 times in a row.

course, the Phillies had no chance against him. Somehow they scratched out two runs, but the Braves got three to win.

Rarely can someone say that he saw a different future Hall of Famer in every game he saw that year. But I can say that I began my big-league baseball love affair by seeing two of the all-time greats—and certainly of my generation—within a week of each other.

—**Dan Lindner**, 55, Clifton, VA, Management Consultant

While I've gone to tons of games with my friends, I've gone to more with my father. I have so many memories of sitting with him in our seats behind the plate at the Vet—keeping score, guessing what the next hitter was going to do, eating hot dogs, playing cards during rain delays, and then walking to our parking spot, which may have been a mile and a half away, but gosh darn it, it was free. My dad taught me pretty much everything I know about baseball, from the importance of working the count to find the best hitting situation to the importance of working the concession stands to find the best deal. Perhaps most importantly, he taught me never to leave a game early—in any sport, but particularly in baseball. Because, well, you just never know.

Another thing my dad taught me is the insignificance of autographs. The idea really is pretty silly—someone writes their name on a piece of paper and it's supposed to be valuable, both personally and monetarily. He taught me that if you do ever meet a true celebrity, it's much more meaningful to have a conversation with them than to have them write their name on a napkin. That said, I did collect *one* Phillies autograph in my life—none other than the immortal Joe Boever. I might need the Elias Sports Bureau to look into this, but I think I'm the only person in history that has Joe Boever's autograph and nobody else's. I might be the only person that has Joe Boever's autograph, period.

My dad has attended hundreds of baseball games in his life and still has never caught a foul ball. He's had them go off his hands, off his fingers, off his face. But he's never actually secured one. So when on August 1, 1998, I snared a Bill Mueller foul ball in my glove, it probably was one of the best days of both of our lives (me and my dad, that is, not me and Bill Mueller). I had waited 15 years to catch my first foul ball. My dad is currently up to 56 and counting. I hope he eventually gets one and I hope I'm there to see it. It would mean the world to both of us.

I really treasure the last game that I attended with both my father and grandfather. It was in 2007. My grandfather was in bad shape physically and we needed to sit in the handicapped seats (which, by the way, are some of the best seats in the house). For a guy with an excellent sports memory, I have absolutely no idea who the Phillies played that day or if they won, but I do remember eating peanuts with my father and his father and knowing that it would be the last time the three of us attended a baseball game together. And it was.

It was also at a game with my grandfather that I was sitting in our seats behind the plate. Maybe the year was 1997. Anyways, I happened to be peering through our binoculars when I realized a foul ball was just hit right at me. The ball landed in the empty seat next to me, but because I had my eyes in those stupid binoculars, I was totally incapable of tracking the ball. As it turned out, it was sitting about one foot from me. Some guy picked it up. I haven't used binoculars since. Dumb invention.

—**Drew Silverman**, 27, Sportswriter, Fairmount PA

My Phillies' memory is my first game at Connie Mack Stadium. It was Tuesday, June 16, 1970. Everything is vivid. My father had gotten the tickets in advance, and I remember the anticipation as we drove down Fox Street, where the light towers came into view. I can still recall walking through the main entrance on Lehigh Avenue. My father bought me a program (which I still have; it has Jimmy Wynn of the Astros on the cover), and my life-long hobby of collecting sports memorabilia began. I was blown away by the green grass and the colorful billboards on the left-field fence. What really got my attention was the Ballantine Beer sign on the scoreboard lit up in red. We had terrific seats in the lower level on the first-base side behind the **PHILLIES'*** dugout. I remember seeing Oscar Gamble coming out of the dugout before the game. I told my dad, "Great seats!" I was seven and had a cast on my right arm. All evening the fans around me asked how I broke my arm. I became a fan of Rick Wise that night, and the Phillies defeated the Houston Astros 2–1 in extra innings, as Doc Edwards knocked in the winning run off Jim Bouton. After the game my dad bought me a pennant, and I felt like the luckiest kid in the world. The next day I told my friends that I had been to a Phillies game, which none of them had ever done to that point. Although the Phillies were a mediocre team in 1970, none of that mattered. I was a Phillies fan, and I saw my team in person. What was even better was that I saw it with my dad.

—**Rich D'Ambrosio**, 48, Philadelphia,
High School English teacher

From 1952 through 1957 (I was 2 to 8 years old), my father watched the Phillies games on TV every Sunday.

He was an avid Phillies fan. He would scream at the players on the TV, which would cause me to tell him "Daddy, that man can't hear you."

Now, I yell just as loudly at Tiger Woods, Allen Iverson, Cole Hamels, etc...

And my soon to be 3-year-old grandson said, just the other day, "Papa, that man can't hear you."

—**Larry Phillips**, 60, founder of The Phillips Group, an
independent investment group in Southern California

---

*The zippered baseball jersey was introduced by the Chicago Cubs in 1937, and the last team to use zippered jerseys was the **PHILLIES** in 1990 when they went back to buttons. On May 19, 1979, the Phillies used an all-burgundy "Saturday Special" uniform that they were going to wear only at home games. They lost to the Expos 10-5 and never wore the "Saturday Specials" again.

My first year and love of baseball came in OUCH, 1964...many decades later as with all first loves I can remember the players, the numbers, and the heartache and it still causes the same feeling it did then. 'What the heck just happened.' No 11-year-old should have to bear the pain at that innocent an age. Being left-handed my first love was, of course, Number 6 Johnny Callison. As I became an athlete I always wore 6 as a tribute. To this day all my email names have 6 in them. Second on my list was Chris Short. As much as it hurt to lose the pennant that year my love of the game grew and grew in spite of it. Every person who lived through 1964 considered it the rite of passage for the true fan. My family could afford only one game a year to attend in person. The 1964 game was late September. Against the Braves. Yes, smack in the middle of horror days. I still have the ticket stub and scrap book from that entire year. I remember walking out of tunnel to a burst of colors. As long as I live I will never forget that emotion. After my dad got the tickets for the game I would check the weather in the newspaper praying for a good forecast. It didn't matter that the game was two weeks off, I still watched for rain. I have to wonder if the other die-hard fans have a hard time remembering the years before and the years after as much as I do. That was quite a time in my life.

—**Tina McElvarr**, Certified Animal Health Technician (CAHT)

The year 1964 marked my first "official" year as a Phillies fan. At that time my Nonna ("grandma" in Italian) had a mom-and-pop store in North Philly—at the corner of Stillman and 25th Street. Every week that year, our family visited Nonna's store—to help Nonna out 'cause that's what Italians do. The only member that didn't work in the store was me—known to family and friends as "Louie in the store." The kids called me that since another Louie—my mom's cousin—also lived in the neighborhood. As soon as the car would pull up on Stillman Street and Allegheny Avenue I would tear through the alley to 25th Street, looking for my friends to play a game of stickball, wire ball, or halfies.

Coincidentally, Nonna's store was located in North Philly just a few blocks from Connie Mack Stadium where the Phillies played. I remember walking to Connie Mack with my dad and my brother Joey to see the Phillies play. Mind you, my brother and I were lucky because Dad was an usher at Connie Mack, and we saw many free games from the left-field bleachers. I remember one time sitting there with Joey and hearing two passionate fans shouting "Merry Christmas, Matthews!" Eddie Matthews was a fine third baseman for the Milwaukee Braves. He was probably the best third baseman in the National League up until the time the Phillies had their own star at that position, Mike Schmidt ("Schmidty").

Sitting in the left-field bleachers was fun. Dad used to sit with us frequently during the game and ask us how everything was. At the time, Joey and I were only interested in the hot dog man, asking repeatedly, "When will the hot dog man come around?" As the catcher, whenever there was a foul pop **CLAY DALRYMPLE*** would flip off his mask, exposing his balding head. I never wanted to be a catcher—not because it was the most demanding position in baseball, but because I didn't want to be bald like him!

Toward the end of the 1964 season, the Phils were riding high. They were in first place by 6 ½ games with just 12 games to play. Mauch decided to use their top two pitchers, Jim Bunning and Chris Short, alternately. That turned out to be a bad call since the Phils proceeded to lose 10 games in a row and

---

*In 1969, catcher **CLAY DALRYMPLE** kept a fielder's glove in his pocket while using a catcher's mitt behind the plate. He would use the fielders' glove on fielding plays at home. The National League office upheld the umpire's ruling disallowing the extra glove on the field.

eventually lost the NL pennant. I remember listening to By Saam broadcast the games every night on my transistor radio. I listened to those last 10 games under the covers and cried myself to sleep each time the Phils lost. My dad even bought World Series tickets. The 1964 collapse was the first time the Phillies broke my heart.

I can't seem to explain my love of and loyalty to the Phillies. I have been a fan now for 46 years. When they lose, I hurt. When they win, I smile. Yet they don't pay me to watch them and I don't work for them. The players are always changing, but those red pinstripes and my feelings for them have always remained the same.

—**Lou Thomas**, NJ, High School teacher

There's one game that just sticks out to me. It was 1968 and I saw Bob Gibson pitch against the Phillies in Connie Mack Stadium. I went with a buddy of mine because we were Phillies fans and because Gibson was pitching. Gibson struck out 12, and pitched a shutout. The **PHILLIES*** barely got their bats on the ball. I also remember that Gibson got a stolen base and homered. He was so dominating. Unbelievable. Now, I'm a HUGE Phillies fan. For some reason, that one game is something that will etched in my mind for as long as I live. Gibson was so dominating, maybe the most dominating pitcher I've ever seen. I feel honored to have been able to witness this in person. Sometimes, when you go to a game, you don't realize what you've just seen. I knew right away after that game. We were talking as

*In 1944, the new owners of the **PHILLIES** held a contest to rename the team. The club had been called 'the Stinkers' and also 'the Phutile Phillies.' There were over 5,000 entries with 635 different names suggested. The winner was awarded a $100.00 war bond and a season pass for choosing the name 'Blue Jays.' Students at Johns Hopkins University in Baltimore were upset because Blue Jays was their school's nickname. There was such an outcry that the team announced that the contest was merely for an "emblem" and "not a name change." The name/emblem survived only one year and was never really used.

we left the ballpark and we were in awe. We were like, 'Did we just see that? Did that just happen?' Yes, it did. Again, unbelievable.

I don't go to as many games as I used to, but I still go. I keep score. I remember as a kid, I used to keep score while listening on the radio. I'm sure a lot of kids did this back in the day, probably not nearly as many do it now. When I go to high school games, youth games, Phillies games, I always keep score. It keeps me into it and I love it.

Going to Citizens Bank Park, keeping score, having some popcorn and watching the Phillies ...it's utopia. And when the Phillies are winning like they are now, it just makes your life better. I enjoy every day anyway, but to have winning Phillies baseball with a chance to win the World Series each year, well it doesn't get any better than this!

—**Brian Thompson**, 73, Mount Holly, NJ, retired

Whenever I think about my relationship with the Phillies and baseball, I always tie it to my father, who was also named Kevin. He was the one who took me to the first Phillies game that I can remember when I was 3 in 1977. My dad saw how much I loved the game and he purchased a 16-game plan after that for both myself and him in the 200 level right behind third base—a prime spot to watch a Hall of Fame career take shape. Of course, my dad—a Philadelphia police officer for 15 years—didn't always appreciate Mike Schmidt. Many nights, he was the guy yelling 'Schmidt...you're a bum." But when Schmidt hit his 500th homer in 1987, he was also the person who admitted that we were darn lucky to see him come through this way. Every summer since my youth, there has been a Phils baseball trip on our schedule—from Pittsburgh to Boston to Clearwater and in 2009, Wrigley Field.

The one interesting story that I'm also embarrassed to admit was that I passed on a shot to go to Game 6 of the 1980 World Series. Being a silly 6-year-old and having seen a classmate who was severely burned in a fireworks accident, I had this fear of anything with pyrotechnics at the time. And when the tickets came in for the Series and I saw they were in the 600 level in centerfield—right under the old Liberty Bell display at the top of the building—I freaked because that was in the fireworks firing zone. (Told you, it was stupid.) So my dad took a cousin of his who lived in Pottstown to those Series games. As it turns out, the guy my dad took was so worried about getting back to Pottstown and the potential chaos on the streets of South Philly that my father ended up leaving in the seventh inning—getting back to the house just around the time of the Frank White foul pop to Bob Boone and Pete Rose in the ninth.

Twenty eight years passed. My fear of fireworks long dissipated and my love of the game turning into an actual occupation, I was fortunate enough to cover the 2008 World Series for the Calkins Media chain. While the job requires you to be impartial and report the events as they happened, there was still that human part kept bringing me back to those days with my dad, who worked almost every night of the '08 Series until 10 o'clock as a security consultant at Philadelphia International Airport. Ironically, at the time when Brad Lidge struck out Eric Hinske, my father was listening to Harry Kalas on the radio, heading home over the Girard Point Bridge and saw the fireworks fly over South Philadelphia. When my stories were done and everything was filed at almost 1:00 a.m., I called him on his cell phone. "Well, one of us finally saw them win it in person," he joked through a crackling voice. "And I didn't run away from the fireworks, either," I replied.

—**Kevin Cooney**, Sportswriter, *Bucks County Courier Times*

Name the Brewers manager
--win valuable prizes!

"Don't tell me I don't know where to play the hitters."
—Phillie pitcher Ray Culp, after a hit ricocheted off his head and was caught by the centerfielder.

"Pete Rose is the most likeable arrogant person I've ever met."   —Mike Schmidt

If a woman has to choose between catching a fly ball and saving an infant's life, she will choose to save the infant's life without even considering if there are men on base.   —Dave Barry

Chapter 2

THE OLD BALLPARK

If God Didn't Destroy the Vet, He Would Have Owed Sodom and Gomorrah An Apology

THE MARQUIS DE SOD

Mark Carfagno

Mark Carfagno was a Phillies grounds-keeper for 33 years and author of Hardball and Hardship. *The book is an inside account of his years working for the Phillies and is available at www.frogcarfagno.com.*

Anyone familiar with the first few years of Veterans Stadium should remember the home run display that was used. It was located just above the 400 level, between the upper and lower decks of the stadium. The level contained, among other things: super boxes, owners' boxes, television and radio booths, and press boxes which housed all of the sportswriters.

The home run display began in left centerfield and ended in right center. Here's how it worked: When a Phillies player hit a home run, huge figures of Philadelphia Phil and Philadelphia Phyllis were set in motion. A series of blinking light representing a pitch was delivered to Phil, who would swing and send the ball toward the Liberty Bell in dead center. The ball would ricochet off the bell and travel over to Philadelphia Phyllis, who was manning cannon. The ball would hit her in the butt, causing her to accidentally shoot off a huge cannon that produced plenty of smoke.

Well, it wasn't smoke created by fire. Actually, it was steam that came from a small boiler system hidden inside the cannon. When a home run was hit, a valve inside opened and released the steam. Believe it or not, the gentleman responsible for starting the extravaganza was organist Paul Richardson. Paul sat in a booth on the 400 level near first base. Whenever a Phillies player knocked one out, Phil just pushed a button that triggered the entire display.

However, there always seemed to be one small problem. Small to most people but gigantic to Bill Giles. When the home run display didn't work properly, Giles would get very upset. The function of the display that often fouled up was the release of the steam. We were always told that the problem was the lack of water in the boiler. It was the grounds crew's responsibility to make sure there was enough water in that small hidden area where the boiler was located.

Getting inside the cannon was no easy task. You have to be relatively small to contort your way into the cannon and locate the boiler. At that time, there were only two small people on the grounds crew: myself and Vic Chavis.

Usually, two people were needed to fill the tank inside the cannon. We would fill up several watering cans with water and remove the sprinkle attachments so that the nozzle would fit into the tank hole. We would haul those cans filled with water up to the 400 level. When it was my turn, Mike DiMuzio or Greg Winter would accompany me. First, I would have to climb out over the stadium façade into a not-too-wide metal walking track. Once down inside the cannon, Mike or Greg would pass the cans to me. Most of the time the inside of this thing would be scorching hot. I don't know why they sent us up there. What the heck did we know about valves, pressure gauges, and boilers? There were times after filling the last boiler with water that we would give Paul Richardson a cue to test the system.

I'd say only about 65 percent of the time the steam came out after the push of the button. During the game, if it didn't work properly, we would immediately get a phone call from Bill Giles to head back up there and check it out. Believe me, it wasn't always a water problem. There were other gadgets in there that didn't work properly.

Now quickly back to Vic. While he was up there one time, the person with him gave Richardson the OK to test the system. Unfortunately, Vic was still inside the cannon and this time the system *did* work. Vic—an African-American—came out white as a ghost. Vic didn't get seriously burned.

After seeing me in there what seemed like the hundredth time, Vic yelled out, "Why don't you just pee in that thing?" It should be noted that Vic went on to become the stadium maintenance supervisor. He was in charge of all the workers. The only person above him was the stadium manager.

Vic continued, "you've tried that water for so darned long and haven't had much success, so just pee in that watering can and fill 'er up." Mike looked at me and shrugged his shoulders. I thought, "It can't hurt. Go for it." I waited a few minutes until I had to relieve myself. Finally, I squirted in the can and then poured its contents into the cannon.

Paul Richardson wasn't around, so we had to wait until the game started to see what would happen. Sure enough, a Phillie hit a home run and the display went off. Mike, Greg, and I were watching from behind home plate when the cannon shot out what seemed like a longer than usual amount of steam. Yes, there were people sitting just above the cannon.

A few weeks after this unusual fueling, I received a phone call at home from a lawyer. He said that he was an attorney for the Phillies and wanted to make sure I was the individual who filled the cannon. He said that a few weeks back a woman claimed she got burned from the steam and was seeking damages! Sure, the one day I pee in the thing it shoots out more than normal and is extremely hot. Thank God they settled out of court. Can you imagine that testimony?

I never realized that so many people were afraid of heights. I found this out while working at The Vet. Somehow in a stadium owned and operated by the City of Philadelphia, the grounds crew was responsible for changing flags on the roof of the stadium. We changed the American flag, the Phillies flag, and also put up the Canadian flag when either the Expos or Blue Jays came to town.

Heights never really bothered me so I volunteered for roof duty when I first started working at The Vet. Most of the time I would go up by myself but occasionally a co-worker would go with me. The stuff you had to go through to get up there was remarkable. First, you needed a key to open a padlock to open a trapdoor that was just below the roof. To get the key, we had to go to the boiler room. Why they kept it in there is beyond me.

The boiler room, near the city's maintenance area, was a gigantic space with all kinds of boilers, valves, pipes, gauges, and a bunch of other stuff that I had no clue about. The key was in the office, which was in the back of the room. There was always someone there, 24/7.

When we finally got into the office we were asked a million questions. What do you need the key for? Who do you work for? Who told you to come here? Who is your boss? After we got through the question we then had to sign our lives away before they would give us the key. Most of the time we used a small vehicle to scoot on up to the stadium's 700 level. With the flags in our possession we headed on up. The drive ended in the concourse area between the 600 and 700 levels. We had to walk up the steps from the bottom of the 700 level to a small ladder that was attached to the back all of the last row of the stadium.

If I were by myself, I would carry the flag and key up the ladder to the door with the chain and padlock. Trying to open that lock was a pain in the butt. The lock was exposed to all the elements, making it almost impossible to open. Additionally, I could only use one hand (and my teeth when necessary). I needed the other hand to hold on to the ladder. There were times that I wondered how in the hell I did not fall. Once the door was open, I cautiously climbed my way to a small landing area. After that it was up a small stairway to the roof and a small catwalk with metal grates and iron railings.

On a clear day, the view was absolutely gorgeous. You would get a great view of the city skyline and Center City and also the bridges to New Jersey, particularly the Walt Whitman. The entire Sports Complex around The Vet was also a nice site. Often people would want to come up to the roof to take pictures. I loved it when someone was never up there before. People would ask me that if they could take a ride with me and go the roof. No problem! When they finally got there, some were scared to death. They would grab the railing tightly and never look down. At times it was comical. They would walk with me to the centerfield area of the roof, where the flagpoles were. The walk began in rightfield, so it wasn't that long. The braver ones would ask if they could walk completely around the roof. That was fine with me.

Hanging the flags could be an issue when it was windy. The rope would get all twisted and, while attaching the eyelets of the flag to the clips on the rope, the flag would blow in your face or wrap around your body. Sometimes it just wasn't fun. However, 90 percent of the time it wasn't too bad.

I came in contact with dozens of celebrities during my 33 years at Broad and Pattison. The most important was former president Gerald Ford while he was attending the 1976 All-Star game at The Vet. I have a rather unique story to tell.

As you can imagine when the leader of our country comes to visit, security is extremely tight as hundreds of Philly's Finest along with the President's own Secret Service unit are mobilized. Before President Ford arrived for the game, the entire place was inspected for several days by the Secret Service to make sure our Commander-in-Chief was going to have a safe visit.

Before the game, Mr. Ford paid a visit to both the American and National League clubhouses. The National League clubhouse was the Phillies clubhouse and was located on the first base side of the stadium. After Ford wished the N.L. stars good luck, it was time for his arrival onto the field. He was to walk down the tunnel from the clubhouse. As you could imagine, there were many dignitaries around. We were told we had to stay in the tunnel behind home plate. About five minutes before his entrance, I had to go to the bathroom. I didn't want to run back to our locker room for fear of missing the President. So what did I do? To this day I'm not sure how I did it but with all the security in place I made my way over to the bathroom in the National League dugout.

After I had done my thing, suddenly I could hear a lot of noise and commotion. I was at the doorway coming out of the bathroom but with security everywhere I was stuck. It appears that nobody knew the bathroom was occupied. I figured if I could just lay low for a couple more minutes I would get an up close look at Mr. President. I stood behind a wall near the doorway so nobody would see me. Then I heard the words very clearly, "Here he comes, here he comes." A Secret Serviceman blocked the doorway, then spotted me, but didn't say a word. He must have figured that since I was outfitted in Phillies garb I was no threat. Yeah, no kidding...Here comes the most powerful man in the world walking down the ramp and here's me, Mr. Frog, about to get a bird's eye view of the leader of our country. I looked to my right and could see him very clearly. As he walked by my bathroom I said "Hello, Mr. President." President Ford acknowledged me with a wave of his hand. How neat was that? Pure potluck. Perhaps pure "potty luck" is more like it.

> As he walked by my bathroom I said "Hello, Mr. President."

Another great experience for the grounds crew was the 1996 All-Star game. Kelsey Grammer sang the national anthem on the field. After he was finished, we somehow managed to get both him and his girlfriend to hang out with us in one of our ground crew locker rooms. They hung out and chatted with us the entire game. What a great guy. Some guys asked Kelsey if he would speak to their wives or girlfriends on the phone and he agreed. Just a genuine "regular guy"....One night, some of the boys ran into Charles Barkley when they went out to a late lunch at one of the local taverns. They sat around and chatted with Sir Charles. Danny DiMuzio asked Charles if he wanted to come to The Vet and hang out while the game was going on. Charles said yes. In fact, he not only hung out, but he put on one of our uniforms and ran out at the end of the fifth inning to change a base.

There were also some in-house visitors who liked to sit with us behind home plate to watch a couple of innings. Those included Sean Landeta, the former punter whose career started with the Philadelphia Stars of the USFL. His head coach at the time, Jim Mora, was also a frequent visitor. Others who sat with us included former Eagles Bill Bradley, Freddie Mitchell, Bill Bergey, Ray Rhodes, and Andre Waters.

We also got peeks at comedian Joey Bishop, actress Jamie Lee Curtis, and singers Bobby Rydell, Pat Benetar, Bruce Springsteen, Lou Rawls, The Lettermen, The Oak Ridge Boys, Patti LaBelle, New Kids on the Block, Boyz to Men and the Backstreet Boys. We also met Billy Joel, Elton John, and the Rolling Stones to do sound checks before their concerts.

Former Sixer Doug Collins was very close with Mike Schmidt and Garry Maddox and could often be seen in the Phillies clubhouse. Blues artist Boz Skaggs was a good friend of Dick Allen and Jim Kaat. He would drop by and say hi to us whenever he was in town.

Greg Luzinski hated sitting on the bench. That made the bench happy.

LATE NIGHT BENEDICTION

Steve Ferenchick

Ferenchick is a towering figure in the social circles of Wynnewood, PA where he lives with his wife, Becca and their three children.

It is hard to pick anything more exciting or memorable than being at Citizens Bank Park for Game 5, parts 1 and 2, of the 2008 World Series. But I spent a night at the Vet that is at least a close second, if not equally memorable: the July 2-3, 1993 doubleheader against the Padres that ended with a Mitch Williams walk-off single in the bottom of the 10th inning at 4:41 in the morning—that hit coming after my friend and I had a hand in retiring the dangerous Derek Bell three times!

I started off the night with a group of 12 or so of my co-workers from a now-defunct Philadelphia bank in the upper reaches of the 700 level in right field. The first game was scheduled to start around 4:35 (a twi-night doubleheader—remember those?), and it was a fireworks night, so there was a big crowd in attendance (54,617, to be precise). With 18 innings of baseball on tap, and a rain delay at the start of the game, much of our group decided not to leave work early, so we arrived in the bottom of the first inning of the first game.

Because of the rain, the areas under cover, including where we sat, were quite jammed, so at some point during the second or third rain delay, a few of us attempted to make our way into our employer's 400-level "Super Box." One of my friends was dating the banker who was hosting clients in there, and he slipped out some spare tickets for four of us to get in. As we showed our tickets to the Phillies employee who sat at the bottom of the elevator leading up there, he asked to see the backs of our hands so he could verify that we had been up there before (as a stamp would show up in black light). When only the one guy had the stamp and the rest of us claimed that the ticket-taker must have missed stamping us when we had left earlier, he said he knew that we were sneaking in—which was pretty much true—and that he would let us go but would report it to the ticket office and that our host would get a call from senior management of her employer. Yikes! Nothing ultimately seemed to come of that, fortunately.

> "Last SEPTA trains leave at 12:00." A mild frenzy swept the crowd...

Well, it was far from "super" in the Super Box. The indoor area that was part of the box was jammed, since rain was blowing into the outside seats and everyone had moved inside. Plus, my friend told his girlfriend about the incident with the lack of hand stamps (bad idea!), and she was then annoyed at him. After a couple free hot dogs and beers, we said goodbye and moved down to lower level seats as play was resuming. As an interesting aside, my friend and his banker girlfriend got married the next year, and in one of the all-time great "two-for-one" deals of my life, their wedding was in upstate New York the day before Steve Carlton was inducted into the Hall of Fame about an hour away in Cooperstown. So that resulted in a great road trip that weekend for the induction and the wedding.

After we left the box, a group of four of us found seats in the 300 level behind home plate. At almost midnight (after the crowd enjoyed watching an obviously intoxicated Phillie fan dancing between each inning on the walkway separating the 200 and 300 levels), the side scoreboards at the Vet flashed the message, "Last SEPTA trains leave at 12:00." A mild frenzy swept the crowd as people quickly had to make up their minds whether they were in for the long haul or at least had a way home before daylight. Two of the remaining four of us—and an equal percentage of the crowd that was left, I'd say—made a run for the subway. I was the only one remaining in our group who had driven and I made it clear that I wasn't going anywhere until the second game was over. So only one of my friends, Jeff, and I remained for the duration.

At the end of game 1—which was quite boring and which the Phillies lost 5-2—there was an announcement made on the scoreboards: "Game Two will begin at 1:20 A.M." The crowd let out a cheer. Despite the fact that it was well-known at the time that the AL had a curfew and the NL did not, it just had seemed likely they would call the game and play it the next day. Fans were quite surprised.

For the second game, Jeff and I moved further down and were sitting in the front row directly behind home plate—just to the first-base side of the tunnel behind home plate used by the grounds crew. There were a lot of empty seats at that point. Plus, all the food stands had closed—I don't know what time that happened, but the few thousand of us left were hungry and thirsty, having to settle for sips of lukewarm water from the Vet's few (and generally unappealing) water fountains for sustenance. The upper deck and outfield seating areas were empty, as the ushers had corralled the die-hards into the infield area so they could relieve some of the security staff for the evening.

Regarding that Derek Bell issue, my friend and I helped the Phillies pitchers **STRIKE OUT*** Derek Bell twice and induce him to pop out as well. Well, at least that's how I remember it.... We led people around us in chanting "Derrr-rek, Derrr-rek,

---

*Between walks and STRIKEOUTS, Mickey Mantle went the equivalent of seven full seasons without putting the bat on the ball.

Derrr-rek" when Bell came up in the 4th with a man on second and Jose DeLeon pitching. This was about a year after the famous episode of "The Simpsons" where the crowd chanted "Darrr-yl" at a cartoon Darryl Strawberry, with Homer saying that he was a professional and wouldn't be bothered by it, while a single tear ran down Strawberry's cheek; so we had inspiration for our chant. "Derrr-rek" struck out and slammed down his bat. He was a noted hot-head even then, long before his famous "Operation Shutdown," and the crowd noticed his reaction to the strikeout. So when he came up again in the 6th with men on first and second and David West pitching, we got even more people to join in, and he popped out. When he came up in the 8th with a man on third and Larry Andersen pitching, it seemed that we had everyone in that whole section and more chanting his name, and he struck out again. So Bell left four men stranded, three in scoring position. Only one of them ended up scoring later in those innings, and that was on an error—and in that nightcap game (morning-cap game?), every run was crucial.

The Phils were losing 5-0 in the 4th, but they battled back to tie it in the 8th. Jim Fregosi had used his whole bench. In the bottom of the tenth with one out, Pete Incaviglia on second, Jim Eisenreich on first, and Mitch Williams due up, Fregosi let **WILLIAMS*** hit for himself. And if you remember seeing the game (or, more likely the highlights later), you'll know that Mitchie-Poo poked the ball to the outfield and Inky hustled around to score the winning run. The crowd went crazy. I had this feeling that we were almost part of the team. For one thing, I don't know that I was ever in those front row center seats before. For another, with the crowd gathered so close, it felt almost like we were part of a movie set, where they only needed people close to the plate for the shots of the batter. Also, the

---

*__PITCHER__ Terry Forster has the highest career batting average for players with over one hundred at-bats....his batting average was .397.

Phillies responded enthusiastically to the crowd, since there were so few of us left and we had stuck it out. I still love seeing highlights from that game.

Most of us there realized we were watching something we'd remember forever. There was a mix of fans in the crowd, including even parents with sleeping kids, but I'd say a large percentage were people like my friend and me—single guys in their 20s who stayed there because we could and because it was such an unusual night. Each time a new hour was reached, a bell rang the time—two rings at 2:00, 3 at 3:00, and 4 at 4:00. Later, when I saw the highlights, I heard **RICHIE ASHBURN**'s* great line to Harry Kalas as the clock struck two: "This is the shank of the evening for you, pal."

Oh, and as has been widely reported, the crowd actually increased in size during the second game. Apparently the Phillies had the broadcasters say that the gates were open and people were invited to come down and watch the second game for free, and when the bars let out at 2 a.m., that's exactly what several hundred or even a couple thousand people did. I always admired the Phillies for that, because they weren't making any money on it as parking would have been free and all the concession stands were closed.

That was the most (or at least the second-most!) memorable night I ever had at a Phillies game.

***RICHIE ASHBURN** once hit the same fan twice with foul balls in the same at-bat.

FOUR PORT-A-POTTIES...NO WADING

Rob Goldman

Goldman is a Philadelphia native and lifelong Phillies fan transplanted to Northumberland, PA. where he is the Program Director/Morning show host for Eagle 107 (WEGH-FM). He has lived all over the state, from Clarion to Stroudsburg to Honesdale to Sunbury to Northumberland. Rob attended his first Phillies game at the Vet in 1971 and made it to at least one home game every year through the World Series championship in 2008.

We decided when Schmitty got inducted into the Hall of Fame, that we'd go up for the ceremony because it isn't that far from Pennsylvania to Cooperstown. I work in radio so I got media credentials for that induction ceremony when Schmitty got in along with Richie Ashburn.

They had a string of port-a-potties out there at Cooperstown. At one point, I walked over, did my business, and when I came out the only person standing there was Harry Kalas. There was no one else around. He was easy to recognize—everybody knew Harry. So I said hello, and he reached out and shook my hand and asked me how I was doing. We walked back together to where the media were sitting by the stage. I asked him if he was going to be introducing either Richie or Schmitty. He said, "No, they both asked me to, but it doesn't work that way for baseball." He just said it in that voice that you get used to hearing. We BS'ed about where I worked for a few minutes, then we shook hands again, and he went his way and I went my way. It just made my day and it was, maybe, a five-minute conversation. Like it says in the book *Remembering Harry Kalas,* he is your best friend as soon as he sees you.

My family was lucky enough to be in the stands for Mike Schmidt's first home run. We went to Pittsburgh for his 500th career home run. It was spring break of my senior year in college. I went to college about an hour north of Pittsburgh and my parents came to visit. We were trying to decide what to do the next day. While we were listening to the Phillies play the Pirates on KDKA in Pittsburgh, Mike Schmidt hit his 499th home run. All three of us looked at each other and decided that he might hit his 500th the next day, so why don't we go to the game?

We drove down to Pittsburgh and got tickets behind third base at Three Rivers Stadium and actually sat in the row right in front of Mike's college roommate—a real nice guy. Schmidt hit his 500th home run in the ninth inning. We saw him hit his first and his 500th home runs in person. I'm sure the odds of that happening are astronomical. It was pretty cool, too, that it was just a spur-of-the-moment thing to go to the game.

But how I first saw Mike Schmidt is a better story. On September 16, 1972, my family headed off to Veterans Stadium for a Phillies game against the Expos. Now, usually when we went to the ballpark we purchased general-admission tickets, since they were inexpensive, and our family of four could enjoy the evening without feeling like we had to cut costs elsewhere.

However, for whatever reason, my dad was able to get us reserved seats in the 300 level at the Vet. We were psyched; they were by far the best seats we had ever had for a ballgame at the Vet, and since they were in the lower level, we had a fair chance of catching a foul ball, at least better than when we were high up in the 700 level.

As we were heading into the ballpark, a Philly police officer was giving us all a very long look when we turned off Pattison Avenue to walk up the ramps. I remember thinking my dad had done something wrong; maybe parking on Darien Street wasn't such a good idea after all. It turned out that the police-man had tickets for four *box seats* that he wasn't going to be able to use, and his wife had instructed him to try to find a fam-ily that would be able to use those tickets, but would *not* run onto the field or cause any problems. I guess we looked like that family, so with a little trepidation (this couldn't be legiti-mate, could it?), Dad made the trade for our existing tickets, and we walked into the Vet from one of the lower entrances.

> ...my favorite Phillies player was third baseman Don Money...

Instead of turning to walk *up* the ramps, a Phillies hot-pants girl led us *down* toward the field. We kept getting closer and closer to the Astroturf, getting more and more excited, until we couldn't go any farther. We were in the *front* row! We could touch the rain tarp! We could easily get autographs from our favorite players! It was a dream come true for all of us, and we settled in ready to soak it all up. Now, back in those days my favorite Phillies player was third baseman Don Money...I was all of seven years old so I thought his name was very cool. However, when we saw the starting lineup on the scoreboard for that night, I saw that instead of starting my Money man, the Phillies were start-ing some guy they had in for a September call-up named Mike Schmidt. I was a little disappointed, since these seats were so close to third base and someone we'd never really heard of would be playing there instead. So I turned my attention to getting as many autographs from both teams as I could. I remember one of the first guys to come over to our seats was the Expos' Ron Hunt, who gladly reached out to grab my base-ball glove and a pen. As he signed his name to it he told me, "Now don't go losing this glove at the playground." We all had a nice chuckle, and I felt so good to get his autograph that later I collected as many of his baseball cards as I could.

Not long after that, my mom noticed that we could walk not far from those seats and be close enough to the dugout that we could call in and see if a player might come out to sign an auto-graph. She saw that Schmidt guy at the corner of the dugout. Mom said, "He's playing for Don Money tonight, maybe he'll sign your photograph of Money." So I shyly walked over toward the dugout and somehow got Mr. Schmidt's attention and asked if he would come over to sign something. When he got to me, I said, "My favorite player is Don Money and you play the same position. Would you please sign Don Money's name on the picture?" I remember a warm smile, and Schmitty said, "I'll sign *my* name on Don Money's picture, I hope that's okay." I must've just shrugged my shoulders, and after he signed it I walked back to my parents and told them what had happened. We all had another laugh, although I was quite embarrassed about the whole thing.

That night Schmidt hit his first major league home run against the Expos' Balor Moore, and I became a **MICHAEL JACK SCHMIDT*** fan for life. I've often wondered if Mike remembered that exchange or ever told anyone about it.

Do you know the difference between B*rry B*nds and government bonds? Government bonds mature.

*In 1977, <u>MIKE SCHMIDT</u> was the first baseball player to earn $500,000 a year. The first player to make a million dollars a year was Nolan Ryan in 1979. The first player to earn $100,000 a year was Hank Greenberg in 1947.

Quick Hits and Interesting Bits

When I was a kid, my father was assistant golf pro and worked at Williamsburg Country Club. The owners of the TV station that broadcast the Phillies at the time, was FOX. They would give out tickets to the people there so we always got seats behind home plate, like 326 at the Vet, right above the concourse, right behind home plate. We would get a lot of foul balls. My friend Frank would be with me, or my mom would take my sister and me. Mike Schmidt was my favorite player.

I always wanted to get a foul ball. We probably got to go to 15-20 games a year. We were always right there, and I would see people all around us getting one. ...but mostly, I wanted a foul ball from Mike Schmidt.

One time we were there, Schmidt fouls a ball back coming right at us. It comes up over the net and heads right for my mom who is sitting next to me. I was thinking, "My mom is actually going to catch a foul ball from Mike Schmidt." The darn thing hits her right in the chest—dead on in the chest. She goes down like she got shot. The ball bounces out on the concourse, and somebody else gets the ball. Of course, I'm upset because first of all my mother's creamed, and secondly because I didn't get the foul ball.

Then we had to go to the first-aid station. There I am with my mother, as she's getting her chest tended to. She had a huge welt—the whole nine yards. She goes home, and the next day she says, "I'm going to see if they'll send us a ball from Mike Schmidt." She knew I was heartbroken because she dropped the ball.

She wrote a letter to the Phillies, "My name is Mary Jane Wheeler. I was at the game with my son and tried to catch a foul ball, but I got hit and had to go to the first-aid station—if you think I'm making this up, you can check the medical records at the first-aid station. Because the ball was from Mike Schmidt, we'd really like an autographed baseball from Mike." We didn't hear anything for weeks.

A month or two later, there's a knock at the door. I opened the door. I'm a huge Phillies fan so I know all the Phillies. It was Ron Roenicke, the outfielder for the Phillies. He said, "I'm Ron. I'm from the Phillies. I wanted to drop this off for you." There was a large envelope and inside was a ball signed by Mike Schmidt. I'm like "Wow!" There was a note from the Phillies inside saying they were sorry about everything and that they hoped this would make up for losing the foul ball. Of course, my sister and I fought over this ball, but I actually do have *the* ball they sent over that was signed by Schmidt.

My mother will probably not be thrilled that I'm telling that story considering the fact that she got hit in the boob with the ball.

—**Andy Wheeler**, 34, Wallingford, PA

It is such a meaningful part of my life—my dad teaching me a love for the game of baseball. He passed away recently so the memory has special meaning.

My Dad would take me to Connie Mack Stadium in the 60s. It was in a run-down area in North Philadelphia, and the stadium was deteriorating badly. Attendance was down, and the stadium was lacking the proper repairs, but it was an old, intimate stadium, the kind they never replicate now but instead replace with all the retro stuff. I remember going to the game and smelling the popcorn and peanuts and seeing that grass when I walked in and being spellbound by it. I was six years old. My dad took me to a number of games at Connie Mack, and between innings he explained the strategy to me—why this guy tried to steal and all the other things that went on. It was great bonding because he instilled in me everything I loved about the game. October 1, 1970, was the last game at Connie Mack and the place was packed. They weren't drawing many people, but on this day it was a full house. It was really exciting. Afterward, the fans were just destroying the stadium. Anything that could be removed, people did. My father even removed a couple of seats and took them with us when we left. It was just crazy. I asked if we were allowed to do this, and he told me, "Sure." It was probably dangerous, but it just captivated me. People were tearing apart everything.

He then took me to the first game of the following year in the new Vets Stadium. I was so impressed at how big and modern it was. But something was missing, and it was that there was no real grass. It was just more sterile.

The last game played at the Vet was in September 2003, 33 years later. Tickets went quickly and I couldn't get one. But my friend was able to get one for me. So I called my dad and told him, and he asked me why I wasn't taking him because he took me to the first game at the Vet. That made me feel really guilty. So, I decided I needed to work it out. I got a single ticket, but we wouldn't be sitting together. But at least we went. I was telling my friend at the game the story about how Dad had taken me to these other games, and it was sad that we couldn't be sitting together, but he was still just happy to be there because we were lifelong Phillies fans. All of a sudden, someone tapped me on the shoulder and said that one of his friends couldn't show up so he had an extra ticket. He said they would shuffle around in the section, so that I could sit with Dad. I called my dad on his cell phone and he came up and we were able to sit together. That was really nice because he taught me how to love the game, and we had now come full circle. He had taken me to the first game at the Vet and it was now my turn, as I was able to take him to the last game.

—**John Lennon**, 49, Business Intelligence Software Sales

I will always miss Veterans Stadium. I'll miss the 700 level. Cheering for the Phillies with my friends in the 700 level was so much fun. The tickets were cheap, the food was average, but the atmosphere was awesome. You can't explain it to others who didn't experience it, but it was awesome. I miss it to this day, even though Citizens Bank Park is a great, great, great place to watch a game. The Vet was Philly. It embodied what Philly was about. Coming in to play the Phillies, you had to bring it. I was sad when the stadium was torn down, though I understood why and everyone understood why. The cats and rats under the ballpark scared so many people. We were like, 'Cool, where are they?' I remember the great Phillies teams at the Vet, most notably from 1976-80. In 1980, my memories are really clear. I was 16 years old and I had just gotten my driver's license. I drove to a number of games in September and five or six of my friends would pile in the back of the car. We had a blast. To be 16 again and rooting for the Phillies. Life was great. We went to as many games as we could. I remember one game where Mike Schmidt went deep twice and the second one was a mammoth shot to left-center field. I couldn't believe he hit the ball that far. The place exploded with cheers. The Phillies fans banded together so well. We knew it was time. And it was. I had tickets to one of the playoff games against the Astros that year. You couldn't take your eyes off the game for one second because you would miss something. I went to the bathroom, came back to my seat, and my friend told me everything that I had missed. I heard the place roaring while I was waiting in line for the bathroom. I stopped drinking soda after that because I didn't want to miss another thing. When they won that series, we knew they were going to bring home the World Series trophy. I skipped school to go to the parade as did many of my friends. I remember one friend whose parents wouldn't let him skip school to go to the parade. He was so upset. Looking back, they should have let him go. It took 28 years to win another World Series. While the 2008 World Series was amazing, I'll always have a special place in my heart for 1980. Maybe because I was a teenager having fun, but it was so much fun. I have a number of DVDs that we watch all the time. That 1980 team got me hooked and I've been a Phillies fan times 100 ever since. Seeing this crop of players like Rollins, Utley, Howard and Hamels is cool. I think they can multiple World Series titles. I hope so, anyway.

—**Ben Leron**, 46, Mount Airy...construction worker

I was at the opening of the Vet back in '71 when they played the Expos. It was incredibly cold. There were four of us. I was attending Cornell Law School—class of '72—and we drove down from Ithaca for the game. We met up with a guy I knew from Villanova Law School. We ended up two rows from the top of the stadium in foul territory on the right field side. We were way at the top. It was so cold and windy, especially in that 700 level. They delivered the very first ball into the stadium by helicopter. It flew in from over the top of the stadium and across right field and then hovered above second base. It was probably a little bit higher than us. Mike Ryan, a reserve catcher, was standing at second base. They were supposed to drop the ball; he would catch it and take it to the home-plate umpire. Ryan's standing there at second base and the ball was dropped. It probably came straight down about 30 feet. Then it started to move directly to third base. Ryan had to sprint between second and third, but he caught the ball. Bunning started that game. The weather was cold, windy, and miserable the entire game.

I watched a doubleheader on TV in 1976 that was pretty interesting—at least the entertainment was. I was back in South Jersey at that time. It was the game at which **KARL WALLENDA*** walked across that wire foul pole to foul pole. It was unbelievable. I could swear someone was playing that song either at the stadium or on TV about how "You'll Never Walk Alone." As Wallenda got very close to the end of the walk, I noticed that there was a woman waiting and holding something. Wallenda gets done and this woman has a full martini waiting for him. He then comes down, and during the second game, Ashburn brings him into the broadcast booth with Saam and they talk for a little bit. Bill Giles was in the booth. Wallenda is holding on to his martini glass. He turns to leave and you hear a loud sound. Saam begins talking again and Ashburn says he can't believe it, but the Great Wallenda tripped and fell over one of the broadcast cables on the way out.

At one point during the walk, there was a slight swaying of the wire. There were, apparently, 20 or 30 people on the stadium floor holding guy wires to stabilize the cable. One of these people had a panic attack and let go. Wallenda bounced a little bit but was okay.

> ***KARL WALLENDA**, the patriarch of the family fell and was killed in San Juan, Puerto Rico on March 28, 1978. The 73-year-old was walking on a cable strung between two hotel towers when he fell.

I grew up in South Jersey, Pennsauken. My high school girlfriend and I used to go to Phillies games. You could catch a bus in New Jersey that took you to and from the game. You had to always bring a coat with you—not for the game—to put up against the windows on the bus because the people in North Philly would throw things at the bus. This was not so much on the way to the game, but always on the way back from the game. The bus would eventually go diagonally over to Lehigh Avenue, and that's where it got very frisky.

—**David Hughes**, 62, originally from Pennsauken, NJ, retired government attorney

One day when Allen Iverson was a 76er he and Aaron McKie were granted permission by the Phillies organization to take a little batting practice. Aaron was a very good baseball player at Simon Gratz High School. I knew Iverson was also a tremendous football player but I wasn't sure about his baseball talent.

The batting cage was set up earlier than usual so these hoopsters could take a few swings. Members of the ground crew were standing around the cage waiting for the two to come on to the field. I am a huge Iverson fan, so I could hardly wait to see him.

They both came out of the dugout with bats in their hands. I don't know what the NBA lists as Iverson's height, maybe 6'1" or 6'2". Well let me tell you: I'm 5'6" and Iverson was maybe only a few inches taller than me. Amazing. That little son of a gun is one tough athlete. At 150 pounds, the pounding he takes while going to the basket and his strong will to bounce back up is really incredible.

As far as the BP session was concerned, it was obvious that McKie had played some baseball. He made some solid contact, while Iverson tried to kill the ball with most of his swings. He did connect and hit a few deep though, although none out of the park.

—**Mark Carfagno**, Phillies groundskeeper for 33 years

The Cardinals were playing the Phillies one weekend. Kids used to always wait around the press gate to watch the players come out. They didn't have the big charter buses in those days; they had the old kind. The players were coming out that Sunday—Joe

Cunningham, Red Schoendienst—and I'm getting autographs. Stan Musial comes out and is signing autographs. There must be 100 kids there and he just keeps signing. The bus driver was telling him they have to go catch a train at North Philly station about a mile from the ballpark. **STAN MUSIAL*** says, "Go ahead. I'll walk." He walked all the way to the train station signing autographs. He had a whole bunch of kids following him down Lehigh Avenue, across Glenwood to the train station, and off he went. You just won't see that today.

Eddie Matthews was the first player I ever saw hit a home run. It was in 1954, and the ball hit the light tower and came back into the ballpark. I couldn't understand how that was a home run but my dad explained it to me. It was interesting at Connie Mack Stadium because they had a corrugated steel fence. When a ball hit it, about a half second later, you'd hear this big boom. First you'd see it hit and then you'd hear it.

—**Walt Stankus**, 63, retired

Jim Brosnan's book *The Long Season* came out before *Ball Four*. Literary-wise, it's a much better book. In the book he talks about the Phillies third baseman, Willie Jones who was there for almost 10 years. It was 1959 and our whole family was at the ballpark. I would be going away to college the next year and my sister was only a couple of years behind me so I guess my dad figured we should do something as a family—so he took us all to a game.

Willie Jones was traded to Cleveland, then a few weeks later was traded to Cincinnati. We were at a Saturday afternoon Phillies game when they were playing Cincinnati. Willie Jones comes to the plate. It took him an such an extra long time to get up to the plate that we couldn't understand what was going on. He's being given a standing ovation. *The prodigal son returns!* Well, later, when I read Brosnan's book I understood—*he was*

***STAN MUSIAL** hit 19 home runs as a grandfather in 1962. When he retired in 1963, he had every Cardinal batting record but one—highest single-season average. That was set by Rogers Hornsby....Hornsby also holds the highest single season batting average for the Braves and the Cubs.

crying. He couldn't hold back the tears for the standing ovation from the Phillies fans.

I was at the game when Steve Carlton got his three thousandth strikeout. Usually you don't feel sorry for the opposition, but I felt sorry for those guys. They had no chance. The first inning Carlton needed three strikeouts to get 3,000...he got them in the first inning! Tim Wallach was the last one. It wasn't even fair—I don't think anybody could have hit him that inning.

In the old ballpark, there was a guy who was a beer salesman. He drove a taxicab during the day and sold beer at the games at night. By doing this, he was able to put his kids through college. If you asked him if the beer was cold, his answer was always, "It's as cold as my mother-in-law's heart." The first year at the Vet, he was there. We remarked, "There's that guy with the cold-hearted mother-in-law," so we ordered a beer from him and asked, "How's your mother-in-law treating you these days?" He said, "That woman just won't die."

—**Fred Shimer**, 68, Lancaster County, PA,
retired high school librarian and bartender

I was at the last game in '81 before the players went on strike, That was the night Pete Rose got his 3,630th base hit to tie Stan Musial for the all-time NL lead. I was also there at the Vet two months later when the players finally returned and the Phils played the Orioles in a 7-inning exhibition game which Phillies won 4-3. The thing I remember most about that night was the game was technically over after 6 1/2 innings with the Phils up 4-3, but the teams decided to play the bottom half of the 7th frame because both teams needed the work.

I was also there in the first official game after the strike ended and watched Pete Rose break Musial's record with a ground single to left off Mark Littell of the Cardinals. The big, old right field message board had the numbers 3,630 in a big, bold font. Then watched it change to 3,631.

Also in that bizarre, strike-shortened season, I went to Game 5 of the NL Division Series against the Montreal Expos. I watched Steve Rogers outduel Steve Carlton in a 3-0 Expos' series-clinching win. Rogers helped himself with a two-run single, I believe. Somehow, I sat in a seat a few rows behind the Montreal dugout and happened to be in the row in front of actor Donald Sutherland, a huge Expos fan who was scoring the game. There was also a small group of Expos fans nearby who kept getting on my nerves by chanting "MVP" every time Andre Dawson came to bat. Mike Schmidt would get the MVP that season with 31 homers & 100-plus RBI. These numbers were better than Dawson's that year. That's what I should've yelled at those Expos clowns.

I watched my first game from one of the business suites at the Vet sometime in the late 80's. I was the only fan in the box that night. I still vividly remember Von Hayes hitting an inside-the-park homer off Nolan Ryan. But what stuck in my mind though was the absolute indifference shown by the other people in the box. An inside-the-parker is one of the most exciting plays in baseball and most of the "fans" in that box just looked up momentarily to see what the commotion was. Apparently they weren't impressed because they went back to eating their appe-tizers and talking shop. I remember seething inside as to how people can go to a sporting event and not care what was going on. I would always fantasize about owning my own stadium and only allowing people in if they passed a sports IQ test. There would also be NO private club boxes. That would be my way of saying that you're there to watch a game, not conduct business!

Also, I remember a Phils-O's game at Baltimore in either 2004 or '05 when the biggest crowd in the history of Camden Yards at the time—49,000-plus—was announced over the PA system and all the Phillies fans in the crowd rose and gave themselves a standing ovation.

—**Vince DiGregorio**, 51, South Philadelphia

In '75 and '76 the Phillies were getting better. Allen came back, and on Memorial Day weekend when I got home from college, Dad and I went to a doubleheader against the Cubs. Between games, the Great Wallenda walked across the tightrope with-out a net. That was something. I had binoculars and looked into the dugout. Usually, the guys would go to get something to eat between games but not this day. They were all watching the Great Wallenda.

People made fun of the Vet—like it being a big concrete bowl—but you never had to worry about getting tickets, even for the playoff games. In '03 we went to one of the last games at the Vet. The Phillies were in the hunt for the wild-card with the **MARLINS***. We were in the upper level so we had to walk down to our seats. They had expansion blocks that allow the stadium to expand a little bit because of the concrete. My wife started down and saw a space, but she didn't realize it was an expansion space and that the drop is from the third row to the first row. She fell against the wall right in front of the front row, and everything she had flew down over the wall. Luckily they got everything back to us—her hat and everything she was holding. I don't think I could have been a baseball fan anymore if something bad had happened to her there.

—**Mark Kanter**, Portsmouth, RI

It's late August 1964...and the times are good for the Phightins' or, as Mets announcer Bob Murphy liked to call them, "The Men of Mauch." While the Phillies were in Pittsburgh for a weekend series, something or some things happened in North Philly to create a race riot. That Friday night (August 28) Bunning went into the 9th with a 2-0 lead, but one thing led to another and Pirates' pinch hitter Smokey Burgess hit a walk-off homer to give the Bucs a 4-2 win. The term "walk-off" was not used back then.

That "Go Phillies Go" team was still comfortably in first but, oh, how we would learn later that every loss would be.... especially one in which the Phils seemed to have the game won. Anyway, for a 14-year old, for his father, and a family friend the weekend was a fun time, as we stayed in the same hotel (the Pittsburgh Hilton) used by the Phillies...and we got

---

*The Florida **MARLINS** have won the World Series twice but have never won their division—the NL East. The Marlins are the only team that travels north for spring training.

plenty of autographs! The next day game (Saturday afternoon) the Phils held off the Pirates 10-8. And that night in a Hilton elevator a **PHILLIE*** rookie OF, Danny Cater, carried an early edition of one of Pittsburgh's dailies. Cater looked quickly at the standings. Realizing that despite winning that afternoon the Phils remained six games in first place, Cater remarked to someone in the elevator, "We didn't gain anything."

—**Dick Mangrum**, 60, radio announcer, Seneca, SC

One of the great events at the Vet occurred on Sunday, August 13, 1972, before a crowd slightly in excess of 32,000. Karl Wallenda, then 67 years old and the head of the world-famous family of high-wire artists, walked a two-inch-wide steel cable stretched from foul pole to foul pole—200 feet above the field. There was no net below the wire and, balancing with a 40-pound pole, Karl walked the 900 feet successfully. The next day sportswriter Ray Kelly wrote about Karl Wallenda's feat in the *Philadelphia Evening Bulletin*, including the comment, "It's a good thing he didn't fall, or the fans would have booed him all the way down!"

During my business career I have lived in cities featuring the New York Mets, the Atlanta Braves, and the Chicago Cubs. A number of time I have been listening to local sports talk radio in these towns when callers were berating the Philly fans that "boo everybody" and "throw snowballs at Santa Claus." I have been successful a number of times in calling into these shows and relating the Ray Kelly story. Each time, the story brings a laugh from the host and usually defuses the false statements about Philadelphia sports fans.

—**Maurie Kring**, 73, Chester Springs, PA

*The **PHILLIES** hold the record for using the same nickname for the longest time. They have been the Phillies since joining the National League in 1883. In early years, the name was sometimes spelled 'Fillies.' Also, the team was sometimes called 'the Quakers' or 'Red Quakers' because of the Quaker heritage of Pennsylvania and the red uniforms the team wore. Early twentieth-century owner Horace Vogel tried to change the team's name to Live Wires. From 1911 to 1930, the team was sometimes referred to as 'the Phoolish Phillies.'

Chapter 3

FANDEMONIUM

Open the Gates and Open Them Wide, Phillie Fans Are Coming Inside!

WE CALLED THE CLINIC ABOUT CHARLES BARKLEY'S CASE...THEY SAID HE'S OVER HIS SHYNESS

CHARLES BARKLEY

Charles Barkley, a former All-Star forward for the Philadelphia 76ers, Phoenix Suns and Houston Rockets, is currently an NBA analyst for Turner Sports. There are four players in NBA history who have compiled at least 20,000 points, 10,000 rebounds and 4,000 assists: Kareem Abdul-Jabbar, Wilt Chamberlain, Karl Malone and Barkley. The outspoken player, who was known as "The Round Mound of Rebound," will forever remain one of the most popular sports figures in Philadelphia sports history.

I've always said that Philadelphia is a fantastic city to play in. There are just a few knuckleheads and nitwits who act out and give the city a bad reputation. The fans, for the most part, are great. You saw that with the Phillies in 2009 and the two seasons before that when they started this run. The fans packed the ballpark every night and really gave them a home field advantage. I was really, really happy for Jimmy Rollins, Ryan Howard, Chase Utley and Charlie Manuel among others for winning the World Series in 2008 and then coming so close again the next year. They have given the fans a team to truly be proud of every day. They have a chance to win every day. The fans are into it and they are given great baseball to watch every day.

I remember spending some time with Jimmy Rollins in New York shortly after the Phillies won the World Series in 2008. He was taping a segment for a show with Bob Costas. You know, Jimmy is like me—outspoken and honest. The fans respect him for that. I think they can relate. Jimmy is the catalyst and the engine that makes that team go. I was really happy for him because I know he had to overcome some adversity. He played great in the World Series and was huge in helping to get the Phillies that ring.

Watching the parade was something. I felt so proud for the Phillies organization from Mr. Montgomery and Mr. Giles on down the road. They all did a great job. The team was put together perfectly and now has multiple chances to win. You could see how happy the fans were. Some people were crying and some were even throwing flowers. There were grown men crying like babies. It had been so long. I know how I felt—if I had more talent around me, we could have won. I got to Phoenix and we came so close when we lost to the **BULLS*** in the Finals. But I had plenty of talent around me. You can't do it alone. You look at the Phillies and you see talent everywhere—up and down the lineup, on the bench, pitching staff—even to the front office. It's a team.

The fans in Phoenix and Houston were tremendous. In Philadelphia, they're probably more passionate, which leads to those few knuckleheads who pop out from time to time. Those Philly fans helped carry the Phillies in 2008. Every night, that ballpark was jumping. It was electric. It was alive. Having them win the clinching game at home was even better. I just felt a major sense of pride for the entire city. I have so many friends in the city of Philadelphia and they deserved it. They deserved all of it. It was great to see.

Being a star athlete in Philadelphia is not easy, but I think the Phillies stars have done a great job.

---

*In 1994, the White Sox recalled **MICHAEL JORDAN** from Double-A Birmingham to play against the Cubs in the Mayor's Trophy Game at Wrigley Field. Jordan singled and doubled against the Cubs.

CRAIG'S LIST

Craig Crotty

Craig Crotty, 68, has retired in Falmouth, Massachusetts. He grew up on a farm listening to the Phillies and any major league baseball game he could find on his old Motorola radio.

Most Phillies fans of my age, when they talk about baseball cards, they always talk about the early **TOPPS*** sets...in their quest to get the Mickey Mantle card. Mickey Mantle was not my quest in those cards because we learned early on he was impossible to get. Three cards we were really trying to get were a Yankee bonus baby first baseman named Frank Leja, Chicago Cubs outfielder Hank Sauer and Granny Hamner, the Phillies shortstop. We would buy dozens and dozens of packs of Topps baseball cards trying to get Granny Hamner and Hank Sauer.

Finally, one day, I had a plan. My parents were away for the day, and I decided I would borrow an idea I'd seen from the comic strips—that was to set up a lemonade stand. I went down to the basement, got a frozen can of lemonade, thawed it out, mixed it up, made a cardboard sign, took a card table and a seat and went down to a corner where two gravel roads intersected near this farming community.

About twenty minutes later, the first vehicle came by. It was a tractor driven by an old farmer named August Stender who was taking a load of grain to the mill. He saw my lemonade

*In the early 1990s there were over 8,000 sports collectibles stores. Primarily because of eBay, there are now fewer than 2,000.

stand and stopped. He jumped off and said, "I need some cold lemonade." I said, "Well, August, today's your lucky day." Then he saw the sign I had made up. The sign said, "Lemonade. All you can drink for one dollar." A bottle of Coca-Cola went for a nickel in those days. My goal was to make one dollar because if I had one dollar, I could go into town to the B&F Grocery and buy a whole carton of Topps baseball cards. I knew for sure that if I did that, I would be able to get the Granny Hamner card. August stopped, hesitated, pulled out his wallet, gave me the dollar and drank about a half glass of lemonade and left. I quickly took the card table, the sign and the leftover lemonade back up to the house one quarter of a mile away. I rode my bike into town to get my carton of baseball cards. I got the carton, but...once again...absolutely no Granny Hamner or Hank Sauer cards. About three days later, my father came looking for me—as irate as heck—and said, "Hey, young man, you need to give August Stender his dollar back." I said, "Why? I had a deal that was all the lemonade you could drink for a dollar. I've already spent the dollar." Of course, he knew what I had spent it on. I just got a good strappin' in the meantime. Today, I could have him arrested for child abuse.

When we grew up, we would go to the ball diamond every spare moment we had and play ball until dark. We didn't need coaches, umpires or soccer moms yelling at us or yelling at umpires. My kids grew up, went to Little League practice, threw the ball ten times, swung the bat ten times and went home. **LITTLE LEAGUE*** has ruined baseball.

Furthermore, in those days, we'd appreciate the one baseball game a week we might be able to see on TV. We all remember the first time we got TV in our house when we'd get up early in the morning to watch 'test patterns.' Our parents may not have liked our music, but they listened to it nonetheless.

---

*The only member of the Rock and Roll Hall of Fame and the Little League Hall of Fame is Bruce Springsteen.

Maybe once a year, we'd be able to get a ride on a train. When we eventually started dating girls, they didn't dress like tarts, and we treated them like ladies. My sons will never know any of those things

Remember how we used to get the *Famous Slugger Yearbooks* at sporting goods stores? They were put out by Hillerich and Bradsby, the Louisville Slugger people. In the fall, we'd get the *Converse Basketball Yearbook* put out by the Converse Shoe Company. Both books were free and worth every penny.

I'm glad I was born when I was 'cause everything has gone to hell in a handbasket lately...I weep for the future. The worst things that have happened to baseball are Bud Selig and Donald Fehr. How the media keeps giving these two guys a free ride is totally beyond me. Selig has screwed up everything from the '94 World Series to the All-Star Game to contraction to expansion to player salaries and, perhaps, worst of all, the total destruction of baseball records. The day Brady Anderson hit his 50th home run was the day that all baseball records became meaningless.

Under Selig's watch, drugs have become rampant—steroids, of course...salaries have gone through the ceiling...records have become worthless. The only thing his supporters have to say is, "But, attendance has gone up." Why wouldn't attendance have gone up? Since I was born in the early 40s, the population of this country has tripled. There are twice as many Major League teams as there used to be. There are more games being played every year—eight more every year by each team. Selig has brought in so many gimmicks that it's going to turn into the World Wrestling Federation pretty soon. Gimmicks like interleague play and the wild card. Another gimmick we can look for him to come up with is something like free beer, naked cheerleaders, and the Beatles singing during the seventh-inning stretch. We've turned the whole thing into a circus with no concern for the records or traditions of the game.

What does the commissioner do all day long anyway? *Seriously*, what does the commissioner do all day long? I don't think he does anything. He doesn't even hand out the fines. He doesn't punish the players. Selig gets paid $14 million in basic "hush money" as I like to call it. He's a total "stooge" for the owners and is one of the worst things ever to have happened to baseball.

Then, he had to embarrass the game further before the congressional committee on St. Paddy's Day in 2005 when he sat there and said that he had never heard of steroids until July of 1998. Well, in 1995, he was quoted in *The Sporting News* as saying he wanted to convene a special meeting of the owners back in 1992 to discuss the looming steroid problems. The most galling thing about Selig is his continual ignorance of the drug-testing in this country. Until they start testing for HGH, the human growth hormone, they have NO drug-testing policy. Who are they trying to kid with this malarkey that they maintain that they have this terrific policy? They say there is no such test—guess what, there is. It's called a blood test. Just ask the WADA (World Anti-Doping Agency), they've been nailing people in the Olympics with steroids since the 1980s.

> We used to get the *Famous Slugger Yearbooks* at sporting goods stores.

A friend of mine suggested that other than Mike Scioscia, there may not be a single good manager in Major League baseball today. I'm starting to think he's right. Why do managers use a five-man pitching rotation? It's absolutely stupid that you would take eight starts from your best pitcher and give them to your fifth-best pitcher. It's equally stupid to take eight starts from your second-best pitcher and give them to your fifth-best pitcher. Why would anyone take eight starts away from Roy Halladay and Cole Hamels?

The fundamentals in baseball today are so bad...so bad...that I'm not even sure they spend any time at all coaching these guys. There are only about five outfielders in the whole game who can throw hard and accurately. None can throw like Johnny Callison. Catchers have just about lost all sight of fundamentals. They don't block the plate anymore. They reach for balls coming in to home plate rather than waiting for the ball to come to them. Outfielders don't catch the ball over the proper shoulder....

You can call me an "old goat" if you want...and I am one—I'm old enough to be a greeter at Wal-Mart. But I love baseball the way it was when I was growing up—sneaking transistor radios in the school to listen to the World Series game, collecting baseball cards for fun—not as an investment—doubleheaders, the special "smell" of the new baseball magazines every spring.

They say that Barry Bonds has never flunked a drug test. Neither did Jose Canseco, Ken Caminiti, or Jason Giambi. You would have to be a blind moron to believe that Bonds was not on drugs. This is not a court of law. This is a court of public opinion. In the court of public opinion, the first three witnesses are logic, history and common sense. Bonds and Roger Clemens will never survive...and where did Clemens find that sleazebag attorney?

Another thing I don't understand is the pitch count. Supposedly we have a pitch count to protect pitchers' arms. But, in reality, the pitch count discourages the development of a strong arm. Walter Johnson, **BOB FELLER*** and Nolan Ryan never had pitch counts. Look at how hard they threw and how long they pitched, and they never had a sore arm. The only way to develop a strong arm is to use it a lot. If you want to protect pitchers' arms, outlaw breaking balls in youth leagues. Even Little League has a pitch count now. When we were young,

---

*Between his junior and senior years at Van Meter (Iowa) High School, **BOB FELLER** struck out 15 St. Louis Browns in a regular season game. Two years earlier, Feller's catcher in American Legion ball was Nile Kinnick, the 1939 Heisman Trophy winner at Iowa.

we'd throw the ball two or three hundred times a day…and these kids have a pitch count. We're developing a nation of wusses. Let's give every human being in America a blue ribbon and a certificate suitable for framing so they don't suffer from low self-esteem. In 1974, the Red Sox were playing at the California Angels—Nolan Ryan versus Luis Tiant. The Angels won in fifteen innings 1-0. Luis Tiant pitched the first fourteen innings for the Red Sox, and Nolan Ryan went all the way for the Angels. That night Nolan Ryan threw 235 pitches, and it ruined his career…because nineteen years later, he had to retire.

One final thing, it is very hard to watch the baseball scores on *Baseball Tonight* on ESPN. ESPN keeps going further downhill every year. I don't know who hires the people up there, but he has to be a jock sniffer. Half of his announcers are ex-athletes who butcher the King's English and have horrible voices for television. But, the worst thing is the music/noise they play in the background during interviews or while giving scores. That violates every principle of communication. Why would you have an anchorman talking and put noise behind him—not only "noise" behind him, but loud noise behind him. It's flat-out stupid. They must have a bunch of kids running that place.

I mean all of this is a positive way, of course.

Go Phillies!

Jamie Moyer cried all during "Jurassic Park." It brought back childhood memories.

PHILLIES FEVER?
NO CURE!

John D. Cantwell, M.D

Dr. John D. Cantwell grew up in Wisconsin, adopting the Phillies as his team during the time of the Whiz Kids. When the Braves moved to Milwaukee from Boston in 1954, Dr. Cantwell switched allegiances to the Braves. He has been the Braves' team physician for the past 35 years and was Hank Aaron's personal doctor. He has done extensive research on the Whiz Kids and their careers and lives following that magical 1950 season.

Heroes, unlike mentors, are often viewed via a child's perspective and from a distance. As William Oscar Johnson once wrote, "they have feet of neither gold nor of clay, but only of flesh." As such, they face the same obstacles we mortals do—bad habits, interpersonal and financial problems at times, aging, and ill health—and often emerge less heroic in the process, but sometimes even more so, as in the case of Philadelphia Phillies pitcher Jack Brittin, who successfully battled Multiple Sclerosis for 38 years.

I was interested in a follow-up on the heroes of my tenth year, the 1950 Phillies. What had become of them, over a half century after their playing days? What health problems have they encountered? How many are still living?

Like the Atlanta Braves of 1991, the Phillies had electrified the baseball world that year by emerging from the cellar to challenge for the National League championship. The "Whiz Kids", as they were called, won on the last day of the regular season. Robin Roberts won his 20th game and rightfielder Dick Sisler hit a dramatic home run in the 10th inning.

Although the Phillies were a relatively young team, many were been battle-tested war veterans. Leftfielder Del Ennis had been in the South Pacific. Reserve catcher Stan Lopata had won the Bronze Star and the Purple Heart. The third catcher, Ken Silvestri, won three battle stars and a Bronze Star in the Pacific. Pitcher Jocko Thompson, a paratrooper, had fought in the Battle of the Bulge. Twice wounded, he won seven battle stars, a Bronze Star, and a Silver Star. Reserve outfielder Dick Whitman was also in the Battle of the Bulge. Jack Brittin had taken part in the invasion of Okinawa.

To find out what had become of the Phillies, I met with Richie Ashburn, their Fall of Fame centerfielder, at the time of our meeting a Phillies broadcaster. Ashburn was generous with his time, very friendly and candid, still radiating heroic qualities 45 years after our first meeting, which he had autographed a ball for me.

I also met with Sharon "Babe" Talley, the daughter of the shortstop Granny Hamner, who was born in 1950. In addition, I communicated with Dean C. Paul Rogers of the SMU Law School, who had written a book about the Phillies in collaboration with Robin Roberts, the Phillies' other Hall of Fame player.

I was especially interested in the whereabouts of Mike Goliat, the second baseman, who had disappeared from my radar screen after the 1950 season.

The catcher, Andy Seminick, was a 30-year-old veteran in 1950. The youngest of ten children of a coal miner, Seminick left the mines at age 19 to pursue a baseball career. A tough guy, he played the last part of the 1950 season with an ankle fracture.

After his playing career ended, Seminick worked as a coach, manager, and scout in the Phillies organization. He retired in Melbourne, Florida and kept involved with the Florida Tech athletic programs until his passing in 2004. Their baseball field is named after him.

The first baseman was Eddie Waitkus. In 1949 Eddie had been shot by a deranged 19-year-old woman who had lured him to her hotel room in Chicago under the pretense that she was from his hometown and had an important message to deliver. The bullet passed through his chest and lungs and lodged near his spine. The woman did have sense enough to call the front desk for help. Five operations were required. Thanks to vigorous offseason rehabilitation, Waitkus played in 154 games the following year and hit .284. He was never quite the same health-wise. He subsequently worked as a floor manager in a Massachusetts department store and married one of the nurses who had cared for his gunshot wounds. He died of abdominal cancer at age 53. His shooting inspired Bernard Malamud to write *The Natural*. Robert Redford starred in the movie.

Willie "Puddinhead" Jones, the third baseman, was a "charmer", said Ashburn, "but you wouldn't want him marrying your daughter". Jones had spent three years in the Navy, returning to baseball in 1946. A power hitter and a good fielder, he had a solid career with the Phillies and later went into automobile sales, living in Cincinnati. He died of throat cancer at age 59. He had been a cigarette smoker.

The shortstop, Granny Hamner, was tough as a street kid who "might have been in prison if it hadn't been for baseball", laughed Ashburn. The Phillies captain, Hamner was a "cocky firebrand who battled and clawed every step of the way." He had signed a bonus out of high school in 1944, at age 17, and was soon inserted into the Phillies lineup.

Hamner became an instructor and a coach in the Phillies minor league operations after his playing days and was considered an excellent judge of baseball talent. A drinker and a smoker, he died of a heart attack at age 66.

The leftfielder, Del Ennis, was a native of Philadelphia, where his father worked for the Stetson Hat Company. Ennis had been an all-state fullback in high school. As the cleanup hitter for the Phillies he his .311 in 1950 with 31 home runs and 126 runs batted in.

Ennis owned and operated a bowling alley in Jenkintown, Pennsylvania after his playing days, and invested well. He also raced greyhounds, naming many for his Whiz Kids teammates. He lost a leg due to diabetic complications. He also had a family tragedy—his wife (his childhood sweetheart) hung herself, as had her mother. Ennis died of a bleeding ulcer at age 70.

Richie Ashburn, the centerfielder, was nicknamed "Putt Putt" by Ted Williams, who observed that he ran "as though he had twin motors in his pants." Ashburn was 23 in 1950, and in his third season. He played twelve years for the Phillies, was an All-Star for four years, won batting titles in 1955 and 1958, and was one of the handful of Phillies to have his number (#1) retired.

Richie was voted into the Hall of Fame in 1995. He worked as a Phillies broadcaster and also as a sports columnist for the *Evening Bulletin*. He developed insulin-dependent diabetes at age 50. A torn rotator cuff limited the tennis, golf, and squash that he enjoyed for many years. He had planned to retire at the end of the 1997 season, but died of a heart attack three weeks prior.

Dick Sisler, the rightfielder, was the son of hall of famer George Sisler. His father was the Dodgers' head scout and instructor in 1950 and was at that final game when Sisler belted his three-run home run in the tenth inning to give the Phillies the National League title.

Like a number of his teammates, Sisler had been a Navy veteran. In 1950, he batted .296, hit 13 home runs, and knocked in 83.

After his playing days, he coached for several major league teams and managed the Cincinnati Reds for a season and a half in the mid-1960s. Dick passed away in 1998 at the age of 78.

Robin Roberts was the Phillies' "stopper" throughout his career, the man you wanted on the mound at the most critical times. He grew up in Springfield, Illinois, where he was a three-sport star. One of six children whose parents had immigrated to the United States from Wales, Roberts played basketball at Michigan State and was once voted the top college player in Michigan.

Over a 19-year career, he won 286 games and made the All-Star team seven times. He is a member of the Hall of Fame. Extremely durable, he once completed 28 straight games—unthinkable in the present era.

The crucial last game against the Dodgers in 1950 was Roberts' third start in five days. It was his sixth attempt at reaching the coveted 20 wins in a season.

At age 41, Roberts attempted a comeback with the Phillies, but he had lost much of his legendary ability by then. He became a stockbroker and a color commentator on the Phillies' home radio network and wrote sports columns for the *Wilmington News-Journal*. In the mid-1970s, he became the head baseball coach at the University of South Florida, a position he held for eight years. Robin purchased a golf course with Curt Simmons in the Philadelphia area and retired to Tampa to work on his golf game year-round. On May 6, 2010, Robin passed away in his sleep. He was 83.

Curt Simmons, the star left-handed pitcher, was a native of Egypt, Pennsylvania. As a schoolboy, he pitched his American Legion team to two state championships and once struck out eleven Phillies in an exhibition game in his hometown. In 1947, when he was 18, the Phillies signed him to a $65,000 bonus—at the time a considerable sum. In 1950 his season was twice interrupted by military obligations yet his record was an impressive 17-8. He missed the end of the season as well as the World Series against the Yankees, which turned out to be a critical loss for the Phillies.

In 1953, Simmons lost part of his left big toe in a lawnmower accident, which may have affected his performance momentarily, but he did make a comeback. His record was 18-9 in 1964 and he pitched in the World Series that year for the Cardinals. His 20-year big league career ended in 1967.

Curt presently lives near Ambler, north of Philadelphia.

The National League's Most Valuable Player in 1950 was the Phillies' relief pitcher, Jim Konstanty. He appeared in 74 games. An all-around athlete while at Syracuse University, Konstanty lettered in soccer, basketball, boxing, and baseball.

Jim mixed speeds well on his pitches and had a great slider and palm ball, as well as excellent control. His personal pitching coach was an undertaker and neighbor, Andy Skinner, who caused the regular coaching staff some chagrin when he came around, but was generally effective in straightening out Konstanty's mechanical problems at the time.

Konstanty owned a sporting goods store in Oneonta, New York for many years and was also a minor league pitching coach for the Cardinals and Yankees. For four years he served as athletic director at Hartwick College in Oneonta.

He retired at age 59 and died the next year of lung cancer. He had never smoked, nor had he used alcohol to any extent. The funeral director for his final service was none other than his personal pitching coach and friend, Andy Skinner.

The manager of the team was Eddie Sawyer, a former science professor at Ithaca College. At Ithaca he had been a football halfback and an excellent student. Sawyer had been described as "dignified, scholarly, tolerant, unflappable, witty, and tough, when necessary." A shoulder injury had limited his own career.

He lost some of his magical touch after the 1950 season. Seminick and Sisler were traded in 1951, when the team finished in fifth place. Midway through the 1952 season they were mired in sixth place when Sawyer was replaced by Steve O'Neill. He did return as the Phillies manager in 1958, but quit after the first game in 1960, saying that at age 49 he "wanted to live to be 50."

He later worked as a distributor for the Plymouth Golf Ball Company and died in 1997 after a brief illness at the age of 87.

And what about Mike Goliat? The least well-known of the Phillie regulars, the second baseman was also the son of a coal miner from Pennsylvania, one of nine children. He had injured his knee the day before the Phillies called him up from their AAA farm team. He agreed to have it x-rayed only when the team doctor promised to let him play irrespective of the findings.

Goliat hit 13 home runs in 1950 and had 13 game-winning hits. His performance trailed off shortly thereafter. He had married during the 1950 season and perhaps due to his wife's good cooking was 25 pounds overweight when he reported to spring training the following year. He was sent down to the minor leagues and was out of the major leagues by 1952. He subsequently went into the trucking business and passed away in 2004 at the age of 82.

Goliat was unavailable when C. Paul Rogers tried to interview him for his book on the team. I tried to contact him by telephone, but his number was unlisted. I did manage to get his address and wrote to him, but never received a reply.

On September 9th, 1997, Richie Ashburn summoned the Phillies trainer at 5:30 A.M. because of chest pain. By the time the trainer and his paramedics arrived, Richie was dead from cardiac arrest.

In reflecting on his life, I recalled a lot of fond memories, including an incident late in his career when he was with the hapless New York Mets. The Venezualan-born Mets shortstop would periodically collide with Ashburn on fly balls to short left-centerfield. Ashburn decided to shout "I got it"—in Spanish. The next occurrence he did so again, hollering "Yo lo tengo." The shortstop veered off at the last moment, but Ashburn was flattened by leftfielder Frank Thomas. Thomas didn't speak Spanish and the ball dropped for a double.

Fanecdotes

Am I a Phillies fan? How can I be a Phillies fan—I worked for the professional basketball franchise in Philadelphia on two occasions for 13 years.

Am I a Phillies fan? Ok, Maybe...

In high school my friend Bob Mounce and I played Babe Ruth and high school baseball together. When we turned 17 and got our driver's licenses we signed up for a Phillies' season ticket package. We were there for the 1976 **ALL-STAR GAME***. We were behind home plate when Tug threw the final pitch in 1980. I can't remember for Bob—but I had a Phillies yearbook and program collection—before memorabilia was an art form. The Phillies were a huge part of our lives. How many 17-year olds have season tickets—of their own?

Predating our season tickets—I'd ride my bike to Keen's Pharmacy in Avalon—everyday—arriving just before the fire whistle blew at noon. Noon was an important time—that's when the *Daily News* arrived. No truck, just a guy with newspapers in his back seat. And I couldn't wait to read Bill Conlin's coverage of the game that I listened to the night before on the radio. I followed everyone of Steve Carlton's 27 victories in 1972 through the eyes of the King of the World.

I was active in photography in high school and college. I had no idea what PR was, but Larry Shenk was a God. Especially the day that he gave me a photo pass to shoot in the dugout. Me. In the Phillies dugout. I had died and gone to heaven. When I ended up in that field after college—I always made room for someone to "get a shot" just as Larry Shenk did for me. I've also credited Larry Shenk as the person that I tried to emulate. And I got to Larry because of my love of baseball and the Phillies.

*Relief pitcher Jeff Shaw represented the Dodgers in the 1998 **ALL-STAR GAME** even though he had never pitched for the Dodgers at that time.

The best part of working for the 76ers (the first time around) is that our offices were in the Vet. We had a door near our kitchenette—open it and you're in right field. From April to October I'd take my lunch (late) and sit in right field and watch batting practice. Is there any better way to spend an hour on a sunny afternoon? Ok, it was great even if it was cloudy.

My wife knows that she shares my love—with the Phillies. She's OK with it. She even facilitates it. For one birthday she sent me to Dream Week. My biggest dream wasn't the games, although they were pretty cool—it was being invited to dinner with Larry Bowa, Dallas Green, Lee Elia, The Bull, Terry Harmon. Are you kidding me? They wanted to ask me questions about Allen Iverson—forget basketball—tell me about 1980. I had to excuse myself from dinner for a minute. I had to call Bob Mounce on my cell. After all, I had to tell someone who would appreciate it as much as me. We celebrated my 50th birthday (my entire family) at **DODGER STADIUM*** watching the Phillies defeat the Dodgers in the NLCS. Best birthday I've ever had.

I could go on, and on but let's just end by saying—I have a Zenith circa 1940 tube radio in my home office where I listen to the Phillies on WCMC out of Wildwood. No better way to spend a summer night.

So yes, I guess that I'm a Phillies fan.

—**Dave Coskey**, VP of Marketing Borgata Hotel Casino & Spa
& The Water Club and former President of Comcast-Spectacor

I was working at a radio station WCOJ in Coatesville when I was just out of college, in 1999. I didn't get to do many cool things—just go out doing regular stories and regular news. I was trying to do as much sports as possible. I get something in the mail from major league baseball containing an application

*DODGER STADIUM—since the day it opened in 1962—is the only current stadium that has never changed its seating capacity. Because of a conditional use permit from the city of Los Angeles, the capacity is always 56,000....Fenway Park's seating capacity is lower for day games (36,984) than for night games (37,400).

for credentials for the All-Star game being held at **FENWAY***. I was thinking, "Wow!" I said to the general manager, "Do we have any interest in this?" He said, "No." I said, "What do you mean—you don't want to send me to the All-Star game?" He said, "Why would I want to send you to the All-Star Game?" I said, "Do you mind if I go on my own?" He said they wouldn't pick up any of the expenses. 'Course I was right out of college and had no money, but I decided to go on my own.

I found the creepiest old hotel in Boston—a Norman Bates type. I stay there. I had all my media credentials for the weekend. The one thing I see is this All-Century team press conference. They have all 100 living members of the All-Century team coming in and answering questions from the media. Everybody is up on the podium, and it's the whole official thing. I couldn't believe I was actually there. It was my first experience as a fan being in a media situation where I had access.

It was amazing to me to actually be there seeing Willie Mays, **TED WILLIAMS***—all these guys. They say, "Okay, everybody. The press conference is over. We're going to break off into a side room where you can interview all these guys individually."

I'm so in awe. I get my tape recorder thinking about who I wanted to talk to. They were all there. I'm looking around and seeing all these guys...but, across the room, I see Mike Schmidt. He must have held court for about 20 minutes while I'm standing there like a star-struck teenager holding this microphone and just staring at him with what I would assume would be puppy-dog eyes. I'm listening and listening, and I asked him a question... and he answered. I think my question was, "Of all the shortstops

*Matt Damon and Ben Affleck made their movie debuts in 1988 as extras in the **FENWAY** Park scenes in *Field of Dreams.*

*Ted Williams and his son John Henry are among 161 frozen bodies world-wide awaiting a cryogenic rebirth...157 are stored in three U.S. facilities...The two Williams men are in Scottsdale, Arizona...In real life many are cold, but few are frozen.

in the game, which would you have wanted to play with?" He answered my question, and I said "thanks" and shook his hand.

I walk out and I call my dad, "I just met Mike Schmidt! I just met Mike Schmidt!" He thought it was amazing. Then... he asked where I was, and when I told him, he said, "Who else did you talk to?" I said, "What do you mean, who else did I talk to?" He said, "You mean to tell me you were in a room with Ted Williams and Stan Musial and Reggie Jackson and all those great guys, and the only guy you talked to was Mike Schmidt." You could hear my mom laughing in the background. I just couldn't help myself. It was the fan in me at that time.

—**Andy Wheeler**, 34, Producer, CBS 3

I have always been a Philadelphia fan, but my senses perk up when it involves either the Phillies or the **EAGLES***. The latter can wait until another day.

I'm not sure if this was my first game, but it sure stands out in my mind. We were a little late getting into the Vet because the line to get $5.00 walkup tickets was longer than my Dad expected. Then we had to climb the serpentine ramps to the upper deck. But what awaited at the top is something I'll never forget. There was a loud roar coming from within the stadium. I had no idea where our seats were but I sprinted through the tunnel to stand at the rail. Everyone was standing and cheering and on the field all I could see where two outfielders laying flat on their backs and with the ball at the feet. And dashing around the bases was Bake McBride. It is still the only inside the park home run I have ever witnessed but it's one I'll never forget.

Many other games followed at the Vet but Game 2 of the '80 World Series was perhaps the best experience. An experience that

*Jim Castiglia was a running back for the Philadelphia **EAGLES** in the 1941 season, then abruptly quit in 1942 to play for the Philadelphia Athletics. Over three years, he played in just 16 games, but he got seven hits in 18 at-bats for a lifetime .388 average, mostly as a pinch hitter. In 1945, Castiglia returned to the NFL, where he played for the Eagles, the Colts and the Redskins.

wouldn't have happened if my dad wasn't as passionate about getting the tickets as he was. He was one of the many that stood in line for hours when they won the NL pennant. When things looked bleak, he heard someone inside the Vet say that there was another ticket booth that had no line but it was inside the building. Not knowing if it was true and figuring it was his only shot to get tickets for us he scaled the fence along the serpentine ramps to get inside. Sure enough the passerby was correct and my Dad came home a hero with right field upper deck tickets to Game 2. The specifics of the game are a blur now but I clearly remember cheering the entire time. I was, and still am, ecstatic to be in attendance to one of the most thrilling events in Phillies history.

As a kid, collecting baseball cards was a rite of passage, a passion kids today just do not understand. Yes they have their Pokemon cards, but those are fictional characters. We felt like we had a real connection to the players of our time. I remember meeting up at my friend Eric Resnick's house and biking to his neighbor who had mystery bags of cards for a $1.00. I can't imagine letting my kids go do that today as our innocence is gone. What fun we had trying to save up for our favorite player's rookie card. Even better was getting it in a pack from 7/11, not to mention enjoyment by chewing the hard stick bubble gum while flipping through the cards.

Being left-handed I was fortunate enough to be able to pretend to be the greatest pitcher in Phillies history, Steve "Lefty" Carlton. I envied him as a player. His quirky off field preparation and uncanny way of striking out any batter was something to see. His hot pursuit of most wins and strikeouts for a lefty was something as well. His nemesis was Nolan Ryan. But there was all of it. I loved it all. Never in a million years would I think I would ever meet him. Well at a builder show in Atlantic City a few years back, I did just that. Not only did I meet him but I got his autograph on a mini-Phillies helmet. What a nice guy. It was small talk but talk nonetheless. Now, my autographed helmet sits in my son's room waiting for its rightful place, the man cave. Someday little helmet, some day.

—**John Marshall**, 40, architect, Haverford, PA

My earliest memory that is crystal clear is from 1972, the year after the Vet opened. I was 10 years old and I went to the game with my Mom and Dad. I was stunned by how cool it was to actually be at the ballpark. I was hooked from there. When we moved as a family to Newark, it wasn't that tough because I would never, ever lose my passion for the Phillies. I go to about 10 games a year and it's the best. When we go down to the Shore in the summer, there are a ton of Phillies fans. We'll be on the beach with our radios playing, eating food and enjoying our families. It's not quite the same without Harry Kalas, but the Phillies broadcast team does a phenomenal job. On a hot summer day in July, eating lunch, playing in the ocean and hearing a friend say, "Utley just went yard!" Or "Howard went deep!" Or "Rollins made a great play at short to preserve the inning!" Oh boy, that's incredible. My two children are huge Phillies fans. In this family, it's all Phillies all the time. A lot of their friends are Yankees fans or Mets fans. We won't have any of that in this household. No way. No how. You will be a Phillies fan.

—**Sue Terapo**, 48, Newark, NJ

October 13, 1993. October 29, 2008. I still have the ticket stubs. The memories of those two evenings in South Philadelphia will last a lifetime. Two different ballparks. The former clinching a pennant, and the latter clinching a world championship. My seats for each game were the same—terrible. But I was in the house (barely), and there was nowhere I would have rather been to see two of the greatest Phillies wins ever.

My dad worked six days a week, with his only off-day being Sunday. My first recollection of the Phillies is going to the Vet every year on a Sunday and sitting with my parents and my two brothers in the 300 level, always down the right field line. My mother was the Vice President of the "Whiz Kids" Fan Club, so as a young boy I knew all about Robin Roberts, Granny Hamner, Eddie Waitkus, Willie "Puddin' Head" Jones, Jim Konstanty, and the throw that Whitey Ashburn's supposed weak arm made to strike down Cal Abrams of the Dodgers at the plate in the bottom of the 9th on the last day of the 1950 season, leading to Dick Sisler's home run in the top of the 10th to win the pennant. I was 11 when they beat the Royals in 1980, and while I remember **TUG*** parading down Broad Street with the "We Win" edition of the Daily News, I don't remember the day-to-day odyssey of that baseball season.

—**Jay Green**, Attorney, 41, Lafayette Hill, PA

As a kid, my favorite player was Mike Schmidt. He was doing a baseball card signing at a mall somewhere, though I can't exactly remember where. I stood in line for a very long time and brought up my Schmidt card and asked for an autograph. You know how some players won't even look up? Well, he looked up, asked my name and chatted with me for a few minutes. He was so honest and sincere and you could see it in his eyes. When I left there, I was just beaming for weeks, months on end. He's a Hall of Famer and he treated me like a friend.

There was another night where I was at dinner at a Center City restaurant and across the room was Juan Samuel. I hate bugging people during dinner. Before I left that night, I wandered over and told him how much I liked his style of play. He asked me to sit down. Me! I did and he ordered a drink for me. It was like a surreal moment. We talked about 30 minutes. I shook his hand and said, "Thanks." What a memory. That doesn't happen every day. It was so cool. Juan was a true gentleman just like Mike Schmidt. I have such fond memories. Looking back, and when I tell people, I realize how rare it is. Juan was the best. I was so happy when he got inducted into the Phillies Wall of Fame. He deserved it. What I remembered was that night at a restaurant where he went above and beyond the boundaries of niceness. He was awesome.

—**Xavier Coyle**, 47, State College, PA, independent contractor

---

***TUG** McGraw got his nickname from his mom because of the "aggressive" way he breastfed. McGraw's famous comment was, "Ninety percent of my salary I'll spend on good times, women and Irish whiskey. The other 10% I'll probably waste."

As a rookie with the Sixers, I threw out the first pitch one night before a Phillies-Giants game. That was really cool because I grew up as a Phillies fan. It was a thrill to be on the mound at the Vet and throwing the ball to the catcher. I obviously love basketball and made it to the highest level in the NBA. I have always liked baseball as well. I watched all the Phillies games as a kid and went to a lot of them, too.

I remember the 1993 team very clearly. I really liked Lenny Dykstra and Dave Hollins. I just liked how they played the game. They played hard all the time. My coaches in basketball taught me that from a young age and that's how I've played basketball—one way and that's hard every possession in practice and in the games.

Being a professional athlete, I have a lot of respect for what other players go through. It's not easy being a professional basketball player or a professional baseball player. I really admired what the '93 team accomplished. They had a lot of heart.

Years later, I had a chance to talk to Lenny Dykstra and he told me how the chemistry was huge. That team just had IT. They had intangibles, and in professional sports, that's as important as anything. That conversation was fun for me, and I understand now what Lenny meant. If you have good team chemistry, you can go a long way.

—**John Salmons**, Milwaukee Bucks, Plymouth-Whitemarsh H.S.

My most memorable Phillies moment is October of 1980. The Phillies had just beaten the Astros in five games in one of the greatest NLCS in MLB history. Manny Trillo had won the NLCS MVP. In that Game 5, he made one of the greatest relay throws of all time and had a clutch triple.

At that time, my dad was working as the Assistant Ticket Manager for the Eagles whose office was located in the Vet. We had tickets for Game 1 of the **WORLD SERIES*** versus the Royals. I was visiting my dad in his office the afternoon before that

*The last **WORLD SERIES** game not played at night was in 1987.

game. I would walk out of his office to watch the teams take batting practice.

As I walked out the door which opened into the hallway in the Vet, I literally ran into Manny Trillo as he was heading down to the clubhouse. Needless to say, I was blown away and the timing was unreal. We shook hands, and he could not have been nicer. I didn't wash my hand for a week.

—**Rob Ellis**, Sports Talk Show Host for 610-WIP & Senior Producer for Comcast SportsNet

I don't remember the date of my first Phillies game. I don't remember the opponent. I don't remember who won. But I will never forget that first sight of the wide expanse of green. That first glimpse you got when emerging from the tunneled entrance into Veterans Stadium. Every summer of my life: sunshine; freshly mowed lawns; and Harry Kalas and the Phils on the transistor radio playing in the yard.

My first autograph was from Tug McGraw, who was my favorite player during my childhood, and who I continued to admire throughout his too-short life. Tug had just been traded to the Phillies, and folks were still trying to figure out this "screwball." Tug was on the cover of *Sports Philadelphia* magazine, and I happened to be the Bond Bread girl in the advertisement just a few pages in. Tug signed the cover of "our" magazine. It's still a treasure.

—**Nancy Scheuer Hill**, 44, Swarthmore, PA

I arranged to interview Richie Ashburn for the Whiz Kids book in Houston during an Astros-Phillies series in 1994. We met at his hotel at the Galleria and in the course of interviewing Richie, I asked him how long he planned to continue to broadcast the Phillies' games. At this juncture he had more than 30 years in the broadcast booth. He told me that the travel was really wearing on him, but that he thought he would really miss doing the games, so he hoped to work a few more years. Then he said to me, "You know, I don't want to end up like Don Drysdale, dying in a hotel room somewhere." Sadly, that is exactly how Richie met his end, suffering a fatal heart attack about three years later in a New York hotel room after doing a Phillies-Mets broadcast.

—**C. Paul Rogers III**, Professor of Law and
former Dean, SMU, Dallas

From the 2010 Phantasy Camp in Clearwater, Florida

Chapter 4

PUT ME IN COACH

The Plays of Wine and Rose's

UP THE DOWN'S STAIRCASE

Rex Hudler

Rex Hudler had a major league career that spanned thirteen seasons and six teams, and included a stopover in Japan. Among his accomplishments is playing every position except pitcher and catcher. He finished his playing career with the Phillies in 1998 and was one of the voices of the Los Angeles Angels of Anaheim from 1999 through 2009. He lives with his wife and two children in Tustin, California.

The Phillies were looking for a right fielder who could do some other things in Terry Francona's first year. He had 13 rookies on the team, and he needed some leadership. He had Curt Schilling. They weren't sure if Dykstra was back or not. They needed another veteran, I'd had a good season, so I was one of their top free-agent signees. It turned out to be a bad thing for Lee Thomas, who lost his job over that because I got injured.

Let me tell you how the negotiations went—My agent, Arn Tellem, from Philadelphia, let me negotiate my own contract. Terry Francona was just coming off the third base coaching job in Detroit when he got hired. He called me himself. I talked to him and told him, "I'm 36 years old, and I don't want to finish up my career on a last-place team. I've never been to the play-offs, and I'd like to go. You're going to have to overpay me to come there." He offered me a nice contract and said he would call me back. He called me back and offered me $800,000 more than the Dodgers.

Here I was in LA with the Angels and didn't have to go far up the road to sign with the Dodgers who wanted me. I called Fred Claire, the Dodgers general manager at the time, and he told me they couldn't go up any higher. I said, "Okay, Fred, I'll see you opening day." The Phillies ended up playing the Dodgers opening day in 1997. I signed with the Phillies. I knew it would be a tough time, but I also knew what I was good at and that was mentoring young players, and I was good in the clubhouse.

After coming to Philly, I blew my hamstring in January. I went into the trainers' room and said, "Hey, I've got to show you something." I pulled my pants down and showed him that I was black and blue from my butt all the way down to my ankle. The guy goes, "Oh no!" I over-trained and tried to be somebody I wasn't.

Before that, Frank Coppenbarger called me and asked what number I wanted. I told him I wanted Pete Rose's old number if it was possible. Robin Roberts wore that number, 14, but they hadn't retired it. I asked, "How come it's not retired?" He said, "Pete Rose wore it last. You've got to be a Hall-of-Famer to retire it." I said, "Robin Roberts wore it." He told me they hadn't retired it yet. I think recently they have.

I had to call **PETE ROSE*** to make sure he was okay with me wearing that jersey. It was the first time ever I tried to call a guy like that. I got him at his restaurant in Florida...he actually answered the phone. I was shocked. I said, "Hey, Pete." I had met him before so he knew who I was. I told him I had just signed with the Phillies and had asked for his old number 14. I said, "What do you think? I hustle. I play hard like you do. I'm going to do it right." He said, "How many bases did you steal last year?" I said, "I led the team. I had 13 stolen bases with the Angels in '96." He said, "What did you hit?" I said, "I hit .317." He wanted my whole stats, and he said, "I don't mind if you wear it, kid, but there's not a lot of hits left in it." It turned out he was right during my year and a half I stayed there.

The interesting thing for me and Jennifer, my wife, personally was that we had a daughter, who was about two-and-a-half when we got ready to join the Phillies. Then two months before we got there, we had our first son, Jade, who was born with Down's Syndrome. After we got down there, we met with Jim Salisbury, the great sports columnist there for *The Inquirer*. I shared with him about my son. We weren't sure how it would affect us and didn't know anything about it. We were brand new at it. We just figured he was our gift, and we would take care of him. They had sent a photographer over to house where we lived in Newtown Square, Pennsylvania. The photographer was taking pictures as I was getting my son dressed.

> "Hey, Dutchie, I'm sorry, man. I don't mean to bring anything personal into the clubhouse…

We played about 12 games on the West Coast before we had our Opening Day in Philly in '97. The day we opened in Philly, there was a big article on the front page of *The Inquirer*. They used a picture they had taken at our house showing my son without a shirt. I was nuzzling him and cuddling with him. It was a real sensitive picture. It was an encouraging article. It talked about my son, and about me being a new player there for the Phillies. I didn't realize what it would mean, but I got tons of fan mail from fans all over the Philadelphia area. They encouraged me and my son, saying, "Hey, my kid's 16, and he's driving. " "My kid's educated. Congratulations on your son." It was really what I needed. So many people when they hear you have a child with a disability, they're bummed like, "Oh, I'm so sorry." I was offended by that. The last thing I expected was to come to Philly with the bad rap fans had there and get encouraged.

I was sitting at a picnic table in the middle of the locker room on Opening Day reading the letters. I was so touched that I couldn't help but weep. Sitting around me was Darren Daulton and Dykstra—a rough bunch of guys. I looked up and saw Darren Daulton looking at me as I was reading the newspaper. I said, "Hey, Dutchie, I'm sorry, man. I don't mean to bring anything personal into the clubhouse that shouldn't be in here. I'm sorry. I don't want to bring anybody down." He said, "Hey, what you have is real, man. We're behind you a hundred percent. Don't worry about it. It's your son. We know you're getting love mail and it's great."

Now, my son is 13 years old, and he's full of life so there's nothing 'down' about him.

That was my beginning in Philadelphia, and it ended up being wonderful—not from a statistical standpoint because of my injury both years. I didn't help them at all on the field, but I did help them in the clubhouse—that was my job. I got and gave encouragement and love and warmth. It was a good experience for me and for my family. The fans forgave me for not being the player they wanted. I had torn my hamstring so bad that it never came back playing on the artificial turf field.

It must have been God's plan for us to go there. Being there with Francona, his first two years as the manager—I'm better for that. I feel better that I got to play for a guy like him. I'm really proud and happy to see what he's accomplished since he's left Philadelphia. Someday I might get to go back to Philadelphia and work with the Phillies in some capacity. I know a lot of people, and a broadcasting spot might be open. I know how to teach the game. The main thing would be able to give back to the community now at this particular stage in my life. After the way they encouraged me, at a time when I really needed to be encouraged, it would be fun for me.

THE WONDER BOYS
GOT HIM WONDERING

Paul Rogers

Rogers is a law professor at the SMU School of Law, where he previously served as dean for nine years. He grew up in Wyoming and for some reason (probably the red pin stripe uniforms with the big numbers) he became a Phillies fan when he first tuned into baseball at age eight. His hero quickly became Robin Roberts, followed by Richie Ashburn and he followed the Phils religiously through the box scores (and still does). As an adult he lived a dream by writing two books with Roberts, The Whiz Kids *and the* 1950 Pennant *(Temple Univ. Press 1996), which gave him the excuse to meet and interview the living Whiz Kids, and Robin's memoirs titled* My Life in Baseball *(Triumph Books 2003).*

One of the highlights of my life was writing a book with Robin Roberts on the Whiz Kids that was published by Temple University Press in 1996. The way that book came about is interesting because Robin was always my hero as a kid. I grew up in Casper, Wyoming and am not sure why I liked the Phillies and why I picked him. I liked their uniforms with the red stripes and those big numbers. When I was 11 years old I got a letter out of the blue from Robin. Since he was my hero, that was a really big deal. I had a grandfather who lived in Jenkintown. He knew somebody who was close to Robin, and that's how it happened—putting two and two together. I wrote him back of course. I was 11 then, but it was 1992 when I contacted him again. From 1960 to 1992—that's

32 years. The **RANGERS*** were having an Old Timers Game. They had a luncheon at Arlington on a Friday, and one of my friends invited me to go, so I did. I had no idea who was going to be there. Bob Gibson was the speaker. So, I'm sitting at lunch in this big hotel ballroom and in walks Robin Roberts. I'd never been in the same room with him, and it was like I was 11 years old again. My palms were sweaty; I even lost my appetite.

After the luncheon, my friend who knew that Robin Roberts was my hero went up to him—I was too excited. He just said, "Mr. Roberts, my friend is the dean of the SMU Law School and you were his boyhood hero. Would you have 10 or 15 minutes to go have a Coke with us?" At that point, I somehow walked up. I was embarrassed. Robin said he couldn't right then because he had a tee time, but his wife was there, too, and they were going to be there tomorrow. He invited us to come out and have breakfast with them. So we did. We both brought our wives and went out and had breakfast with him and his wife, Mary. We probably spent about an hour and 45 minutes and it was really a lot of fun.

> I always thought when I retired I might write baseball books because I read a lot of them.

I always thought when I retired I might write baseball books because I read a lot of them. And a few months later, literally while I was in the shower, it occurred to me that I could try to write a book on the Whiz Kids because no one had ever written one. Now that I knew Robin Roberts, I could try to write one with him—like through his eyes, since he was on their pitching staff—that would be really cool. There were all these books on the Yankees and Dodgers but none on the Whiz Kids. I called

*Nolan Ryan, president of the Texas **RANGERS**, is the first Hall-of-Famer to be a club president since Christy Mathewson in 1925.

Robin up, as I had his home number, and he immediately said let's do it. I was kind of like the dog that chases the car and then catches it. I just thought, what do I do now?

Then I talked Robin into letting me write his memoirs with him, so I've actually done two books with Robin. The coolest thing was his wife, Mary, and how nice she was to me. She died a couple of years ago. But when she was alive, I got the biggest thrill because when I'd call she'd always visit with me and want to know how the kids were. They've stayed with me in Dallas, and I've stayed with them in Tampa a couple of times when we were working on the book. We got to be friends. He came out here and made some appearances and stayed with us. The best ever, though, is still my calls to Robin. Mary would usually answer the phone and want to check on us and the kids. Then she'd offer to get Robin. She'd always say, "Robin, it's Paul". Not "Paul Rogers" or "that guy from Dallas"—just "Paul." That always gave me the biggest thrill to be on a first-name basis with Robin. Like I was the only Paul.

> That always gave me the biggest thrill to be on a first-name basis with Robin.

There's another bizarre story. While I was working on the book there was a big card show in Philadelphia with a reunion of the '50 Phillies and '80 Phillies. That was in '93, and the poor promoter just lost his shirt. They had this huge weekend. Robin was there and it was a great opportunity to talk to a lot of the guys. I flew up and ended up interviewing Putsy Caballero and Ken Heintzelman. One guy that I really wanted to talk to who had been pretty unresponsive was Granny Hamner. He was a shortstop on that team and had sort of a rough streak. He was signing at this show, and there was a dinner for the players and dignitaries on Friday night that I was invited to. So I went to the dinner, and at the reception before the dinner, Bubba and Robin made sure that I met Granny Hamner. I'll never forget this. I was standing with Bubba, Granny, and Robin, and they told Granny that he needed to meet with me because I was writing this book. Granny said, "Fine, how about tomorrow at 11:00 at my hotel?" The promoter had players in hotels all over downtown. Granny was talking about his health with these guys. He recently had a checkup and the doctor told him he was healthy as a horse. He didn't quite understand it, because he was still smoking and drinking.

The next day I interviewed Putsy Caballero at 10:00 and, having Granny at 11:00, I race over to his hotel. Granny said just to call his room. If he wasn't there, he told me to check the coffee shop. I call the room and he's not there. I check the coffee shop and he's not there. So I fooled around and called the room again. Finally, I actually remembered his room number and thought I'd just go up and knock on his door. I went up and there was no answer. I heard either a radio or a television playing very low. That doesn't always mean that there is somebody in the room, but it does mean someone had been in the room. There was still no answer.

Granny was supposed to sign at the card show at 1:30. He was not known as dependable and didn't always show up. But surely, I thought, he'll show up at the card show because he's getting paid for that. I thought I could talk with him a little bit while he's signing autographs. I go to the card show and there's a line of people there that want him to sign, but he never shows up. Robin says Granny is probably on a bender and that he'll surface in a few days.

I flew home to Dallas that afternoon, and I'll never forget this. I was in my office on Monday morning and about 8:30 in the morning Robin calls. He says he found out why Granny never showed up—they found him dead in his hotel room. He was sitting in a chair probably waiting for me to come. I guess what happened was that shortly after I'd been there, housekeeping tried to get in but couldn't because the door was locked from the inside. They got security to open the door and they found him in there. He was 64 and had a heart attack. It was very bizarre. This was September of '93. The book was published in late '96. Some experience...

James Michener was Robin's choice to write the foreword for our *Whiz Kids'* book. Michener was a big Robin Roberts' fan and had dedicated his popular *Sports in America* book to Robin among three people. He also had pushed very hard for Robin's election to the Hall of Fame, which finally occurred in 1976. Robin asked me to contact Michener, who lived in Austin, so I did, writing a letter and explaining Robin's involvement in the project. After I received no response, I tried again. Still no response.

> Robin and I flew to Austin and took a cab to Michener's home to present him with a copy of the book.

Then Robin wrote him, to no avail. We knew that Michener was in frail health, so we finally decided he just was not going to be up to it. Our second choice was Pat Williams, vice-president of the Orlando Magic. Pat had been a childhood friend of Ruly Carpenter, son of Phillies' owner Bob Carpenter, and had often been in the the Whiz Kids' locker room while growing up. He knew and loved the Whiz Kids and readily agreed to the foreword.

One day well after I had Pat's foreword in hand, I received a manila envelope with an Austin return address. It contained a typed essay on Robin Roberts from James Michener. No cover letter, just the typed essay. Now we had two introductory pieces for our book. What could have been a problem was not, however. Mr. Michener had slightly misunderstood, and thought the book was Robin's autobiography. So his piece fit nicely as a tribute to Robin while Pat's essay was indeed an appropriate foreword for a book celebrating the Whiz Kids. So we happily used both.

When the book was published in late 1996 Robin and Andy Seminick flew to Dallas for a large book signing party three of my friends had set up at the Dallas Country Club. The next day Robin and I flew to Austin and took a cab to Michener's home to present him with a copy of the book. It was a very moving visit. He was undergoing daily kidney dialysis by that time.

He signed a *Whiz Kids* book for each of us and was delighted to see Robin one last time. Less than a year later, he made the decision to stop the dialysis and passed away.

"Garland them with timeless lilies!
Although they are a bunch of dillies
Who give honest men the willies
We still love them for their sillies
Hail, the Phillies."

A poem by James Michener written while on an airplane headed for Bangkok after he heard that the Phillies had won the 1980 World Series.

WHY CAN'T SUGAR BE AS SWEET AS HOWARD ESKIN?

Howard Eskin

Howard Eskin is a long-time radio/ television personality in Philadelphia. Eskin began at WIP Sportsradio 610 in August of 1986 and he has been going strong ever since. Over a storied career, he has always worked at various other AM and FM radio stations as well as television stations breaking sports news in the Delaware Valley.

I remember one day in 1981, the strike season, when Dallas Green just went off on the team. He was so mad at how they were playing. If you knew Dallas, he was trying to motivate them. We, in the media, knew what he was doing. It was intentional. I really remember this one day. The Phillies were the best team in baseball and probably would have won another World Series if not for the strike. Anyway, the Phillies had lost a few in a row at one point and Dallas was mad. So, one day after a loss, Jayson Stark asked the first question to Dallas in the manager's office at the Vet. Dallas was so mad that he said 47 ½ bleeps in one interview. I know that because I listened to the tape over and over and there was a half bleep at the end. I actually counted the bleeps and it was 47 ½. At one point, I started laughing because I knew what he was doing. So I walked out of the room, composed myself, walked back in and he was still bleeping. It was classic. The next day in the clubhouse, I brought my tape recorder and I was playing it for a lot of players like Pete Rose and Mike Schmidt. They were laughing. They got a real kick out of it. Once that was over, it was over. Dallas went back to his everyday self the next day. He was just trying to get them to play. But those bleeps I had that tape recorder for a long time. Somewhere, I might even have that tape, but I'm not sure. I'll never forget 47 ½ bleeps in one relatively short interview basically off the first question from the press. Dallas wanted to go off and he sure did.

Another thing about Dallas Green—many of the players didn't like him. **GARRY MADDOX*** didn't like him. Pete Rose really didn't care for him. But Dallas got them to play for him. He was a great motivator. To this day, I still say that Dallas Green is the best manager in Phillies history, even better than Charlie Manuel. That's not a slight on Charlie at all. I just think Dallas got them to play. Those players bonded together from the start and were cohesive as a unit. If not for the strike in 1981, the Phillies would easily have won another World Series. They were the best team in the first half and Mike Schmidt was playing at such a high level. They just had it. The strike happened and we'll never know just how good they could have been.

Since I've been covering the team for so many years and I'm around them every day, you have your run-ins with the players from time to time. I had a brief one with John Denny once in St. Louis. I had a fairly big one with Tug McGraw after some comments I made following the 1980 World Series season. I said Tug was getting too caught up into the celebrity circuit instead of becoming a better relief pitcher. Well, Tug was not too happy with my comments. He took offense to them and said I was way off base. Well, one day I get a telegram from the Singing Banana Telegram Company. This person in a hat comes and sings to me and sings, 'Bye, Bye Birdie.' Then I get a pie thrown in my face. The players laughed. It was from Tug. I guess it was his way of breaking the ice. We never had another problem after that. We had a great relationship from there on out. That

"He's really turned his life around. He used to be depressed and miserable. Now he's miserable and depressed." Harry Kalas, on **GARRY MADDOX.**

was his way of saying everything was cool. It definitely wasn't something you expect.

Then there was a time when Mitch Williams joined the Phillies. As you know, he was wild which is obviously where his nickname of "The Wild Thing" came from. Mitch wanted a three-year contract extension. I went on the air and gave my reasoning why I thought the years were too many. Money is money and that's fine, but I didn't like the Phillies thinking about three years. One day, Mitch approached me before a game at the Vet and asked me about it. I said, 'If I said something, I'll tell you. If it's accurate, I'll tell you that as well.' So he says, 'How about if I just punch you in the face?' I said, 'Go ahead. Let's go outside and you can take the first shot.' It was over the next day and forgotten about. The thing about Mitch was he was wild and he didn't have many clean innings. He rarely went 1-2-3. The next night against Pittsburgh, the Phillies have the lead and Mitch comes in the game. He gets the first two outs, then walks two and gives up a double and the Phillies lose. He says, 'I guess you're going to kill me now, huh?' I didn't kill him on the air. It was just my objective opinion based on how he was pitching. He just didn't have many clean innings and I said it. As a reporter and talk show host, you have to be honest sometimes and players don't like it. I can take that. As long as players come to me, that's all I ask.

Back in the day, Steve Carlton hardly ever granted an interview request. He just didn't. Had a line, "policy is policy." He almost always stuck to it. One time, I was getting some work for the Associated Press radio. I wasn't making a lot of money at the time. I walked up to Lefty's locker because he had pitched a one-hitter the night before. He said, 'policy is policy.' I said, 'Come on, Lefty, you threw a one-hitter. Plus, this is for a radio feed no one will hear.' So he granted the interview request for me. The next day, Bob Boone comes walking through the clubhouse and said he heard my interview with Lefty. So Lefty says, 'Howard, I thought no one heard it?' I didn't think they did. Anyway, he was fine with it, but it was ironic because he never granted interview requests. He wasn't that type of talkative guy. We went to Mike Schmidt, Pete Rose or Larry Bowa or others. Lefty was unique.

Lenny Dykstra was nuts. Wow, was he nuts. One time, I was playing with him on the golf course. You have to understand that Lenny played golf like he played baseball. He was intense and even a bit crazy. One time on the golf course, he had a 90 yard shot to the pin from the rough. He takes the driver out. I'm like, Lenny, "you can't use a driver here." But that was Lenny. He was crazy and nuts. He was smoking a cigarette on just about every hole. He was so fidgety with the golf clubs, like when he used to be with his batting gloves. He would take them off, put them, take them off, put them on. He was so fidgety and anxious all the time. It was the same thing on every golf shot. You were nervous and anxious playing with him on the golf course. It was something, though.

In Philadelphia, you tend to find more passion with the callers on my radio show. Now, I haven't worked in Boston, and we know how Red Sox fans are. The Phillies fans are passionate. They aren't always objective, which is why they're fans. Some are overzealous and many of them are knowledgeable. They just don't know how to be objective, so sometimes they get annoyed at me for being objective and honest about what I see.

John Felske wasn't a very memorable Phillies manager. The team was just terrible. He used to wear a toupee. He would rarely go out and argue with umpires. He never would get that crazy. I think it was because he didn't want his toupee to come off. It's funny what you remember, but I never remember him ever getting that crazy. I never remember that toupee coming off. He just didn't get into it with umpires all that much.

As a kid, I was a Phillies fan and I went to games at Connie Mack Stadium. My favorite player and my hero was Sandy Koufax. Years later, I got to meet Sandy Koufax. I was working the All-Star Game in 1985 getting live shots for Channel 3. An old friend of mine, who was a PR person for the Dodgers, set me up with an interview of Koufax. He didn't do many interviews, but he talked to me and he couldn't have been nicer. I got my picture taken with him after the fact, and it was an honor for me because he was a boyhood idol of mine. Sandy was a friend of Billy Cunningham's. One other time I got to meet Willie Mays. It was done through Mike Schmidt because they knew each other. Willie was so nice, too, and told stories. I never forgot that. Those types of memories are special because they really do take you back to when you were young.

Many people don't remember the all-around game Mike Schmidt had. He could hit home runs and everyone remembers that. One year, he was one stolen base away from the 30-30 club. People don't remember the type of speed he had and what a smart baserunner he was. He had a chance for steal No. 30 and Greg Luzinski was at the plate. Schmitty took off for third and had the base stolen easily. Well, Luzinski interfered with the catcher and was called out and Schmidt never got that 30th steal. That's how good Schmidt was. He adjusted all the time. If he wanted to, he could have hit for a higher average. He was paid to hit home runs and he did that extremely well. He was technically sound in the field, and he did everything so fundamentally sound. There are good third basemen who have played for the Phillies. But there hasn't been one as good as Mike Schmidt. If he's considered the best third baseman in Major League Baseball history, he has to be considered the best third baseman in Phillies history. Don't you think? No one did it better. Schmitty had all the tools offensively and defensively and he was a team leader.

There was another good story where without me, Ryne Sandberg would never have been a Chicago Cub and one of the greatest players in Cubs history. I was doing a show one night on an FM radio station in 1982. I called Larry Bowa in Seminole, Florida, during one of my commercial breaks. Bowa told me he was being traded and he went on the air with me to tell me of the trade which also included Ivan DeJesus and Keith Moreland. The Cubs loved DeJesus and didn't want him included in the deal. Anyway, Dallas Green was with the Cubs at the time. He went to the Cubs after leaving the Phillies. Both franchises were mad at me for going on the air and reporting the deal. So the deal doesn't take place and people are mad at me. Three weeks go by, and the Cubs decide to re-work the deal. They put Ryne Sandberg into the deal that involved Bowa like I originally had reported. If I hadn't called Larry Bowa during that one commercial break, and he hadn't gone on the air with me, that trade might never have happened. It took three weeks, but it did happen.

I remember another thing about Lenny Dykstra. I was down in Spring Training, and I went to talk to him. He had gained like 30 pounds. I said, Lenny, 'How did you get so big?' He said, 'Vitamins, dude.' He said it with such a straight face. That was Lenny. He was nuts, crazy...pick a term. There won't be many like Lenny. He was unique.

Through the years, I have covered so many good players through good years, great years and some very lean years like the John Felske era. I have always tried to maintain a professional relationship with the players. If they had a problem with me, they usually came and talked to me. Occasionally, like Charlie Manuel's dustup a few years ago—and I thought he planned it—they'll pop off. I treat people with respect. I say what I say based on professionalism and knowledge. They don't always agree, and that's fine. I don't have a problem with that. I try to give players and coaches the respect they deserve. In professional sports, it's a business. They have a job to do and so do I. Many times, after a player's career is over, and I'll see them, we'll laugh and joke and talk about a lot of things. I've made a lot of great friends through the years like Mike Schmidt, Pete Rose, and so on. There are so many players who have come through here. I know how fortunate I am to have worked for so many years in a job I really love.

THIS PHILLIES FAN IS FROM SAN FRANCISCO, NOT THAT THERE'S ANYTHING WRONG WITH THAT

Terry Daily

Daily, 67, was born in Wilmington, Delaware and grew up in southern New Jersey. He has been practicing law for over 40 years and was an assistant District Attorney in Manhattan prior to moving in 1976 to Santa Clara, CA to become a public defender and ultimately start his own private practice. Daily has been the mayor of Los Gatos, CA and coached youth baseball for nearly twenty years. His wife is also an attorney. They have three sons, all of whom played baseball growing up and one of whom is a presently head baseball coach at Menlo College in Northern California.

One of my earliest memories growing up was going to a Phillies game with my dad. I remember parking our car, walking up to the game, and a couple of young kids saying, "Hey, mister, want us to watch your car?" My dad would always say "Sure, yeah." He'd give them fifty cents—a big thing then. I remember asking Dad what that was all about—how come we do that. You parked on the street; they didn't have any special parking lots. "Son, you're basically paying security so that your car is okay when you come out of the ballpark. You need to give a little tip or something or when you come out of the ballpark your car could be sitting up on four milk cartons." I thought we were paying extortion money. Then he told me, "When you're leaving the ballpark and someone comes up and asks if you want them to wash your car windows, you want to always say yes. You want to give them a buck or so for whatever it was. You never know what can happen." I have to laugh—I hadn't thought about that for a thousand years. I don't know if I ever saw a car on milk crates or whether I envisioned it. That was one of my first memories. The park was in a nasty location with no parking, and a lot of people were afraid to go there. That's why they moved out to the Vet. You just learned that that was a part of what you pay to go to the ballpark. I don't remember anything ever happening to our car, but I do remember paying "protection" money.

This is a fun story. I have three sons. The two oldest both had their picture taken with Steve Carlton. This is how that came about. The place where we lived was Los Gatos, between San Jose and Monterey. A little town of about 28,000. I was mayor of Los Gatos from 1985 to 1986. There was a friend that had a restaurant. We got to shootin' the breeze one time, talking sports. He said he went to spring training every year. One of his best friends was **TIM MCCARVER***. Timmy Mac was playing for the Phillies then.

My friend said, "I'll tell you what I'm going to do. When I get to spring training this year, I'll have Tim call you to say hi." One Thursday, I was in a meeting and all of a sudden the clerk came in and said, "Terry, there's a long-distance call from Florida for you. It's a guy named Mr. McGovern or McGivern or something like that." I asked him if it could be McCarver. And he said, "Yeah, that's it, Mr. McCarver." I walked into a little side office and picked up the phone. I know McCarver's voice, being a baseball addict and a Phillies junkie. When I get on the phone I hear, "Hello, hello?" My buddy that owns the restaurant tells me, "Terry, this is Jimmy. I got someone that wants to say hi to you." So Tim McCarver says, "Hey, Mr. Mayor, how are

---

*Brent Musburger was the home plate umpire when **TIM MCCARVER** made his pro baseball debut for Keokuk, Iowa, in the Midwest League in 1959.

you?" I could tell right away it was McCarver's voice. He said he'd heard that I was a big Phillies fan.

> Someone then comes over and cuts Steve Carlton's tie right in half.

McCarver then said to me, "I'll tell you what. We're going to be playing the Giants in San Francisco next month in a weekend series. We're going to have a few drinks and eat dinner at our friend Jimmy's restaurant. How about if you join us for dinner?" I'm thinking *holy cow*. I just died and went to heaven. I was 42 years old and my kids by that time had become baseball junkies. I coached baseball for about 18 years. My two oldest sons were about 11 and 8. I couldn't believe this whole thing was happening, but we set up a date.

I touch base with the owner of the restaurant and ask him if it's really going to happen. He tells me it is. So I ask him who was coming. He said, "Well, Mac can't make it, but Steve Carlton, Lefty, is coming." I was surprised because he was an enigma—real private, didn't talk to the press, and all that. The other guys who would be with him that night were a guy they called Dutch or Double D—Darren Daulton—and another guy, a young pitcher named Don Carman. Then another guy that is now the manager of the Pittsburgh Pirates. They called him JR, John Russell.

The day comes and my boys are so excited. The night was supposed to start at 6:30. The deal was that I was going to take the two boys, they'd have their pictures taken with Lefty Carlton, get a card signed, and then my wife and I would take the kids back home, come back, and join the players for dinner. I still can't believe this whole thing is happening. The time comes, we go to the restaurant, and, sure enough, there is Carlton sitting at the corner of the bar. Not too many people would know him. I come in and introduce myself. He acknowledges me as the mayor and has me introduce my sons to him. He has his picture taken with both the boys—gracious as all get out. Great smile, nice guy. He had the boys on each side of him. The boys still have that picture and also the signed ball he gave them.

The dinner was fun and in a private room. My wife doesn't know any of the other guys except Lefty. The booze is flowing—lots of booze and these little appetizers. These guys are living like princes. As the night goes on, we're talking about baseball and life and the wine keeps coming. They're bringing in wine that's probably $300 a bottle—and that was 25 years ago. The wine is flowing and the guys get a little buzzed. One of these players starts taking these bottles, shaking them up and squirting everybody. Now they're squirting these bottles of $300 wine, and someone pours it over another guy's head and the fight is on. My wife and I are sitting there dumbfounded.

No one pours anything on us, but we still can't believe it. Someone then comes over and cuts Steve Carlton's tie right in half. This is a nice silk, expensive tie. Then everybody is cutting their ties. I can't believe the world they live in. Then they start throwing food. It's like they're all 10 years old, but if my wife wasn't there, I'd be doing the same thing.

The next day, thanks to these guys and my friend, we got primo seats—first-row box seats on the Phillies side for a double-header. Double D—Darren Daulton—is down in the bullpen warming up the starting pitcher. When they're done, he comes running up from the dugout and he has to run right by us. I didn't know he was called Double D, but I yelled that to him, "Hey Double D." He's wearing sunglasses, and he says, "Hey Mr. Mayor, how ya doing?" I asked if they all had a good time last night and he says he really doesn't remember but "I know somebody drove us home about 5:30 this morning, and I've got to catch a doubleheader today on about two hours of sleep."

Ah, to be a big league player!

ROOTING FOR THE PHILADELPHIA A'S WAS LIKE GETTING MARRIED FOR THE SECOND TIME: HOPE WINS OUT OVER EXPERIENCE

Carl Goldberg (right) with Harry Kalas

Carl Goldberg

Carl Goldberg, 64, currently lives in Upper Gwynedd, PA. He attended his first Phillies game in 1948, has been a season ticket holder for 25 years, and has attended 19 All Star games. Goldberg is on the board of the Philadelphia Athletics Historical Society.

I collected Perez Steele cards. They were really nice cards, whether they were the postcards or the great moments. I was fortunate enough to get an uncut sheet from Frank Steele, who lived not too far from me. I thought this would be a great piece to get signed. It featured Earl Weaver, Steve Carlton, Mike Schmidt, a couple of other Phillies, and Richie Ashburn. I decided I should get this thing signed and framed. It was a nice piece. I knew some people at the Phillies, so I finally got one of the girls upstairs to get me up into the booth so I could get Richie to sign it. Richie was always available to everybody. If he did a show it was always $5 or $3. He wasn't one of these expensive guys, and he'd do it anytime—after a game, before a game—so I didn't have to be in a rush to get it. But I wanted to get it signed because he'd just been admitted to the Hall of Fame not long before. I got upstairs to the radio booth and Harry and Richie were there. Richie was very congenial, very nice, and he signed it. This was at the Vet. I already had everybody else I wanted sign it. The artist had signed it; Mike Schmidt and Lefty had signed it. I just needed Richie.

I got it over to this guy to get it framed and he said it would be ready in about three weeks. You may know what's coming—two weeks later Richie was dead. When I moved there was a lot of memorabilia I couldn't keep; I had a big room of baseball memorabilia. I had things like Andy Seminick's Phillies uniform that he wore in the 1950 World Series. A lot of other good things I gave to an auction, but I had to keep this framed piece, and to this day it's over my bed. I kept it because of Richie. He was a very congenial guy.

Some of the past memories I still hold on to because I'm on the board of the Philadelphia A's Historical Society. One of the A's players I talked to last week—I still have his picture on my desk—was Gus Zernial. We bring these guys, like Lou Brissie, in for our big breakfasts. Recently he was there signing his book *The Corporal Was a Pitcher*. Lou had his leg blown up in Italy in WWII. The doctors wanted to amputate the leg, and Brissie said, "No, you can't do that to me. I'm going to be a pitcher in the majors." Connie Mack told him, "When the war is over, you come back and I'm going to have you with the team." He came back, tried out, and went on to appear in the All-Star Game. These are the guys that are really fantastic to talk to—like Eddie Joost. The A's only had three managers—**CONNIE MACK***, Jimmy Dykes, and Eddie.

It all goes back to **SHIBE PARK***. We have a store back here that sells memorabilia. I have one of the original turnstiles from Shibe Park. I was a little kid at the time and we went to the A's and Phillies games. I'd go out shopping or to dinner with my

*CONNIE MACK, Jimmy Reese, and Wayne Terwillinger are the only baseball people to wear a major league uniform (Mack normally wore a suit) for fifty years.

*SHIBE PARK was the first concrete and steel park in major league history. It opened in 1909 and seated 20,000 people.

parents. Occasionally, after that we'd be going home and if my dad made a turn up Lehigh Avenue, that only meant one thing—I'm going to a ballgame I'm going to see the Phillies tonight! What a big thrill!

Parking the car was another experience—you parked your car behind another car and you couldn't get out of there until the guy in front of you left. That's the way the parking went back then. Most of the parking at Shibe Park was in this one lot or you'd park in the neighborhood and a kid would say,"Hey, watch your car for you, mister?" They'd watch it for a quarter or something. You certainly gave it to them because how would you know what they were going to do to your car?

Anyway, they didn't have the space for parking. They had that one lot. But, that was also where I had my first experiences of meeting some of the ballplayers. Once of the first ballplayers I ever met was Harry "The Hat" Walker. He was with the Cardinals and came over with the Phillies. The players would park their cars in this lot, too. But they'd be up front because they'd get there at 2:00 in the afternoon. We'd stand around their cars and wait for the guys—they have to come out for their cars—and that's how we were able to get some autographs. Harry would always say, "Don't lean against my car or push and I'll sign an autograph." I still have a ball that he signed "Harry 'The Hat' Walker." When he got injured, it was Richie that took his place.

I met **ART MAHAFFEY*** and some other ballplayers because they parked their cars there. But a lot of the players lived in the neighborhood, and some would walk home after the games because their homes were near the ballpark.

> ***ART MAHAFFEY** bragged that he would pick off the first baserunner he saw in the major leagues. In his first game in 1960, at Busch Stadium in St. Louis, he picked off Bill White in the seventh inning. He also picked off the second batter after he reached base. In his very next game, Mahaffey also picked off the first baserunner he allowed, Jim Marshall.

But the real thrill for a little kid like me was going down to the ballpark. It was like a palace. It was gorgeous. You'd walk in through the turnstile and then up about six or seven steps behind home plate. Then, right in front of you was this green pasture—it was euphoria—you were in another world. No matter how many times I did it, it was always a thrill. I remember Frank McCormick and Emil Verban. I didn't get to meet them, but years later I got to meet a number of the ballplayers like Robin Roberts. In 1950, I was very fortunate to meet Andy Seminick at a show. I asked him if he had something to sell, and he told me he had his uniform that he wore in the 1950 World Series. I worked out a deal with him, and he gave me a letter declaring that I was the owner of the uniform that he wore in the 1950 World Series. Andy Seminick was a great, great guy who has since passed away. Some of these guys are still alive, just like the A's, who left in '54 and went on to Kansas City.

They didn't keep good records back then. Bob Feller wrote to SABR, The Society for American Baseball Research, trying to find out the first guy he struck out. He didn't even have a record of who his first strikeout was. Now, I was born in '36 and he came up in '36. I had purchased all the *Sporting News* newspapers for 1936. I went to town and attacked those papers and the Cleveland papers and came up with the answer. In appreciation, Bob sent me a plaque. He gave out plaques to certain people for things they had done for him in baseball, and Bob sent me a plaque thanking me for getting him the information. I saw Bob in Philly in late 2009. The A's Society brought him in for a show and signing of his book, and I discussed it with him again. In fact my wife and I were at a private dinner the night before and I've got a picture on my desk of Bob and my wife. I've met some great guys from the A's Society.

When I was a kid, I would hang out at a couple of hotels in town. There was the Warwick and the Ben Franklin. I got friendly with the girl behind the counter—her name was Joan—at the Ben Franklin. She would tell the ballplayers when they came up to get their mail, "There's a little boy on the third floor by the drugstore inside the hotel. Will you sign his book for him?" They didn't want kids running around in the hotel lobby. Today players sell their autographs. I was getting them in my book. I got some good autographs—Howie Fox—I was told he was a very tough autograph. I met Luke Appling there and Johnny Vander Meer. I saw one guy at the hotel and asked him to sign. He told me he wasn't a ballplayer, and I said, "C'mon, sign my book" because I saw him signing for someone else. So he signed my book and guess what?—I was stuck with Benny Goodman. I still have it in my original autograph book. I met a lot of ballplayers in the hotel. It was a great chance to meet them. The one guy that I got really friendly with was **TOMMY HENRICH***. Tommy passed away in the past year or so. Tommy was in the outfield with a guy named DiMaggio in center.

My relationship with Bob Feller was through SABR. But with the Phillies, the best way to meet the guys was after the games. They'd sign our books, and back then they signed with pencils. It was great to meet these guys and they had time for you. Even in later years they'll sit and talk to you. I met Enos Slaughter at an All-Star Game. They all have a story to tell. I was invited to Willie Mays' 70th birthday party. Stan Musial sat at the table behind me. Bobby Shantz was there and even Mayor Giuliani. I got to meet a lot of interesting players and people.

One of the biggest thrills was when I was invited into the Phillies dugout in 1983 when they brought back the 1950 team for an **OLD TIMERS GAME***. It was under one condition—you don't ask for autographs. I remember that Willie Jones was there. I'm

---

***TOMMY HENRICH** hit the first walk-off home run in World Series history...Dennis Eckersley coined the term "walk-off home run."

---

*In an **OLD-TIMERS GAME** at Shea Stadium in the 60s, Bobby Thomson homered into the left-field bullpen off of Ralph Branca.

sitting in the dugout with Robin Roberts on my right and Seminick on my left. Dick Sisler was the coach or manager of this team they were playing. I said to myself, "God, if you could just stop the clock right now." What a thrill sitting there with my idols. With Roberts on my right and Seminick on my left and Sisler and Willie Jones there. I was able to meet some of the 1950 Phillies. I promised I wouldn't get autographs, so I just sat there and enjoyed the games. What a thrill—like freezing time.

I don't think the players today are as sociable. Back in the old days, they rode trains and played cards and they went out together. I don't think there is the togetherness there was in the old days.

Eddie Sawyer, former manager of the Phillies, was another great, great man that I met. I had some things I wanted signed by him and didn't know if he was alive. I called somebody and they said he was. I eventually got his phone number and called him and he acted like he knew me all his life. He said, "I'm up in Valley Forge, but you probably would have a hard time finding my house. How about next Tuesday if I meet you behind the Valley Forge post office?" I went up there and next to a car was standing Eddie Sawyer. He was great to me. His team played in the 1950 World Series against Casey Stengel. He had a picture of himself and Casey and he signed it for me. Whenever I saw him after that at shows, he would stop signing autographs and just come over and hug me.

It's all been great, but maybe the best part was walking down Lehigh Avenue and seeing those light standards and walking in and seeing that grass.

There was a "win chill" factor at Connie Mack Stadium

PHILLIE HEROES, LIKE PHILLIE MEMORIES NEVER GROW OLD

Burt Penn (right) with Jim Bunning

Burt Penn

Penn's baseball career started as a batboy at the age of five. He played until he was 59 years old. In between he had a lengthy career in semi-pro ball. In addition to baseball he has officiated football, basketball, and soccer. Penn, 74, resides in Glen Mills, PA, with his wife of eight years—his high school sweetheart, although she didn't know it back then.

I went down the first time the Phillies had the Dream Week in 1984. I went down actually to cover it. The head guy running it came over to me and said, "I understand you've played ball." I said, "Yes, I've played." He said, "Would you like to play here at our fantasy camp?" I said, "I'm not giving you $3,500 to play here." He said, "We need some guys who can catch—somebody told me you caught in high school." I told him that I had and that I had also caught in semi-pro. I also told him I was over 50 years old. He said, "Well, if you'll play, I won't even charge you."

When I was down at Dream Week, I was talking to Ashburn, and he was a pretty nice guy. I wrote an article for the Phillies Report, which is what I had gone down there for. We used to stay in a motel facility in those days. About the third day, the former big leaguers came up to the motel one afternoon. Richie was standing with this beautiful blond girl. I had umpired in

Legion ball and high school ball where his sons played. I knew Richie, Jr. and the other son. His daughter was still alive then, but since, unfortunately, was killed in an automobile accident. I get out of the car and said, "Richie, I know your boys, but I've never met your daughter." Well...if looks could kill I'd have been dead! The next day I'm at my locker putting on my stuff. He came over and said, "I thought we were friends." I said, "We are, but I want you to know something. You were always my favorite Phillie, but now *you're my idol!*" He smiled, and he took it the right way.

A lot of the Phillies are funny. I loved Larry Bowa. I went down there for ten years. One year, I helped with different things. Bowa came over and I asked him to sign a ball for me. I needed a single-signed ball. Unfortunately, I pulled a ball out of my bag that Bobby Wine had already signed. Bowa actually got angry that I handed him a ball that was already signed by Wine. I said, "What the hell are you getting mad at? You get mad at everything. I think they're right when they say you're nuts."

This is going back a lot of years now. One day I was talking to John Vukovich in the runway at the Vet. Bowa walked up. I had played for him for a couple of years. I said, "How you doing, Skip?" You know how you always call your manager "Skipper". He walked by me like he didn't even know I was there. I said to Vukovich, who was also a nice guy by the way, "What the heck is the matter with him?" He said, "Are you coming down here later?" I said, "Yeah, I've got to talk to somebody in a couple of days, and I'll be down then." He said, "Oh, he'll probably be all over you like he's your long-lost buddy." I said, "What are you talking about? He didn't even say anything to me." He said, "Oh, you mean Sybil. He's a whole bunch of different people."

Two days later, I'm down here talking to Greg Luzinski and Vukovich. Bowa came up and jumped on my back from behind. By the way, Bowa is not as small as people think he is. He said, "How you doing, Big Guy?" I said, "Who the hell are you?" He told me in no uncertain terms what I could do to myself—which was impossible. I like the guy because he was a winner, but he did not know how to handle the new ball players. I was very happy to see how it's worked out with Charlie Manuel managing. I didn't like him in the beginning because he let these guys do just about anything they wanted...but, evidently, that's the way you've got to handle the new ballplayers.

I like Bowa's attitude. We were undefeated, and one day, when we were playing, I was catching. There was a pop-up, and all the guy had to do was catch it, and we'd have been out of the inning. We end up losing the game. I'm yelling at the top of my lungs—and I can yell pretty loud having umpired for 49 years— "shortstop, shortstop, shortstop." They let it drop, the next guy got a hit, and we lost the game. Bowa calls these old men—some of them are in their sixties—over to the corner of the locker room, and he rips the s--- out of them. He said, "I don't expect you to play like big leaguers, but anybody could hear that big mouth back there behind the plate yelling 'shortstop.' You guys let it drop in. I don't want to see anymore of this stuff at all. I'm staying way in the back, and he comes out, and he says, "It's a good thing you didn't laugh." I said, "You don't know how hard it was to keep from laughing." He actually had these guys scared. He wants to win at everything...*marbles*—I don't care what it is. He never wants to lose, and I love a guy like that.

They had women down there every now and then. They had this woman come in and she was writing an article for a magazine. She said to me, "I understand you're a writer." I said, "I free-lance." She said, "You wrote an article for *The Village Report.*" I said, "Yeah, Rich Westcott's a nice guy. I still have the check framed. I never cashed it." That was the first time I ever sold anything. She said, "Maybe you can give me some tips." I said, "First of all, I'm an old-fashioned guy. You don't belong in this locker room. These guys are walking around naked." She said, "I change in the equipment room." I said, "But, you're in the locker room, and there are guys walking around naked, and you don't belong in here. I'm sorry if you don't like that but that's the way it is." She said, "Suppose a naked guy walked up to me, how would I interview him?" I said, "Look him right in the eye. Don't look anywhere else." Later she calls me and leaves a message on my answering machine telling me, "The article is coming out. I took a little literary license in writing it." ...which, to me, means she lied. Sure enough, she lied. She said, "No sooner did he walk away from me, when a naked guy walked right up to me and said, 'Do you want to interview me?' It was obvious he put the guy up to it." Which, I had not done! I got about ten calls from females I know—relatives and others who couldn't believe I'd do something like that. Because *I wouldn't do anything like that*. When I did see her at the reunion down at the ball park, I tore her a new one. I said, "This is why you shouldn't have been in the locker room. Poetic license my butt, you were lying."

Another time, we were playing. I had an old judge pitching to me. We were tied with Granny Hamner's team. Granny was a piece of work. He'd say anything to anybody. Especially when he was drinking. We were playing against the Phillies, they brought in Howard Eskin to bat. I was told I had to give him a hit. I thought bulls---, so I threw him three curve balls, and he struck out. They came out and said, "This is going to be on television. You've got to let him hit the ball." So I lobbed it underhand, and he got a single. He got around to third base on a couple of hits. My catcher was a 68-year-old, if you can imagine. I was probably 50-something at the time. I threw a wild pitch that just about reached the plate. It was the last day of the Dream Week. My arm was shot—in fact it's never returned. Eskin comes running in from third so I run in to cover the plate. Well, when you're playing in Dream Week, you're not allowed to advance on passed balls and you're not allowed to steal. Eskin is running, and they've got the camera on. I ran in and the old catcher couldn't get to the ball so I gave Eskin a hip as he went past me, and he went rolling. Of course, it never showed up on television and Hamner runs out and says, "Where the hell did you learn to do something like that? What the hell's the matter with you?" I said, "I learned it from watching you play." ...which was the truth.

When we were playing his team this time, this woman came up who had won a trip. It was one of those games that went 11 innings, and this was the 10th inning. Hamner comes over to me and says, "Would you mind letting her get a hit? What the hell! Give her a break." I walked out to the pitcher, who was a judge from down in Turnersville or somewhere—a good pitcher. I told him, "He wants to give her a hit. Throw it down the middle... as hard as you can...three straight pitches." He struck her out on three pitches. Hamner comes out to me and says, "You're a jerk." I said, "Just like you." I like Hamner—don't get me wrong.

Hamner got up at one banquet and was cursing so bad Jim Bunning and his wife got up and left the room. He was a politician of course. He's saying, "I had the worst team there ever was, and they were all Jews." I'm thinking, "What are you doing?" He says, "Not only that, they all look alike." One guy walked up to him and said, "Will you knock it off. You can't say stuff like that." He says to him, "What the 'f' are you going to do about it?" He was never allowed to speak up there again, but he did say something funny at the end, "By the way, they all want to come back next year, and I've already made arrangements to have the plane hijacked to Cuba."

Andy Seminick could still hit the hell out of the ball. He was an old man who couldn't even run. They'd have somebody run to first base for him. Smoky Burgess could hit line drives all over the place, and he couldn't run. Tony Gonzalez was in as good shape as he was when he played. Pancho Herrera still had a big gut but he could still hit the ball off the wall. Del Ennis couldn't hit anymore. Johnny Callison couldn't hit, but [Bobby] Wine could really hit—he hit a grand slam against us one game. Chris Wheeler said it was the only grand slam he ever hit in his life.

I tell you the truth it was a treat to meet all these different guys at Dream Week. Chris Wheeler is a great guy. Chris Short was a fantastic guy, really great to talk to. The only guy I didn't like was Bake McBride. He's just a miserable character. I said to the left fielder on his team, "What do you think of this guy, Bake McBride?" He says, "He has the personality of a peanut." The guy was a psychiatrist so I guess he knew what he was talking about. I played for his team one time, McBride was supposed to introduce us, but he wouldn't even come to the banquet.

The guy who ran this outfit said to me, "Don't you do public speaking? How about introducing the team?" I said OK, so I got up and everybody was looking at me, wondering what the hell I was doing up there. I said, "The reason I'm up here to introduce the team is that George Culver had some business to take care of, and Bake McBride's attending a seminar on *How to Win Friends and Influence People.*" Everybody laughed but Bowa. He didn't think that was funny.

To tell you how bad Bake was, I'm catching a guy about 70 years old, and he's not even reaching the plate. I went over and got a first-baseman's mitt so I could try to scoop the throws from behind the plate. Instead of saying something to the guy, which I was really glad he didn't because the guy had paid his money, and if you pay your money, you play. That's the way it is). McBride says to me, "Catch the ball." More balls were hitting me than I can catch, but I'm scooping a lot of them up. Even the umpire turned around and said, "He's doing a good job back here." Finally I called time out. I looked around and there were no ladies present, and I said, "Hey Bake." The umpire said, "What are you doing?" I said, "Watch." McBride turned around, and I said, "Are you listening? Go f yourself."

Most of the Phillies guys down there were terrific guys. Luzinski was a cool guy. I got to know him a little better. Every year, for the last ten years of my aunt's life, on or around my her birthday, I took her down to see a Phillies game. We were down there when she was 91 years old, a real little lady and a life-long Phillies fan. She saw this stand where Luzinski sells all his memorabilia. I went over and said to him, "My aunt's over here, Greg. She's a big Phillies fan. Can I take her picture with you?" He said, "Sure, bring her over." You know what he did— he picked her up and sat her on his knee. She thought that was the coolest, greatest thing that ever happened. I was using a Polaroid camera, if you can imagine, so I pulled the picture out and let it dry and asked him to sign it to her. She died about eight years later, but she had always treasured that picture.

The first year I played down there, I was on **TONY TAYLOR'S*** team. He was another great guy. The umpire called something. They were using umpires that were being trained. I used to argue with them, but Tony would just sit there so I'd take it on myself to argue with them. He said to me, "What the hell do you want to do—be a baseball player or a coach?" I said, "I want to be an umpire. These guys don't know what they're doing." Lee Elia, another nice guy said, "Why the hell are you always telling the umpires what to do for?" I said, "You know, and I know, that they're not calling the game right. They don't even know the rules." He said, "What the hell are you, a rules expert?" I said, "Compared to these guys, I am." I've been umpiring for over 40 years. I started umpiring at 14 years old and umpired for 49 years.

I made more money umpiring than anything else. It's the next best thing to playing. Coaching doesn't even rank, especially if you're coaching kids' teams. Last year, I was asked to help coach my grandson's team, seven to nine year olds. Can you imagine? I did take over as the batting coach. I had to hold my tongue. The parents all should be shot. They don't know what they're talking about.

***TONY TAYLOR** was the first batter in the first regular-season game at the Houston Astrodome in 1965. Richie Allen hit the first regular-season home run. During a previous exhibition game, Mickey Mantle hit the first home run ever at the Astrodome.

Short Stories from Long Memories

I remember that I cried. I cried a lot. On Jan. 5, 2004, I cried like a child. I couldn't believe it. Tug McGraw had been taken from us after a fight with brain cancer. Now, I was 45 years old when the Phillies won the World Series in 1980. I have two boys and they each got to meet Tugger at a baseball card show in the Philadelphia suburbs. I'm trying like crazy to remember but the name of the town escapes me. We got in line and waited for what seemed like forever. When my boys got to the front of the line, Tugger was engaged with them like they were best friends. Tugger gave me the club's address and told them to send more pictures if they wanted autographs. Well, about two months later, we got a letter in the mail from the Phillies. It had four tickets in a club box at the Vet, parking and VIP passes to meet Tugger and some other Phillies afterward. I thought it was a hoax so I called the Phillies to confirm. No, this was true. I was in disbelief. That night was one of the best in my entire life. My boys were so excited, they couldn't sleep the night before. The tickets were great and we spent about 20 minutes with Tugger, Garry Maddox, Larry Bowa, Mike Schmidt and some other players afterward. It left my kids and me, frankly, on cloud nine for a long, long time. It was something not many people, especially pro athletes, would do. They just wouldn't.

When I heard that Tugger was sick, I cried. I couldn't believe it. When Tug died, I had tears in my eyes the entire day. It just brought me back to that day with my boys and the cherished memories they'll have for the rest of their lives because of that man's unselfishness. When I called my oldest son, he hadn't heard the news yet and he was screaming in tears over the phone. You just never forget what Tug did. He was a true gentleman and a true person.

He'll never, ever be forgotten. I know he's up in heaven smiling down on all of us. When the Phillies won the World Series in 2008, I poured a glass of champagne, toasted the

Phillies and then raised my glass to the sky and thanked Tug. And then I cried tears of happiness and sorrow all at once. I still miss the Tugger.

—**Jonathan Cullenwolder**, 75, Phoenix, Arizona, retired

I grew up in Wilmington, Delaware, and was very fortunate to have a friendship with Ruly Carpenter, whose father, **BOB CARPENTER***, was owner of the Phillies from the World War II period until they sold the club in the early 80s. Ruly and I were classmates all through Tower Hill School in Wilmington. We started there in kindergarten and went all through high school together, playing football, baseball, and basketball on the same teams. Ruly was a terrific athlete, an all-state end in football and an outstanding pitcher in baseball. Every spring when we were in high school, we'd take the train to Clearwater, which was, of course, the Phillies spring training site. What a thrill. What an opportunity to spend a week in March during spring training with the owner of the Phillies' son. Through that I got to know many of my Phillies heroes—Robin Roberts, Richie Ashburn, etc.—and still have those wonderful memories today.

In March of our senior year, 1958, we went down to Clearwater, and the Phillies in those days were struggling terribly. The glory days of the 1950 Whiz Kids were long gone. One afternoon we went over to Tampa to Al Lopez Field. The Phillies were playing an exhibition game against the Reds. The last three hitters in the lineup, numbers six, seven, and eight, collectively

***ROBERT M. CARPENTER, SR.** once made a famous comment that he was going to write a book on how to make a small fortune in baseball. The answer, he said, was to "start with a large fortune." When Carpenter bought the team, the reins were handed over to his 28-year-old son, Robert, Jr., better known as Ruly. Ruly was the first baseball owner ever drafted into the military. After playing football at Duke, he entered the service in 1944. The Carpenters also owned the Wilmington Blue Rocks of the Inter-State League. The Carpenters owned the club until 1981 when Bill Giles' group paid over 30 million dollars for the team. Carpenter had paid $400,000 in 1944 for William D. Cox's interest in the team.

went 0-for-12. I remember them well: Joe Lonnett, Woody Smith, and Roy Smalley Sr. That night at the Carpenter's home in Clearwater, Ruly was needling his dad, incessantly saying, "Even I could get those guys out, Dad." And his father—I will never forget—listened and said, "All right, you're on. I accept your challenge." The next thing we knew, Bob Carpenter had set it up two days later, after an exhibition game, for his son Ruly to pitch against those three guys. I would be his catcher. Ruly could name any defense he wanted from among the Phillies major league players, which he did, and there we gathered. It was about 4:00 p.m., after the game. Bob had bets everywhere. The bet basically was that they would score more than four runs in a three-inning exhibition. Ruly was pitching just against the three guys drafted into this. Ruly pitched well. He gave up a home run to Joe Lonnett, got the rest of them out, and his dad lost the bet. I often wondered if he wasn't paying off those bets gleefully. His 17-year-old son had excelled. Joe Lonnett did hit a two-run home run over the right center-field fencing. Every time I saw Joe after that, he'd say, "I ripped it, kid. I ripped it."

Roy Smalley Sr., whose baseball card I collected when I was a little kid, was on the bubble trying to make the team that year. I can still hear him saying when he struck out, "What a way to leave the big leagues." A few years ago, I wrote a book called *How to Be Like Jackie Robinson*, and I tracked down every living major league ballplayer, like 800 former ballplayers, to see if they had a memory or reflection on **JACKIE ROBINSON***. I tracked down Roy Smalley Sr. in California. I knew he would have no memory of me. After I got his thoughts on Jackie Robinson, I said that I would like to ask him about something that happened almost 50 years ago. I asked him if he had any memory of that day in Clearwater. He said, "Oh, I remember

*What major league player has a street named after him in Cairo, Georgia, **JACKIE ROBINSON**'s hometown? Willie Harris, currently of the Washington Nationals. Harris scored the winning run in the 2005 World Series and in 2007 had six hits in one game for the Braves.

it. I've thought about it many times. That was a terrible thing they made me do that afternoon. To have big leaguers put in a position like that was not good at all." So that March afternoon in 1958 still reverberates, and I don't think Ruly will ever forget it.

—**Pat Williams**, co-founder of the Orlando Magic, former Philadelphia 76ers GM

I loved everything about Philadelphia from the moment I got here. The fans. The passion. The excitement. The expectations. All of it. I didn't mind the pressure. I truly never did. It was a lot of fun being a part of the '93 team. I signed in January of 1993 and the way the whole community treated me and my family is something that will remain with us forever. We consider Philadelphia our second home. We love coming back whenever we can.

For me to keep playing was close to a miracle. I broke in with the Twins in 1982 and in my first three seasons, I played maybe 50 games because I was fighting Tourette's Syndrome. It's a neurological movement disorder and I couldn't get it under control.

I never minded the pressure or expectations because I had my own battles in life as I conquered Tourette's Syndrome early in my Major League career. I have spent countless hours trying to help others with the disorder. As a Phillie, I hosted groups of children with the disorder and their families before games in the visiting football locker room at Veterans Stadium. I would answer questions and assure everyone that a normal life can be lived. One-on-one meetings with people afflicted with the disorder took place often. During my final year with the Phillies, I established the Jim Eisenreich Foundation for children with Tourette's. I wanted to be able to reach out to help others.

I also got cheered because I had four very good years with the Phillies, capped by a .362 season. I remember someone telling me it was the highest average by a Phillie with 300 or more at-bats since Smoky Burgess hit .368, I think, in 1954.

I signed with the Marlins after the 1996 season and won a World Series in 1997. I was thrilled to get a World Series ring but I would have liked to have gotten one in Philadelphia, too.

I mean, that would have been great. I felt like we had it in 1993. We were right there. We were so close.

It took a while but The Tourettes' eventually got under control and I was able to play 15 wonderful seasons in the Major Leagues. What a great ride it was. I'm in the business world now, but I still stay connected to the game. I kept a close eye on the Phillies in 2008, and I was so happy for the fans. They have stuck with the team through good and bad. They deserved it. Maybe no city deserved it more than Philadelphia. I actually cheered when Brad Lidge got the last strikeout. I just felt so good for the fans there. They treated my family and I so well the entire time we were there. I hear so many crazy things about the Philadelphia fans. You won't hear any of that from us. We love the fans and always will.

—**Jim Eisenreich**, member of 1993 Phillies

I remember being stopped at the border when I was coaching with the Baltimore Orioles. I forget exactly, but a custom agent asked me if I played major league baseball and I said, "Yeah, for several teams." The agent recognized me and remembered that I played for the Phillies. I told him there were others, too, but I had the most enjoyable time with the Phillies. Those fans were the greatest. They supported me, cheered for me and truly pulled for us every single night.

When the Phillies told me they were inducting me into their Wall of Fame, I was so thrilled. It's a tremendous honor for me to be a part of the Phillies Wall of Fame with so many greats—ex-teammates and guys who I saw play when I was in the minor leagues who were part of that 1980 championship club. Growing up in the Dominican Republic, and finding myself here now is tremendous. I never really knew where my career would take me. I loved being in Philadelphia. It will always be special to me.

When I was traded, I cried. I never wanted to leave. I understood there was a business side to this game. I remember getting called to go to the manager's office. I thought, "What did I do?" When they told me, I was shocked, because I loved it here and thought I was going to be here for a long time.

When I got the call to come back, I was so very happy. I saw so many friendly faces when I arrived. I almost cried tears of happiness. When these guys won the World Series in 2008, I was thrilled for the city. They deserved it maybe more than any other city in the Majors.

—**Juan Samuel**, 47, Former Phillie and Member of the Phillies Wall of Fame

There is nothing quite as unique as the Phillies fans. They'll boo you if you stink. They'll cheer for you if you do well. I love my time in Philadelphia. I always felt like I was one of them. I was a hard worker and pretty much a regular guy. I had a great run here. Every single day, someone will ask me about giving up the home run to Joe Carter in Game 6 of the 1993 World Series. They'll also say, "We love you, Mitch. The manager should have taken you out because you were overworked." I always enjoy talking to the Phillies fans because of their passion. They're the best. You have to understand where they're coming from and I do. They knew I gave it everything. I had nothing left in the tank. Nothing. They've been great to me ever since. They all say, "Mitch, we love you. This World Series (in 2008) is for you. You deserve it Mitch." It brings a tear to my eye. I was sorry we couldn't bring it home for them in 1993 but we gave it everything. I felt like we were the better team than Toronto. We had a few lapses and give them credit because they took it from us that year. We didn't just hand it over to them. They went out and took it from us. They deserved the World Series. I remember the whole season and it was great. The Phillies fans supported us, and, I think, drove us to the pennant. They were unbelievable. We had such an unbelievable home-field advantage at the Vet. Teams did not want to play us there. The clubhouses were dingy and dark. There were **RATS*** and cats under the stadium. It was

*The Yankees once had a bullpen car (Toyota) that fans constantly bombarded with trash. The trash attracted **RATS** that ate through the engine cables. The car was scrapped in favor of a golf cart. Both the Toyota and the golf cart were used to transport the relief pitcher to the mound.

not an ideal place to play. But it was us. It was who we were—a bunch of guys playing to win. We weren't the prototype athletes. I mean we had John Kruk, myself, Lenny Dykstra and so on. We went out and played as a team and got the job done. And the fans were awesome. Man, they drove us to some victories. I'm convinced of that. They would get on the opponent so bad and psych them out. Conversely, they drove us to a number of wins. The fans haven't changed through the years. They have the same passion, probably more. I was so thrilled to see the Phillies bring home the World Series in 2008. The parade was awesome. Those fans had been longing for a title and they got it. That team just had it. Even though it took an additional 15 years from 1993, they got it. No one was happier than I was.

Mitch Williams, Former Phillies closer,
now an analyst with MLB Network

There was a rookie outfielder for the Phillies in the late 80s who was a real speedster. His name was **JEFF STONE***. He led the minor leagues in stolen bases one year. I had the occasion to be with him at winter baseball in Venezuela and we became quite good friends. This kid was a little naïve. He was playing for the Phillies, and when the season ended, he was packing up his things to go back to South America to play winter ball. His next-door neighbor was Al Holland. Jeff was packing and moving out of his apartment to head to the airport. He's carrying a big television set with him. Al Holland asks him what he's doing with the television set. Jeff tells him that he's taking his set with him to Venezuela. Al Holland explains that they have television sets in South America, but Jeff tells him that he needs his own because his TV speaks English. That's the kind of kid he was. He had 11 siblings and his mother died when he was very young. He was a young black man, and after he lost his mother, he was

---

*Tonya Harding's husband was Jeff Gillooly. After her debacle with Nancy Kerrigan, her husband changed his name to **JEFF STONE**.

raised by a white woman. He told me a lot about his experiences in the minor leagues. He was a patient of mine.

A lot of these players played for the Phillies, and they went down there because of their connection with Ruben Amaro Sr., whose son is now the GM of the Phillies.

—**Myron Eisenberg**, 81, Philadelphia, retired

Connie Mack Stadium—oh, how I loved that place. The sightlines were spectacular. It was a true experience at the ballpark. I wish I could go back in time to the way it was. Well, I remember one game against the Reds and this guy next to me—I think he had been drinking—was all over Del Ennis. He went crazy the whole game. Finally, I said something to him and he said something nasty to me. I told him if he didn't have anything good to say not to say anything at all. I know people pay their money and they think they're entitled. But this guy was a jerk and he wasn't representing Phillies fans in the proper way. There's a line and he went way over it. Anyway, years later, I was having dinner and who was there but Del Ennis. I stopped at his table—I hate to do that to people but I wanted to—and I told him that story. He smiled and bought me a drink. Then he asked if I had friends with me. He ended up buying a round of drinks for like 10 people. We even sat and talked for a while. Best experience of my life. What a class human being. That night taught me something about being a fan. You can get on players for not performing. That's what fans do. Del Ennis was a classy guy and a regular guy. He didn't deserve a lot of the booing he got when he played. He said he blocked it out mostly, but it had to be hard. Anyway, I thought that was a great experience and I've mentioned it to people, especially when they start to get on players.

For me, baseball is like family. I have five grandchildren and they all play baseball. They all love it. Some of that comes from me because of my love for the game. I have passed that down to my kids. I'm glad to see it because baseball is a bond that can last forever. We get together as a family sometimes and have cookouts and the kids play baseball out back and then come in to watch some of the Phillies game. It's a great way for a family to spend a day. I even go to my grandkids' games when I can. Imagine that thrill for me. It just takes me back to my childhood. Baseball has changed but not that much."

—**Kiley Smith**, Phillies fan for 86 years

We all got along, for the most part. Because nobody expected us to do anything, we were just baseball players who went out there and played the game like it was supposed to be played. We had a common goal and that was to have fun. It was a crazy group of guys. I mean, a really crazy group of guys. It was maybe the most fun I ever had playing baseball because we were a family. You know how families are nuts? That was us from top to bottom. When it came time to play, we did that. And we did it really, really well.

In my first full season with the Phillies in 1991, I threw a no-hitter against the Expos in Montreal's Olympic Stadium on May 23, striking out 10 batters in the process. In my next start, on May 28, I threw another complete-game shutout, this time blanking the Expos on three hits in front of a home crowd at Veterans Stadium. What a start. It was almost an out-of-body experience. That's a heck of a lot of success early. I saw how the fans responded to me. They were awesome. I had a great time in my years with the Phillies. Back to my no hitter, it was only my 15th career start. I was a little erratic, which may have helped. I struck out a career-high 10 at the time but I walked seven. I remember getting into a good groove in the third inning or so, and then just when I was sailing, I'd get wild. Maybe they didn't know what was coming. Around the seventh inning, I knew I could do it if I just settled down and didn't put batters on base. It was tougher to pitch out of the stretch because you're worried about the runners now as well as the hitter. I focused on my job and just got it done. The last batter, Tim Wallach, hit a very hard one-hopper right to me. I grabbed it and flipped the ball to Ricky Jordan. We hugged and my teammates went crazy. They soaked me with beer in the clubhouse. It was an awesome day. I knew the second he hit it that I had it.

—**Tommy Greene**, former Phillies pitcher

I had Philly tickets going back to 1971, the first year at the Vet. I got mad with them and canceled them briefly. I said, "How dumb can the Phillies be—trading Rick Wise for Steve Carlton... Wise is a guy who has pitched a no-hitter and hit two home runs and is the ace of our staff." I just gave it to them something awful. That was one of my big boo-boo's with the Phillies. I got back in with them and got my tickets back after that was over. ...

I had Johnny Callison's glove one time. The first year he was with the Phillies, he came running in, and he tried to be smart and throw his glove into the dugout. It landed on top of the corrugated metal roof that covered the dugout...and slid right across the top of the dugout and landed right in my lap where I sat in the first row. He said, "Hey kid. Come on now. Give me my glove." He was calling me a kid, and he was less than two years older than me. I thought it would be a good laugh for us. I gave it back to him, but I'll never forget holding onto his glove for a few minutes....

I had a Little League banquet one year, and we were supposed to have Willie Mays as our speaker. The crowd got so large I had to move it out of our town of Laurel and move it to the Convention Center in Delmar. Less than nine days before the big day, Mays' agent called and said he couldn't come. I said, "What do you mean he can't come? You can't do this to me. I've got 865 people coming." He said, "I'm sorry. You're not paying him...and this other group is." That was the end of it.

We ended up getting Dallas Green. He forgot it. I called him at home where he was sitting on a Saturday afternoon reading the paper. He said, "I'll be there in a few minutes." I said, "No, you won't. It's two hours to get down here." He said, "I'll make it in an hour." He got two speeding tickets coming down to our banquet....

I talked to Rich Westcott, the writer, a couple of years ago and said, "Rich, there's one thing that has never been touched on about the Phillies that I think would appeal to the real Phillies fan. That is a story about guys like Joe Coppock, Mel Roach, Marv Blalock—the unknown player that only a Phillies fan would know. How their career ended up, where they are now." He said that it would take a lot of work to do that. I said, "Yeah, it would, but I would read it ten times over." He said, "You would, but that doesn't mean a lot of other people would." I don't guess he was sold on the idea....

Pancho Herrera was a first baseman for the Phillies in 1960. It was the last game of the season, and I reached over as they're going into the dugout. This other kid gets his hat. After the game I pestered the kid to death. Back then, a dollar was about like $5 now. After we got outside the ball park, he sold it to me for $1. Tony Taylor and Herrara were loading their luggage up. There was a bunch of kids around them. He said, "How'd you get my hat? You took that off my head." I said, "No, I honestly didn't, but I did buy it for $1." He just laughed. I wore that hat for a large number of years and now wish I had kept it. It was the last game of the season, and 2,900 people were all that attended that day....

St. Michael's, Maryland is a very upscale area, right on the water. The whole Murphy clan, about 30 of us, were there for a dinner to celebrate my parents' 50th wedding anniversary. I was sitting there looking out the window and said to my wife, "Kay, Mike Schmidt just walked by." She pointed and said, "That guy?" I said, "That's Mike Schmidt. I'm telling you. I know what I'm talking about." He had an old scruffy shirt on. He'd let his beard grow out. It was right after he retired. He had this yacht in there—the fanciest thing you've ever seen in your life—with jet skis on the front and everything else. I went outside, but he had gone into an enclosed swimming area where his wife and kids were. I looked through the slats and said, "I think I know you." He said, "You do?" I said, "Yes, I do. You hit your second home run off Bob Gibson on Easter Sunday in 1971." He said, "You do know me, don't you?" I said, "Yeah. You're Mike Schmidt. How can I ever forget you?" He said, "Please don't tell anybody I'm here." I said, "I won't but I've got a tremendous favor to ask of you. It's my mom and dad's 50th anniversary. Would you allow them to have a picture taken with you?" He took a great big deep breath and he said, "Sure, meet me down at the bottom of the dock. But, I'm telling you—don't you tell anybody." So, we did, and we got his picture. It was very nice, and he even shook hands with everybody.

The following year my dad said to me, "Oh, I'm so glad we're going out. I can't wait to see who we're going to meet this year." I said, "Well, it ain't going to be no Mike Schmidt, that's for sure."

—**Pat Murphy**

The player I remember the most is Tony Taylor. When we were kids at Connie Mack and hanging over the rail hollering for autographs, Tony Taylor always made a special effort to come over and sign a couple of autographs during warm-ups.

When we moved to Washington it was really a treat to be able to root for the Senators and the Phillies, even though they both stunk. With the Senators it was great to see these guys in the twilight of their careers—guys like Dale Long and Gene Woodling and **JIMMY PIERSALL***, who was my favorite player.

When we lived down there, we would go up to Philly twice a month to visit my grandparents. Coming up from suburban Maryland to the inner city of Philly was like day and night. It was a whole different atmosphere. We'd hop a trolley and go out to the Phillies games. On the weekends we'd go to the Sunday game. On Bat Day they'd give you a full-size Phillies bat—a Johnny Callison or Richie Allen bat or whatever. But you couldn't get it unless you were with an adult. We used to stand outside the stadium, get our tickets, walk up to the guys that were walking in, tug on their arms, and ask if they'd be our dad so that we could get a bat. It was a nice time—everything was so much more accessible. It's different today.

—**Sky Brady**, 56, Georgetown, DE, Musician / Disc Jockey

***JIMMY PIERSALL** hit his one hundredth Major League home run off Dallas Green. To celebrate, Piersall ran the bases backwards.

Chapter 5

THE SOUNDTRACK OF PHILADELPHIA

Harry the K and His Buddies

HIS MEMORABILIA COLLECTION IS AMAZING...HE EVEN HAS A BALL NOT AUTOGRAPHED BY PETE ROSE

Tony Mowen

Mowen is a professional musician. He has played with Les Paul, Mark Farner, and Pete Best, the original drummer of The Beatles. Tony has won two Harry Kalas sound-alike competitions on 610 WIP Sports Radio and 93.3 WMMR-FM in Philadelphia. Tony performs at McFadden's at Citizens Bank Park and he was also featured in an NBC-10 tribute to the passing of Harry Kalas.

I've amassed an amazing autograph collection. I've never bought any autographs. Every autograph I have from the Phillies and their staff has a backstory to it. They're all personal to me—Robin Roberts, Richie Ashburn, Mike Schmidt, Pete Rose, Larry Bowa. I have every Phillies autograph personalized to me except for Chuck Klein and Grover Cleveland Alexander. I've got Andy Musser. He actually wrote me a personalized note that I still have. I have a huge passion for all of this.

My Harry Kalas imitation came about when I was a little kid. I worked on it, perfected it, the whole nine yards. I ended up competing in Harry Kalas impersonation contests. The first one was held on WIP, and they must have had about 50 callers calling in and doing Harry. Joe Conklin was the judge of the contest. I called them and did the Harry impersonation and, out of all of the people that did Harry, I ended up winning the contest. That was in 2003, and it was the last-hurrah weekend for the Vet. They took me up to the Vet, and I got to go to three games that weekend, but the grand prize was that I got to go up into the broadcast booth and meet Harry Kalas. My dad was sick at the time, so I took my mom up with me. She couldn't have been more excited. They took us into the broadcast booth, and all the guys were there, and they asked me to do some "Harry" for Harry. Of course I did the imitation, and he said to me, "Tony, that's really, really great." Then, it was Opening Day at Citizens Bank Park and Joe Conklin was working as one of the Phillie guys at WMMR. They had a fierce competition of Harry Kalas soundalikes, and I won again. I won a second time! They gave me all kinds of prizes like Aerosmith tickets and other good stuff. I was named on Opening Day of Citizens Bank Park as the Harry Kalas soundalike winner.

> I was named on Opening Day as the Harry Kalas soundalike winner.

On April 13, 2009, Harry died. I was devastated, and unbeknownst to me, one of my dearest friends sent an e-mail to Channel 10. Doug Shimell, the Channel 10 reporter, came down to my house for what I thought was going to be a little man-on-the-street piece about Harry Kalas. They ended up doing a full news story on me. You can find it on YouTube. Just type in my name and click on the Harry Kalas thing. They ran that news story twice on Channel 10 in Philadelphia. When I play at McFadden's, I always do Harry and do a Dan Baker imitation as well. It goes over like gangbusters. I was actually approached by a gentleman that owns a radio station in Jersey to come and do voiceovers and imitate Harry. At the time, I didn't feel it was appropriate. It was just a respect thing that I had for Harry Kalas.

Honestly, for me, Harry Kalas was the voice of the Phillies. I was a little boy that grew up listening to the crackling of an AM radio, listening to Harry call the games. He was my best friend. I graduated with a degree in communications and worked at Delmarva Broadcasting—at WSTW and WDEL. I've done voiceovers for radio and TV commercials. I've wanted to be a broadcaster *because* of Harry Kalas. That's my love for the Phillies.

One of my first jobs out of college was working at the Leukemia Society of America, Delaware chapter. I was in charge of all their promotions and special events. My executive director was working on the Leukemia Golf Classic, which was a huge event. They had all kinds of celebrities coming in. Our secretary asked if I was busy Thursday afternoon. I was about 23 years old, pretty green and just out of college. She said they had this lady flying into Philadelphia International Airport. She's some kind of celebrity and is coming to the golf tournament. I asked who it was, and Joyce told me that her name was Robin Roberts and she had something to do with the Phillies. Are you kidding me! "Joyce, Robin Roberts is not a woman," I exclaimed. "He's one of the most decorated Phillies ever. He's a Hall of Fame pitcher. You want to know if I can pick him up from the airport? Are you kidding?"

As God made green apples, I swear I drove my 1984 Honda Accord from Wilmington to the Philadelphia International Airport. I stood there with buckling knees—I could hardly contain myself. I'm standing in the airport when he comes out of the tunnel. I just said his name, and he looked at me like, who's this young kid? I just told him I was with the Leukemia Society and there to pick him up. I carried his luggage and put it in my hatchback and we talked all the way to his hotel. I will never forget that as long as I live. He signed a picture and gave me autographs. It was really cool.

I SAW IT ON THE RADIO

Jay Tidwell

Tidwell, formerly an aspiring broadcaster and presently a custom tailor, grew up in Yeadon, Pennsylvania. His highlights include attending Game 1 of the 1993 NLCS, Curt Schilling's last home start as a Phillie in 2000, the last Vet home opener in 2003, Jim Thome's 400th home run in 2004, and the last game of the four-game sweep of the Mets in 2007 during their collapse.

When I was about 12, I decided that I wanted to be a broadcaster. Back in 1997 when I was a freshman in high school, we had an occupational project. My teacher encouraged me to call the Phillies and try to get an interview with Harry because I wanted to do baseball.

I called the office, and they said they'd see what they could do, because he was in Clearwater at spring training. About two weeks later the phone rang, and someone says, "Hello, Jay?" I said, "Yes," and all he said was, "Harry Kalas." I was so excited and it especially blew me away because he called from Clearwater. We talked for about 20 minutes or so. After the interview the public relations lady from the Phils called me and asked if there was anything else that she could do for me. I told her that I'd like to meet him, if I could. She asked me to call her back in two weeks and she'd see what she could do.

April rolled around and I called her up. She asked me to pick a game that I could come to and she'd leave two tickets. She'd come down to get me and take me up to the booth to meet Harry. So my brother and I went to the Vet, and we got to go up and meet Harry about a half hour before the game. He said, "How you doin' Jay?" He was the greatest guy and hearing that voice of his in person—wow! He treated me like I was an old buddy of his. We talked with Harry and Andy Musser, and five minutes before the broadcast started, when we were on our way out of the booth, Richie Ashburn came in. Whitey came in with his pipe and he's eating a bowl of grapes. I was nervous enough talking to Harry, but I was really nervous talking to Whitey because of who he was. I was at a loss for words, so I just said, "It's really nice meeting a Hall of Famer like yourself." He asked if I was having good time and I told him I was. I pulled out this old baseball that was a game ball from a **BABE RUTH*** league I was in. He says, "Boy, this ball sure is dirty!" Everybody was laughing, and I didn't know what to say, so I just told him that in our league baseballs stay around forever. He signed it and gave it back to me. We went back to our seats and watched the game—good game.

Interestingly enough, six years later, I had to interview Harry again for a similar project when I was at Temple. This was after the season and the Vet was closed. I took the subway down to the ballpark and the first person I saw when I was walking across the parking lot was Larry Bowa. He was driving out. That was interesting. Then I went to the front office and Harry himself met me. That was a surprise. We were talking all the way up to the press dining room about the Phillies' season and the Vet. I interviewed him for about 45 minutes or an hour. He got into the little minutiae about his routine and how he uses the old score sheets instead of the modern scorecards. He talked about who his favorite announcers were among his contemporaries. He really looked up to Bob Prince, and everyone looked up to Vin Scully. The thing that blew me away at the end was when I told him that I'd like to keep in touch with him. He gave me his home phone number. I couldn't believe it.

Harry had no ego. He treated everyone like they were a close friend. He was a great man.

***BABE RUTH** was the first player ever to hit 30 home runs in one season, the first to hit 40 in one season and the first to hit 50 in one season . . . and he accomplished those feats in the same season.

I NEVER MET HARRY KALAS BUT I'VE KNOWN HIM ALL MY LIFE

John Miley

Miley, a 79-year-old retired businessman, owns perhaps the world's largest sports audio library, about 100,000 highlights of complete sporting events taped from radio on 24-hour reels stored in rows of filing cabinets in a temperature-controlled room. He has perhaps the only existing copies of the entire seventh game of the 1955 World Series—the Brooklyn Dodgers' lone championship; the fourth quarter of Wilt Chamberlain's 100-point game against the Knicks in Hershey, Pa., on March 2, 1962; and the first of Nolan Ryan's 5,714 strikeouts in his debut with the Mets in 1966. Miley and his wife of 53 years, Carole, live in Evansville, Indiana.

I first met up with Harry Kalas when he was with the Astros, and I liked him there. When he got with the Phillies, he just seemed to come into his own. Perhaps it was working with **BY SAAM*** that helped him to adapt to what he finally ended up being. Of course, he was one of the great announcers of all time. Saam was one of my favorite announcers—I don't know whether he would be in the top five, but he certainly would be in the top 10 announcers I remember down through the years. He had a great voice and a great delivery. Among my favorites was his call of the Willie Mays catch in the 1954 World Series.

***BY SAAM** broadcast 4,935 losing games during his 49 years and never saw a pennant by either the A's or the Phillies. However, the Phillies won the pennant in 1950 when Saam was exclusively with the A's for the first time. In 1976, the Phillies brought Saam out of retirement to broadcast the late-season game in which the Phillies clinched the Eastern Division title.

Really, he did a great job on almost everything he did. I caught a game or two of his when he was in the twilight of his career and thought he was still announcing very well at that time.

I don't dislike the current Philly announcers. They may be some of the best of today's announcers—I just don't like, in total, today's announcers versus yesterday's. Is that because of my age or some other reason? I just don't think they make announcers anymore like they used to.

I thought Richie Ashburn was an outstanding announcer from the standpoint of being a former ballplayer. I generally don't appreciate the former ballplayers coming into the broadcast booth. They are not announcers; they are players. If they're going to sit there and tell their stories, that's fine, but don't do any play-by-play. I don't recall Richie ever doing play-by-play, although I bet he did some.

One name who comes to mind as a great ballplayer as well as a great announcer is **PHIL RIZZUTO***. He may not be the most-liked announcer in New York—although a lot of people from New York do like him. I think he did a great job. Recently, I just rel-istened to the 1964 World Series. I've been transferring games over from cassette to CDs for my business. In doing so, you're forced to listen to the games as they go into the computer. I was listening to Rizutto and Garagiola, two announcers who would not be necessarily my favorite play-by-play announcers because most of them are more accustomed to color than doing play-by-play, but I mean to tell you...I was enthralled by the stories they told. They did a fairly good accounting of the games, too. Ballplayers have a lot of stories. I wouldn't say that I don't necessarily like the old ballplayers coming into the

***PHIL RIZZUTO** is the only baseball person to earn a Gold Record... his game calling was in the background of Meat Loaf's *Paradise by the Dashboard Light*....Rizzuto was also the first-ever "Mystery Guest" on *What's My Line*.

booth, but maybe I'm mellowing a little bit in my old age as far as that's concerned, too.

Chris Wheeler was not a former ballplayer, to my knowledge. I believe he had been a writer. I didn't appreciate him to start with because I didn't think his voice was good enough and he didn't blend well, as far as I was concerned, with the announcers around him, such as Harry Kalas. But who would blend with Harry Kalas...really...because Harry is so good. As time went on, I appreciated Wheeler more and more, especially the stories he told. He did a little play-by-play but did mostly color and did an outstanding job of it—to the point where I saved some of his material. I think Scott Franzke is one of the better announcers of today. I love to hear his delivery. It's really good. The Phillies have been blessed down through the years with a really outstanding talent base of announcers.

Another guy with the Phillies was By Saam, who was the lead announcer when Harry Kalas came on. I first caught Harry Kalas when he was with the Houston Astros with Gene Elston. Gene pretty well controlled the booth so to speak, so you didn't hear much of Harry Kalas. I think Kalas was wise to move on to Philadelphia. When he moved on to the Phillies, he became another person. Each year he improved, to the point where, well, he's deservedly in the Hall of Fame. I just loved his delivery.

Today, instead of placing the shortstop or first baseman, or telling you what's happening in center field, or whether the outfield is swung to the left or to the right, the announcer will tell you what they're going to have for supper or tell you what they had for lunch. I don't want to hear that stuff. Just give me the ball game—a good description of it so that I can close my eyes, sit back, and think I'm right there in the ballpark. They don't do that anymore.

Andy Musser was a sensational announcer who worked with Harry Kalas for several years. I loved him on football when he was on one of the networks, as well as baseball. He and Harry Kalas together, with Richie Ashburn—that tandem right there was one of the best in the history of baseball announcing.

THE LAST GUY IN THE WORLD TO LET YOU DOWN

Brian McCafferty

Brian McCafferty is the President of McCafferty Sports Management, representing over 40 minor league baseball players. Prior to that he was Vice President of Chase Manhattan Bank, three times winning Sales Manager of the Year. His family owns James A. McCafferty Funeral Home located in Northeast Philadelphia, which had the honor of handling the funeral service for Harry Kalas in 2009.

It's April 13th, 2009 around 12:30 p.m. and I just left Frankford High School where I was helping Wander "Dominican Sensation" Nunez fill out his Florida Marlins questionnaire. I was listening to Anthony Gargano, sports talk show host on 610 WIP. Gargano interrupted, "We have just received word that Harry Kalas collapsed inside the Phillies broadcasting booth, in the Washington Nationals Stadium".

It's 3:00 p.m., and there is nonstop Harry Kalas coverage on all local, national, and radio stations especially WIP. Howard Eskin started his 3 p.m. talk show on 610 WIP in tears over the passing of Harry Kalas. A very dark cloud was cast over the City of Philadelphia. This was one of the biggest stories to hit Philadelphia in decades, some say bigger than the Phillies winning the 2008 World Series.

The phone call I was about to receive at 3:10 would be life changing for my family's funeral home business. "Hello", I answered. "Brian?" "Yes." "This is Dion Rassias." Dion Rassias is Harry's attorney and is also a friend of my wife Melissa, a criminal defense attorney in Philadelphia. Dion was placed in charge of funeral arrangements. "The Kalas family would like to have Harry buried through the James A. McCafferty Funeral Home."

Wow! We were going to bury Harry Kalas? I immediately drove to my family's funeral home. My brother Mark was in the middle of funeral arrangements with another family. I interrupted Mark and told him I needed to speak with him immediately. Mark was upset. "Brian what are you doing?" "We are going to bury Harry Kalas." "What?" "What are you talking about?" "Dion Rassias just called and the Kalas family wants to use James A. McCafferty Funeral Home."

On Tuesday, April 14th, accompanied by Police Captain Frank Bachmayer, I started on what would be a three hour trip to Virginia to pick up Harry Kalas. Harry had passed in Washington, D.C. but a Virginia licensed funeral director was contracted to pick him up. Frank and I didn't say much. We were traveling on I-95 and as we approached Citizens Bank Park. I heard Harry Kalas' voice. "Here's the 0-2 pitch". Okay, now I'm freaked. I yell, "Frank, do you hear that?" Frank then apologized and disclosed to me that Harry Kalas' 2008 World Series final out call was his incoming ring tone. When we arrived to pick up Harry we didn't say much. I was asked to identify him. I couldn't believe it. This was very upsetting. We left Virginia with Harry Kalas on our three hour journey to bring back a Philadelphia icon. Out of respect for the Kalas Family, no one, with the exception of their immediate family and close friends knew where Harry was.

I understood the magnitude of this event and told my brothers, "We have to have the funeral service at Citizens Bank Park!" The Kalas family and the Phillies agreed. Harry Kalas would become the third person in baseball history to have his funeral service held in a stadium. The other two were Yankees great

Babe Ruth in 1948 and St. Louis broadcasting legend **JACK BUCK*** in 2002. And, of course, legendary Detroit announcer Ernie Harwell joined that elite group in May 2010.

Harry Kalas would be a closed casket. I would be one of the last people along with my brothers to see the legend. My brother Mark ordered a white velvet blanket embroidered in red with Harry's name, the year of his birth and death, four baseball players, and his famous "That ball is outta here". That blanket was custom ordered and covered Harry. We closed the casket and put Harry into the hearse. We had a presidential motorcade ready to escort us to Citizens Bank Park. There were four police motorcycles and five police cars.

We entered Citizens Bank Park at 6 a.m. We backed the hearse up to home plate where Harry's coffin was placed on a stand. We met Chris Long, Dave Montgomery's assistant. Chris informed me that moments before we arrived, Phillies employees and ownership were up in the suite level when they saw our motorcade coming. They stopped. Speechless! They couldn't believe it. Then someone recognized me from the Philadelphia Phillies Scouting Department. "Brian, what are you doing here?" "My family owns James McCafferty Funeral Home." "Wait a second you're an agent and you own a funeral home?" "Well, yes!" "Oh my God!" they responded. "You guys can't get away from me," I laughed.

Former players, employees, ownership just looked at Harry's casket in disbelief. I watched Scott Palmer (formerly of Channel 6, now employed by the Philadelphia Phillies) just stare at Harry's casket for about ten minutes. I was told fans started lining up the night before. At 8 a.m. the first of 9,000 fans entered Citizens Bank Park to pay their final respects to this legend.

*In late 1953 the Cardinals chose **JACK BUCK** for play-by-play over Chick Hearn from Peoria, Illinois. Buck got the job because he had done excellent Budweiser commercials that summer while broadcasting the Rochester Red Wings, the Cardinals' AAA team in New York. The Cardinals had just been purchased by Anheuser-Busch.

They entered on the third base side and came onto the field and filed past Harry Kalas' casket for over five hours. Fans left cigarettes, beer cans, and personal messages they wrote Harry on top of the casket. **ESPN***, Comcast, Fox, and all local stations were live. This was truly an unbelievable outpouring of love for the "Voice of the Phillies." That day I also realized that Harry Kalas was bigger than any player that ever put on a Phillies uniform. He WAS the Phillies.

There was one fan that had a sign that read "There's no crying in baseball...until now". I later found out his name was Michael Albridge, of Blackwood, NJ. He went through the line three times.

At 1 p.m. the memorial service began for Harry Kalas. The Kalas family, along with former players, and friends filed by Harry's casket saying their final goodbyes. They were then seated behind home plate in the Diamond Club section. The Harry Kalas family sat in the first row. Then the 2009 Philadelphia Phillies team came out of the Phillies dugout led by Charlie Manuel. They filed past Harry Kalas' casket. Jimmy Rollins, Ryan Howard, and Jamie Moyer took longer than others. They were dressed in game uniforms. The team sat behind home plate in the Diamond Club Section joining the Kalas family and former players.

Also in attendance were Steve Carlton, Robin Roberts, Mike Schmidt, Dickie Noles, Larry Christiansen, Mitch Williams, John Kruk, Dick Allen, and many other former players; Governor Rendell and Mayor Michael Nutter. The memorial service had nine public speakers. I watched with my brothers Mark and Kevin from the visitor's dugout. I was sitting next to Bud Black manager of the San Diego Padres. On Friday night Mike Schmidt told the fans if you could look past Ben Franklin and

*****ESPN** debuted September 7, 1979. ESPN2 debuted October 1, 1993. **ESPN** The Magazine made its first appearance on March 11, 1998.

William Penn, Harry Kalas might have been the greatest to ever grace Philadelphia. I would agree.

Around 2:45 p.m. the Harry Kalas Memorial Service was over. Earlier in the morning, when we arrived, Chris Long disclosed to us that her boss had a "vision": When the memorial service concluded, present and former players would form two parallel lines starting where the coffin was and end at the hearse. They would pass Harry Kalas' casket to one another until he got to the hearse. When the memorial service concluded, starting from home plate, next to where Harry's coffin was, everyone formed parallel lines leading to the hearse. Starting with Bill Giles and Dave Montgomery, the casket was passed down the line from former to present players. As Harry's casket was being passed, "Bridge over Troubled Water" by Simon and Garfunkel was being played. As Harry's casket was being passed, fans were cheering. When the coffin reached the end of the line, Ryan Howard, Charlie Manuel, Jimmy Rollins and Brett Myers helped place Harry's casket into the hearse. As the hearse drove away, Harry's favorite song was played, "High Hopes".

The police motorcade was ready to leave Citizens Bank Park once the hearse left the field. It was disclosed in the media that Harry was going to be buried in a private ceremony on Tuesday. That was to throw everyone off so the family would have some privacy. Harry Kalas was going to be buried that day in Laurel Hill Cemetery. There were six limousines waiting outside Citizens Bank Park for the Kalas family. The police did a marvelous job coordinating the motorcade. We traveled north on I-95 and then we hit bumper to bumper traffic on 676. What I witnessed was amazing. Somehow the police were able to clear a path that was barely wide enough for our cars to get through. People figured out what was going on and started cheering: "Go Harry!" "We love you Harry!" It was an unbelievable tribute to an unbelievable man.

Hear Me Now, Listen to Me Later

My father had a steak of orneriness in him that makes a human barnacle like me look like St. Francis of Assisi. When Richie Ashburn, the Hall of Fame center fielder who saved the 1950 season by throwing Cal Abrams out at the plate in the ninth inning of the final game, died of a heart attack in 1997, I mentioned to my father that I had never met anyone who didn't like Whitey, far and away the most beloved Phillie of them all.

"I never cared for him," my father muttered bitterly.

"Why not?" I asked.

"I never liked his attitude."

For his career, Richie Ashburn hit .308, winning the batting title twice. Despite a weak arm, he led National League outfielders in put-outs, assists and double-plays in the same season twice, leading the league in put-outs a record-tying nine times. His final season, when he was banished to the **NEW YORK METS***, he batted .306. Even though he knew that he belonged in the Hall of Fame long before nonentities like Phil Rizzuto, he did not spend the rest of his life whining about it. In 1995, when the Special Veterans Committee finally voted him in, the entire Delaware Valley rejoiced.

My father never liked his attitude.

No wonder I turned out the way I did.

—**Joe Queenan**, 59, Tarrytown, N.Y.

I grew up in Southern Jersey so I couldn't make it to a lot of the Phillies games. Even when my parents took us to games, we still brought radios to the game. To sit in the stands, watch a game, and still hear Harry, that's the perfect evening.

---

*Richie Ashburn received a boat from the **NEW YORK METS** for being their most valuable player in 1962, the first year of the Mets' existence. He later said that the boat sank and the salvage operator who bought the remnants bounced his check to him.

My older brother is three years older than I; we grew up as die-hard Phillies fans. We started listening to Phillies games as soon as we were born. We were both born in June, so I'm sure the first games we heard Harry on the radio were some of our first days alive. My parents would always tell us how Harry was the only thing that made us fall asleep during our first few months. If there wasn't a Phillies game on TV that evening, then they knew they would have a long night.

> "She's my daughter, of course Harry can keep her calm."

We became little boys, and our parents gave us a little sister in the summer of '92. It was then that I realized what the Phillies meant because my sister was the same as us. She would scream and cry on the nights when no Phillies game were on and fall asleep as soon as she heard Harry. They actually had a taped Phillies game to use for the nights they didn't play.

So now, years later, my brother and I both have children of our own. The stories of us as children have been forgotten and not talked about for at least 15 years. My daughter was born in October—actually on the first day of the 2005 World Series—and her initials are M.L.B. (Mackenzie Layla Bartleson), so she is bound to be a baseball fan, but more importantly a Phillies fan. Anyway, she was six months old before she got to hear Harry for the first time. I remember every moment of it; she was sick and crying one night. The Phillies were playing the Dodgers in L.A. so the game was late. I had tried everything to get her to sleep and had gotten so frustrated that I had to watch some Phillies action just so I could calm down some. It was almost immediate—as soon as she heard Harry, she stopped crying. All the memories of when I was young hit me, and I thought, "She's my daughter, of course Harry can keep her calm." She fell asleep within five minutes of the game starting. I stayed up half the night and watched the Phillies beat the Dodgers. I thought it was funny that when I was a child Harry would calm me down and help my parents, and now that I was a father he calmed my child down and kept me awake.

I never got to meet Harry, and that's my loss. Regardless, my family always had a strong connection with him. You can tell when someone is great; they don't ever have to come in contact to have a great impact on you. Harry was great. I don't think people outside of the Philadelphia area will ever understand it; it's just something you need to feel, need to experience. Harry put the love in "Brotherly Love." Most importantly, he brought all of us together, brought a connection to all Phillies fans that no one will ever be able to explain. He was just great.

—**Matthew Bartleson**, 24, Cape May, NJ

My wife and I were at the Nationals Park the day Harry Kalas passed away. When you go to a Phillies-Washington Nationals game, it's almost like being at a Phillies home game. There are at least as many Phillies fans as there are Nationals fans. When they announced that Harry Kalas had passed away, it was just overwhelming—there were tears and just a stunned silence in the crowd.

I knew the Phillies official scorer at Washington, and he told me well before the game started that Harry had collapsed. He called me on my cell phone to let me know about his death just before the announcement was given to the stadium. That was a tough day.

—**Wayne Voltz**, 60, Stafford, VA, Intelligence Specialist for the Department of Defense

Six or seven years ago, I used to go with my friends to Benny the Bums to hear Skip Clayton do his talk radio show. He would have on a former Phillies player or an executive or coach. One time Harry Kalas was a guest. I wanted to meet him so badly. I love the Phillies. I grew up battling a learning disability and eventually overcame many problems to go on to work toward my Ph.D. When I could not get to a game, I listened to his broadcast. When the show was over, Harry signed autographs and the line was long. I had three items for him to sign and I wanted a picture with him. He was so patient and did not mind signing all of my items and graciously posed for a picture with me. That I treasure the most. At the time I was discouraged that I was not going to finish my Ph.D. because I was having trouble writing the dissertation. Harry encouraged me and made me feel that I could reach the major leagues of academia with the highest degree granted. I thought that he would find me to be a nuisance and talk too much because of my disability, but he did not. He made me feel like I was his best friend. I decided not to give up after hearing him encourage me. When I went to the **ALS*** benefit a few years later, I was lucky to be matched with him because I wanted Harry to sign a major league baseball that I did not have when I first met him. I wanted him to put the Hall of Fame inscription and the year. He signed it with the inscription and graciously asked if I was satisfied with the autograph. I was and I love the baseball, as it reminds me of him. I told him that I did not give up on my dissertation. I was sad to learn that Harry passed away before I graduated. I wanted Harry to say at a future Phillies game something like, "Congratulations to Louis Teller, who earned his Ph.D. As far as his time at Walden University, he is outta there with his Ph.D. in psychology."

—**Louis Teller**, 38, Holland, PA, Behavioral Specialist

It all started when I was 10. I loved baseball. Played it every chance I could. My dad was a Phillies fan and took me to a game here and there. Dad was a big stickler about getting outside and not sitting around watchin' television. He always wanted me to help him outside with some chores. He loved to listen to the Phils on the radio, but I hated it. Too much static, I thought. Both Mom and Dad were from Philly, but at the time we lived near McGuire Air Force Base because of his job. You see, the

*Jacob Javits, Charles Mingus, David Niven and Catfish Hunter have all died of **ALS**—Lou Gehrig's Disease.

SPORTS ILLUSTRATED

March 7, 1960

America's National Sports Weekly

25 CENTS

BASEBALL
The camps in the sun

OLYMPICS
Climax at Squaw Valley

SPORTING LOOK
A spring preview

Sports Illustrated

NEW HOPE
IN PHILLY

PITCHER ART MAHAFFEY

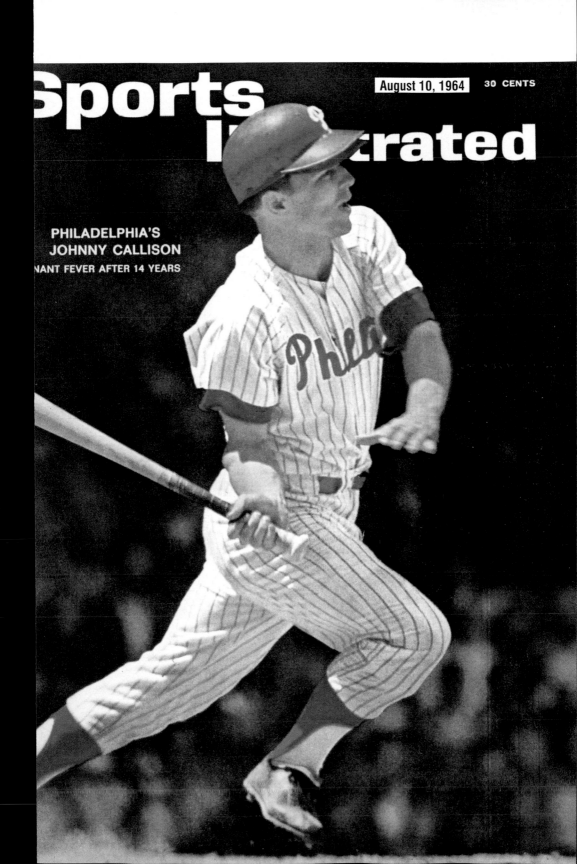

Sports Illustrated

August 10, 1964   30 CENTS

**PHILADELPHIA'S
JOHNNY CALLISON**
NANT FEVER AFTER 14 YEARS

March 1, 1965

Sports Illustrated

THE PHILLIES—OLD AND NEW—TRY AGAIN

JIM BUNNING
AND BO BELINSKY

BASEBALL 1966

Sports Illustrated

April 18, 1966   35 CENTS

In Color:
Scouting Reports on Both Leagues

DICK GROAT AND THE NEW PHILS

Sports Illustrated

April 9, 1973   60 CENTS

Baseball 1973

PHILADELPHIA
MIRACLE MAN
STEVE CARLTON

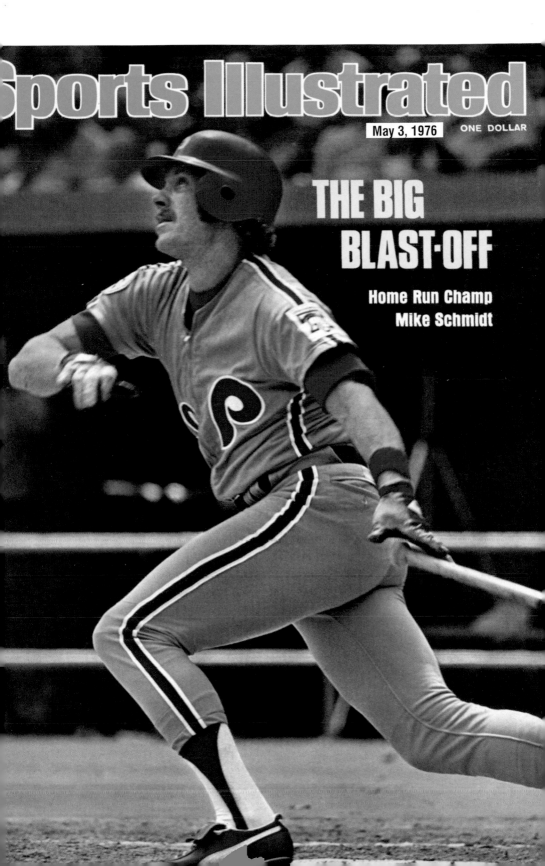

Sports Illustrated

May 3, 1976   ONE DOLLAR

THE BIG BLAST-OFF

Home Run Champ Mike Schmidt

Sports Illustrated

August 29, 1977 ONE DOLL

THE PHILLIES BULL AHEAD

Muscle Man
Greg Luzinski

Sports Illustrated

May 28, 1979 $1.25

ROSE HAS THE PHILLIES ON THE RISE

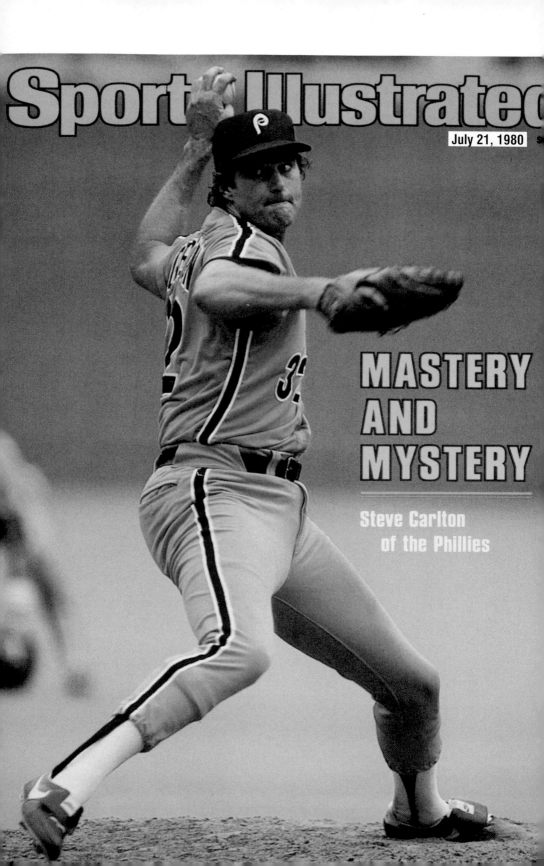

Sports Illustrated

July 21, 1980

MASTERY
AND
MYSTERY

Steve Carlton
of the Phillies

Sports Illustrated

October 27, 1980 $1.50

THE WORLD SERIES

Philadelphia's
Mike Schmidt

724454

SPECIAL BASEBALL ISSUE

Sports Illustrated

April 13, 1981

HOTSHOTS
AT THE HOT
CORNER

MVP
George Brett

MVP
Mike Schmidt

Sports Illustrated

July 19, 1982 $1.50

THE OLD MASTERS

ete Rose

Carl
Yastrzemski

29

Sports Illustrated

March 14, 1983

A ROSY REUNION

Tony Perez

Pete Rose

Joe Morgan

Sports Illustrated

ber 3, 1983 | $1.75

HEY LEFTY, TELL US HOW YOU WON No. 300

Steve Carlton Of The Streaking Phillies

Sports Illustrated

THE MONEY GAME: BASEBALL'S MILLIONAIRES

MIKE SCHMIDT	Phillies	$2,130,000 *
JIM RICE	Red Sox	$2,090,000
GEORGE FOSTER	Mets	$1,950,000
DAVE WINFIELD	Yankees	$1,745,000
GARY CARTER	Mets	$1,728,000
DALE MURPHY	Braves	$1,600,000
BOB HORNER	Braves	$1,500,000
RICKEY HENDERSON	Yankees	$1,470,000
EDDIE MURRAY	Orioles	$1,380,000
BRUCE SUTTER	Braves	$1,354,000
OZZIE SMITH	Cardinals	$1,300,000
JACK CLARK	Cardinals	$1,300,000
ROBIN YOUNT	Brewers	$1,284,000
PEDRO GUERRERO	Dodgers	$1,270,000
RICK SUTCLIFFE	Cubs	$1,260,000
FERNANDO VALENZUELA	Dodgers	$1,200,000
RICH GOSSAGE	Padres	$1,200,000
TIM RAINES	Expos	$1,200,000
STEVE KEMP	Pirates	$1,170,000
STEVE CARLTON	Phillies	$1,150,000
ANDRE DAWSON	Expos	$1,136,000
KEITH HERNANDEZ	Mets	$1,100,000
MARIO SOTO	Reds	$1,100,000
ANDRE THORNTON	Indians	$1,100,000
FRED LYNN	Orioles	$1,090,000
JOHN DENNY	Phillies	$1,083,000
TED SIMMONS	Brewers	$1,050,000
STEVE ROGERS	Expos	$1,050,000
JASON THOMPSON	Pirates	$1,030,000
JOAQUIN ANDUJAR	Cardinals	$1,030,000
WADE BOGGS	Red Sox	$1,000,000
GEORGE BRETT	Royals	$1,000,000
NOLAN RYAN	Astros	$1,000,000
JERRY REUSS	Dodgers	$1,000,000
KEN GRIFFEY	Yankees	$1,000,000
LaMARR HOYT	Padres	$1,000,000

*Figures Indicate Guaranteed 1985 Compensation

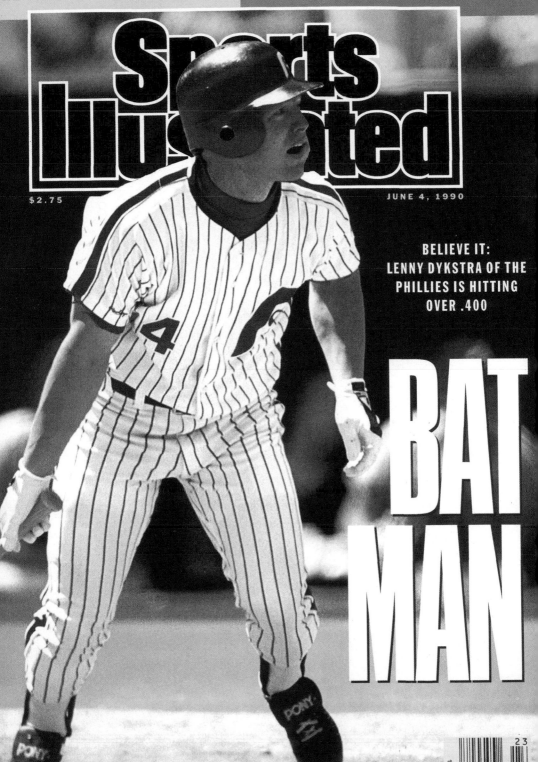

Sports Illustrated

$2.75

JUNE 4, 1990

**BELIEVE IT:
LENNY DYKSTRA OF THE
PHILLIES IS HITTING
OVER .400**

BAT MAN

0 724454 6

23

10094

NFL MELTDOWN

CAN CHARGERS, BEARS AND SAINTS SAVE THEMSELVES?

Sports Illustrated

www.SI.com

421 A RECORD
4-0 A STUNNER

October 8, 2

PLAYOFF PHEVER

J-Rollin' In Philly

Why Jimmy Rollins Is MVP

BY TOM VERDUCCI

Led by shortstop Jimmy Rollins,
the Phillies completed their amazing
comeback to win the NL East

2007–08
NHL PREVIEW
FINALS FORECAST
RANGERS vs. S
PLUS
THE PERFECT

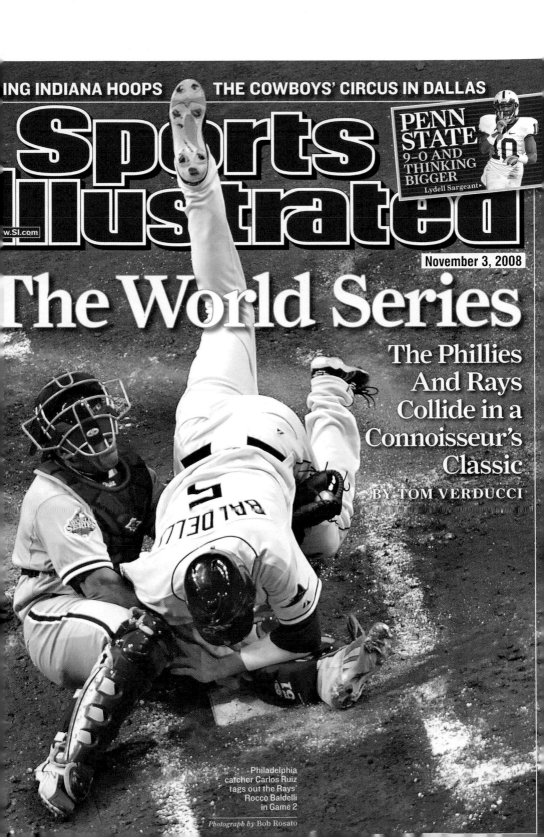

Sports Illustrated

w.SI.com

November 3, 2008

The World Series

The Phillies And Rays Collide in a Connoisseur's Classic

BY TOM VERDUCCI

Philadelphia catcher Carlos Ruiz tags out the Rays' Rocco Baldelli in Game 2

Photograph by Bob Rosato

Albe
Hayr

THE BIG MAN: Best of the Massive Tackles
DR. Z's ALL-PRO WATCH • PLAYOFF FORECASTS

92

Sports Illustrated

www.SI.com

November 10, 2008

Phillie

Phillies Win!
(But it was cold, wet and late. They deserved better)

To: Bud Selig From: Tom Verducci Subject: World Series

Dear Bud,
The season was memorable, but the World Series needs to change. The game has never been healthier but not for the fans. It's your job to fix it. . . . (Page 36)

Reliever Brad Lidge and Carlos Ruiz
helped bring Philadelphia its first
pro championship in 25 years

WORLD CHAMPIONS

Sports Illustrated

PRESENTS

PHILADELPHIA
PHILLIES

PHANTASTIC!

HOW THE PHILLIES WON THEIR FIRST
WORLD SERIES IN 28 YEARS

by Tom Verducci

PLUS

COLE HAMELS, RYAN HOWARD, CHASE UTLEY
and the ALLTIME PHILLIES TEAM

Sports Illustrated

February 23,

THE FABULOUS NEW LIFE

Of

COLE HAMELS

(Maybe it is as easy as it look

By BEN REITER

The World
Series hero
brings the
buzz to
the start
of spring
training

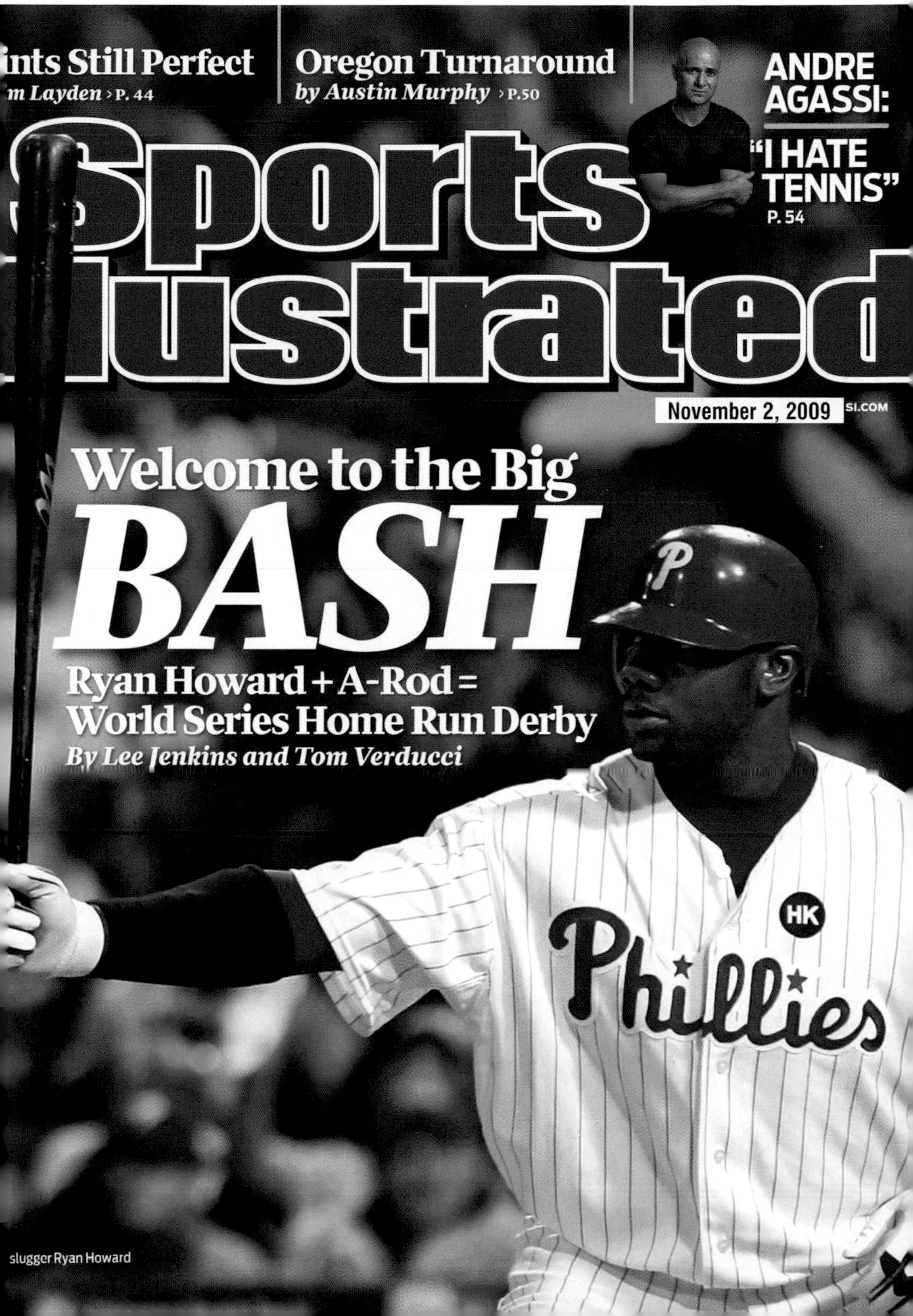

ints Still Perfect
m Layden › P. 44
Oregon Turnaround
by Austin Murphy › P.50
ANDRE AGASSI:
"I HATE TENNIS"
P. 54
Sports Illustrated
November 2, 2009
SI.COM
Welcome to the Big
BASH
Ryan Howard + A-Rod =
World Series Home Run Derby
By Lee Jenkins and Tom Verducci
HK
Phillies
slugger Ryan Howard

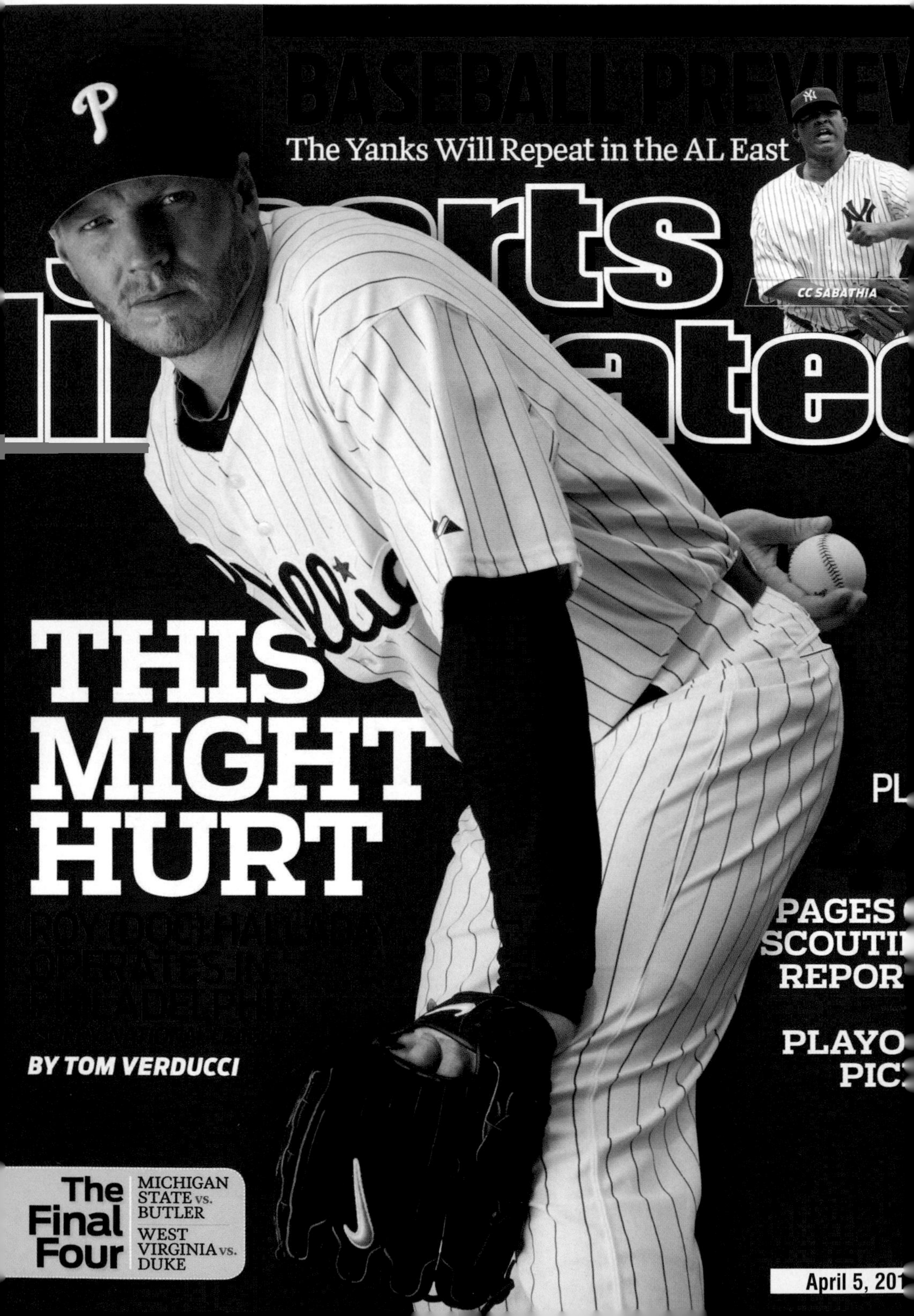

BASEBALL PREVIEW

The Yanks Will Repeat in the AL East

Sports Illustrated

CC SABATHIA

THIS MIGHT HURT

BY TOM VERDUCCI

PL

PAGES
SCOUTI
REPOR

PLAYO
PIC

The Final Four

MICHIGAN STATE vs. BUTLER

WEST VIRGINIA vs. DUKE

April 5, 201

air force base interferes with the radio to a certain degree, and that's why the radio was a little annoying to me.

Something magical happened though. Being forced to listen to the Phils was startin' to grow on me. I started finding myself imitating Harry while practicing around the house. I'd say, "Full-count pitch from Lefty—struck him out..." or "3-0 pitch to Schmidt—swing and a long drive." I imagined that was me striking someone out or hitting a long ball. I would say that from 1978 until Harry left us that he was a comfort and a friend to me although I never personally met him. By the time I was in my late teens, listening to Harry on the radio was an addiction. I just couldn't get enough. Some friends and family wondered why I chose to listen to the Phils and not just turn on the TV. They just didn't get how Harry painted the picture. You could turn on the radio and within minutes Harry would let you know where the game was. Harry never left me hangin'.

My most memorable game was a **CUBS***-Phils afternoon game. Dad and I were out and about, and when the other team started to get the better of us, Dad and I would just switch the station for a little while, looking for a change of luck. We seemed to write this one off. To our surprise a long time later, turning the radio back on, the Phils were in a slugfest in a game that ended with both teams scoring over 20 runs apiece. Harry kept my dad and me close and helped use my imagination and made me a person who always has "High Hopes." Thank you, Harry.

—**Alan Pennell, 41**, Hightstown, N.J., U.S. Postal Service

Here is something I heard during a radio broadcast of a Phillies game. It had to be around the mid-to-late 80s; either a businessperson's special or a day game in Chicago. This happened during a lull in the game and is "nearly" word for word:

*When **CUBS** manager Lou Piniella played minor league baseball in Aberdeen, South Dakota, the team's batboy was Cal Ripken, Jr.

Harry: *Due to pressure from the top, from now on...[pause] [Harry chuckling], I wasn't supposed to read that on the air.* Then Harry tries to go on to something else.

Richie: *Now wait a minute, Harry, wait a minute. Now that sounds interesting!*

And Harry tried to laugh it off and get back to the game, but Richie keeps it up. Obviously it was some edict that worked its way down indirectly from Bill Giles or whomever. I was on my way home from work and laughed about it a good part of the way.

It was either later on in the game or possibly the next day when I heard something like this:

Harry: *This is really a pressure situation.*

Richie: *Yeah. Pressure from the top! [more laughter]*

Some readers may have heard about this exchange before, and if so can fill in some of the blanks about the note comment.

—**Tom Holland**, 59, Northeast Philadelphia, PA

I am a long-time Phillies season ticket holder as well as an avid amateur photographer. I frequently take my camera to games, especially if there is to be a special event. On one such occasion, I took a picture of Mike Schmidt in civilian clothes, throwing out the first pitch at his last game at Veterans Stadium. The photo turned out very well, so I had it enlarged to 20 x 30 and sent it to Harry up in the booth at the Vet.

I never heard whether or not he liked the picture or, for that matter, if he had even received it. One day at an event for season ticket holders I ran into Tug McGraw and related the story to him. I asked if he knew anything about the picture and whether Harry liked it. Tug said, "Well, Doc, who did you do this for, him or you?" I realized he was right and didn't think about it any further.

A few years later, I got a call at my office from Harry's wife asking if I had a negative of the picture. She said that Harry had framed that photo and hung it on their playroom wall. But, while some guys were horsing around, the picture was hit, the glass was broken, and the photo was destroyed. The reason for her call was because she was interested in having the picture duplicated. I told her I was glad to know that the photo had been received and very pleased that he liked it enough to have it framed, because I had never heard anything back. She was shocked and said that she would take care of that since he had liked it very much. I was able to find the negative and sent her an identical print.

A few weeks later on a Friday, a letter from Harry was sent to my office. I put it on my desk, unopened, just prior to conducting a group therapy session. My wife came in and admonished me for the sloppy appearance of my desk. I quickly gathered papers and straightened up before my patients arrived for the session. Afterward I left for the weekend in a hurry, not realizing I'd forgotten to take the letter with me. When I returned I couldn't find it. While straightening up it must have been discarded, and the cleaning crew took out the trash. Despite an exhaustive search it was never seen again.

Sometime later I sent Harry a photograph of Whitey leaning out of their broadcast booth. Apparently it was the last photo of Whitey taken at the ballpark, and it was shortly before he died. This time I did hear from Harry. He thanked me for the picture and said it was very meaningful to him. He also sent me a mass card from Whitey's funeral.

To this day, I wonder what he said to me in that lost letter...

Arnold Gadwin, M.D., 83, Cherry Hill, NJ, Neuro Psychoanalyst, co-author *Conquering Chronic Pain After Injury*

When Harry and Whitey were broadcasting a Phillies game in the summer of '93, Whitey said he remembered when Art Mahaffey struck out 17 batters at Wrigley Field back in the 60s. Harry agreed with Whitey. Well, I happened to be lucky enough to be at that game, and it took place in old **SHIBE PARK*** (Connie

The Phillies first played at **SHIBE PARK in 1939 as tenants of the A's for night games. They became the sole occupant of the ballpark, later known as Connie Mack Stadium when the A's left for Kansas City after the 1954 season. The Phillies then purchased the ballpark and played there through 1970.*

Mack Stadium). I wrote the boys a note telling them about where the game had been played.

Lo and behold, about two weeks later I received a nice note from Harry. He actually said he was glad I pointed their error out and enclosed five box seat tickets for a Phillies/Pirates game. My sons Ed and Tom, my friend Andy, his son Christian, and I went to the game. The boys printed a large sign that simply said "Thank You Harry" on it. Between innings we held the sign up and during one of the breaks Harry leaned out of his broadcast booth and smiled and gave us a big wave!

Later I had the privilege to sing *The National Anthem* at Veterans Stadium. It was a memorable moment for me. When I came home I said to my wife, "I wonder if I could get a tape of that to share with the family." I wrote a short note to Harry, and about a week later there it was, a tape of my *National Anthem*. The biggest and best part of the whole thing is at the end when Harry says over the loudspeakers, "That was Ted Andrewlevich from Sunbury, PA, with a fine rendition of our *National Anthem*." I will always remember that comment and that moment.

Yes, Harry was quite the guy. A down-to-earth real person, awesome announcer, and a true Phillies fan. So I leave you, or as Harry would say, "I'm....outta here!"

—**Ted Andrewlevich**, 70, Sunbury, PA

Harry Kalas was a huge part of the Phillies experience. When I was in high school at about age 15, I wrote to Harry that I was interested in pursuing broadcasting as a career. He sent me a really nice letter that I probably still have. I was so impressed because it was a real letter about the path that he'd recommend, not a form letter. He answered the specific questions that I asked. At that age, it so impressed me that he had answered my letter right away, too. I saw him at college basketball games as a kid. He was such a humble fan with such a nice way about him. Having opposite experiences with other announcers that weren't necessarily that friendly made him even more impressive. He was the genuine thing.

—**John Lennon**, 49, Horsham, PA

I was very close with Harry Kalas for many years. The thing that always stands out is that Harry loved the fans and the team. He loved people—no matter what he did he got a lot out of what he could do for people.

When Harry was inducted into the Hall of Fame, it was a big weekend. I was lucky enough and very honored to have credentials to attend all the things they had planned for Harry. Watching all these people like Stan Musial and Hank Aaron come up and hug Harry and tell him how much he deserved to be in the Hall of Fame was really something to see. At the big dinner they had where Harry was one of the honorees, his son Todd all of a sudden got up from the table and left. When he came back a couple of minutes later, he came over to me and said to eat up quick. He said the same thing to his brother, Brad, and the others. We knew the Phillies had a big contingent of people there for the weekend. But all Todd told us was that we were going to take a ride. It was a very class act. The Phillies had this huge party going on that night. They had a big place about a mile outside of Cooperstown set up with a big tent, a band, and all the works. Todd then told Harry to finish up because we were going to go see the Phillies people. Harry was so happy about that.

That year I was told that 68 Hall of Famers had returned for that weekend. It was the biggest group ever. Harry was being honored, and we're sitting there having a great time with all these great players and their families, but Todd knew that his dad would want to be with the Phillies people. By this time it was near the end of the dinner anyway, so sure enough we all walk out and a van takes us off to the Phillies party. It was one of the neatest things I had ever seen. We were driving down this dirt road where all these cars were parked and a band was playing. There were about 200 people there. When Harry walked in they were just mesmerized. They were so happy and excited to see him. I think Todd might have said something to his dad like, "I'm sure you want to be at that Phillies party tonight, so

I've arranged it." He was loved by the Phillies organization, but he loved the Phillies back.

—**Jeff McCabe**, long-time close friend of Harry Kalas

I first saw Harry Kalas at Connie Mack Stadium. Then I saw him on a couple of road trips, in Pittsburgh and Chicago. I ran into him again at the Vet. But the first time I *really* met him was in 1984 when I was dating my wife. I was a bartender at the time at Scoogi's, and we had box seat tickets at the old Veterans stadium right on the fence. My brother and his girlfriend went with us. This probably wasn't a good thing to do, but we had parking with these tickets inside the confines of the stadium. I had packed a cooler full of beer. So, I told my brother that after the game, we'll sit around and wait for the traffic to go and have a beer.

We're sitting on the grass where the Phillies come out and drinking Moosehead beer. We were watching Daulton come out and those guys. People were chasing around for autographs. Nobody was bothering us and we were having our own fun. Pretty soon, here comes Harry Kalas wearing a fancy jacket with a cigarette in his mouth. He had a cup of beer in his hand. My fond memory was that my kid brother and I went over and said "hey" to him. Harry was never snobbish so he was friendly. My kid brother, Patrick, then walks up and puts his arm around Harry, and they're walking together. We go back to where we were sitting on the grassy hill, and I asked Harry a little bit about Andy Musser, who was a broadcaster at the time, before Chris Wheeler came on the scene. He acted like we were old buddies. Harry shook our hands, met our girlfriends and then heads to his car. The next thing you know he and his wife go by—she's driving—and they honk and wave at us. What a thrill.

Fast forward a few years to 1992. I took my wife on a Phillies trip to Wrigley, and we all stayed at the same hotel as the Phillies team. We go to the Friday game and end up in the hotel lounge with Phillies fans all over the place. It was a Phillies excursion—mostly beer bums; not a lot of couples. We're sitting there at our table and here comes Harry into the room. He was staying at the same hotel. Everyone says hello and then he stops at our table. We make eye contact, then he looks away, and we make eye contact again. He recognized me from back in '84 when I was with my brother. He said, "Hey, John" to me and it blew our minds and everyone at the table almost fainted. He said he had to get out of there because he was meeting someone for dinner. He and Bowa or someone took off then, but it dropped all of us that he remembered me. It was amazing that he remembered after all those years—like eight years later. I never forgot that.

But the greatest thing was the night with my brother with his arm around Harry and they're walking up to the car. Harry's got the cigarette hanging out of his mouth and he's signing an autograph for my brother. Then the fact that he remembered me and my name eight years later in front of all those beer bums sitting at the table. They were all shell-shocked. Those are my fondest memories.

I have another Phillie memory of Lennie Matuszek that's pretty good. In September of '83 when they had the call-ups, they put Pete Rose on the bench. He was still a Phillie that year. They benched him in favor of Matuszek. Matuszek hit like nine home runs and knocked in 30 runs in September. It really was him and Schmidt that won the division for them. I got to meet him the day after the Orioles beat them. I worked as a bartender at a place in northeast Philly called Ye Olde Ale House. Matuszek shows up there. I wasn't married yet so when I got done at 6:00, we end up going out with my cousin. Just the three of us—me, my cousin, and Lenny—go to watch some of our buddies play softball. The thing about him that I thought was really nice was that two months later he sent me a personal letter and a bunch of signed stuff. That was really nice that he took the time to do that. He ended up broadcasting for the Cincinnati Reds.

—**John O'Mara**, 56, Somerton, PA, retired

I met Harry Kalas once in my life. I bumped into him at a catering hall when he must have been having dinner in another room. And true to his reputation he was the perfect gentleman and said hello to me and shook my hand. But I have a policy that I do not do anything more than say hello to celebrities in their off time.

I have met many Philly sports celebrities in my time—Buddy Ryan in the men's room at the Merriam Theater when he was the celebrity 13th body buried in the basement at *Arsenic & Old Lace*. I asked how the team was doing and he said, "Don't count us out." And when he came up out of the basement as the "body", I was shocked. I met Bobby Clarke at my neighborhood McDonald's one morning with a friend of mine. I just went over and shook his hand and said hello. The same with Jaromir Jagr in the Sands Casino one night when he and his lady friend were sitting next to me and my wife. My wife went over to him and asked him if he was actually Jagr and, when he said yes, my wife said that I was a big fan. I said I wasn't *his* fan but a *Flyers* fan and we had a big laugh.

I seem to meet celebrities in bathrooms. I met Bobby Taylor in a bathroom in a now-defunct Mexican restaurant in New Jersey the same night that Buddy Ryan was there. Taylor was being constantly hassled and people wouldn't let him eat. I felt sorry for him. My biggest thrill was the day that we were hanging around the Vet for autographs, and all the kids started chasing Willie Montanez for his autograph. My friend and I stuck by the door and were both lucky to get Steve Carlton's autograph. That was his first Cy Young year, the year he went 27–10. I shook his hand and thought I was to blame for that five- or six-game slump he had before he went on that tear that led to him winning the **CY YOUNG***.

My wife attended a few baseball 101 clinics for ladies. The last one that she went to she was able to meet Harry and had her picture taken with him. She made Harry cry because she told him that she missed him and Larry Andersen together on TV.

—**Fred Weber**, 57, Blackwood, NJ

*As a young boy in Newcomerstown, Ohio, Woody Hayes was a batboy for a semi-pro baseball team managed by CY YOUNG.

Chapter 6

PHILLYPALOOZA

Experience Is What You Get When You Don't Get What You Want

UP IN THE AIR ABOUT THE PHILLIES

Tim Herlich

Despite moving away from Philadelphia at the age of five, Herlich has been a life-long Phillies fan. Tim grew up on Long Island and has lived in Seattle since 1982. He is a member of the Society for American Baseball Research and is current president of the Northwest chapter. Tim thanks his Dad Ken, wife Leslie, and daughters Wendy and Jamie for their enthusiastic support of his passion for the Phillies and the game of baseball.

To know why I'm such a Phillies fan is to know something about my dad. He was born in New York City and grew up in the Glendale neighborhood of Queens, close to the Brooklyn/Queens line. He grew up with everybody around him being a Dodger, Yankee, or Giants fan. He wanted to be different, so he rooted for the Cardinals and the Gashouse Gang. He remembers the first pennant race he followed in the newspapers in 1934 when he was 11 years old. It was his Gashouse Gang in that pennant race. His favorites were Dizzy Dean and Pepper Martin and some of the guys on that team. He probably would have remained a Cardinal fan if World War II hadn't intervened. And if that hadn't happened, I might be a Cardinal fan now, too. He tried to enlist in the service three times early in the conflict, but he was rejected all three times because he had a punctured eardrum from a childhood illness. He was declared 4-F and not allowed to serve in the armed forces.

He wanted to do something to support the war effort so signed on with the fledgling commercial airline industry and went to work for a company called Trans World Airlines, now known as TWA. He started working in New York and was ultimately transferred to Philadelphia. He married my mom and had us three kids—I'm the youngest—all born in Darby, PA. I was born in 1950 after the Whiz Kids pennant. The Whiz Kids captured my dad's imagination. His favorite player was Robin Roberts, and for some reason, I liked Granny Hamner as well as Roberts. That's what turned him into a Phillies fan—being in Philadelphia in the late 40s as the Whiz Kids formed. I followed in his footsteps as a Phillies fan. We moved back to the New York area to be closer to the family on Long Island in 1956. My brother and sister rooted for the Dodgers and the Giants, but I kept my rooting interest with the Phillies. The Dodgers and the Giants moved to the West Coast after the 1957 season, so there was no National League team there to root for anymore. And my dad raised us all to hate the Yankees. He hated the Yankees, so we all despised the Yankees—and do to this day. I continued to be a Phillies fan even when they became a **CELLAR-DWELLER CLUB*** with their four last-place finishes beginning in 1958. My dad worked for TWA, and at one point we said, "Let's travel and see our favorite team, the Phillies." They were showing a few Phillie games on television in New York since the Dodgers and Giants had left but not enough, and we wanted to see them in person. We had to go someplace where TWA flew so that we could go and get back in the same day. Unfortunately, Philadelphia was not on a direct route for TWA, so in 1961 my dad and I took a trip to St. Louis. That day we flew on the newest commercial jet in service, the Convair 880, a four-engine jet that handled almost like a military fighter jet. We flew to St. Louis during the Phillies' record-setting 23-game losing streak to watch a doubleheader. Dad thought that no one would come out to watch the Phillies, but the place was packed—Sportsman's Park in St. Louis—because there was a reunion of the Gashouse Gang between games, enabling my Dad to see his

*From 1918 through 1949, the Phillies never finished higher than third. They **FINISHED LAST** 16 times between 1919 and 1945.

old team. The Phillies dropped both games and kept their losing streak intact. I was ten years old at the time so I don't remember a lot, but I do remember Bobby Gene Smith running into the outfield wall and having to be taken out of the game with an injury. But that whetted my appetite to see my Phillies team, if I at all could. So the next year, 1962, we began going to one Phillies game a year. But I wasn't content going on the road. I wanted to go down to Connie Mack Stadium and see people rooting for the Phillies. I didn't want to always go to hostile territory. When the Mets came into being with the National League expansion, we were able to go to the **POLO GROUNDS*** when the Phillies played there beginning in 1962. So I was able to see a couple of those games. I saw Jackie Davis, a rookie outfielder who played only one year for the Phillies, hit the only triple of his career. It was a line drive over the center fielder's head in the Polo Grounds. They probably could have sent him home, but they held him up. I also went to a game where Art Mahaffey hit two home runs and pitched a complete game against the Mets.

In 1963 our sojourn to Connie Mack Stadium was to see a doubleheader against the pennant-leading and, eventually, pennant-winning Dodgers. Koufax and Drysdale were scheduled to pitch the doubleheader. We planned to fly down and then, since we couldn't fly back, take the train home. So we flew down, stood on line for the Koufax/Drysdale doubleheader, and never got into the stadium. It ended up a real disappointment because the one day of the year we planned to go to the home game, we got shut out. Koufax won the first game, but the Phillies actually scored two runs against him. I remember thinking, when reading about it, that they did pretty well. They beat Drysdale the second game—about as good an outcome as you could hope for at that time.

*The lights from the **POLO GROUNDS** are used today at Phoenix Municipal Stadium, the spring training home of the Oakland A's.

In 1964 we went down to watch a doubleheader against the Cubs. Dick Ellsworth was pitching for the Cubs at the time and beat the Phillies the first game. The Phillies came back to maul the Cubs in the second game, something like 10-2. Of course that was when pennant fever for the National League was in full swing. During that time, we would also take trips if we could. We flew out to Wrigley Field to see the Phillies play a couple of games—once early in the season, and I can't ever remember being colder than I was that day in Wrigley Field in April. We made a couple of trips to Wrigley because that was an easy trip to get out and back in one day. And in those days at Wrigley, they were all day games. During the summer you could go out during the day and be back home in bed that night. It was during that time living on the south shore of Long Island that I discovered that, then and now, I could get the Phillies on the radio. I'd turn on the radio and hear **BYRUM SAAM*** and Bill Campbell announcing. It was crackly and the signal went in and out. It was like I was in a time warp listening to a Phillies game, but it was *my* team going for a pennant for the first time since I was born. It was enthralling to listen to a live game and hear Roy Sievers hit a home run, or Bobby Wine make a great stop and start a double play, or Tony Taylor do something, and of course Callison and Richie Allen. In those days, Richie Allen, Bunning, and Chris Short were the guys—it was just a great team. And that was my team and still is to this day. Even though they didn't win the pennant, they are all my heroes—every one of them on that team.

*"Hello there, **BYRUM SAAM**, this is everybody speaking." Byrum "By" Saam's first words on his first broadcast for the Phillies. Saam was known as "the man of a zillion words." He first broadcast Phillies games in 1938 and worked simultaneously for the A's and the Phillies from 1939 through 1949. He broadcast exclusively for the A's from 1950 through 1954. After the A's left for Kansas City, he went back to the Phillies for 21 years before retiring after the 1975 season because of cataracts.

In 1965 we went to Milwaukee to watch the Braves. I remember seeing Hank Aaron and Eddie Mathews and being scared every time a Brave batter came up because they had the type of lineup where any batter could change the outcome of the game with just one swing. They had five or six guys that hit 20 or more home runs that year. But the Phillies won that game behind Bunning and Gary Wagner in relief. Then in 1966 we made our last trip to Connie Mack Stadium. Robin Roberts was in his last year and was pitching for the Cubs. And of course he was my father's idol. We flew down and even brought my mother. We took the subway to Shibe Park and watched as Roberts got bombed. He didn't even last the first inning. The place was packed. You didn't always have a packed house in the 60s, even for a good game. But, of course, Roberts was coming back. It bothered my father so much to see him lose that game and basically end his career.

By that time I was 15, and the next year the summer jobs started, because that's a rite of passage. I didn't have as much time to make those trips to see the Phillies as I wanted to. We made one trip down to Veterans Stadium in 1971 before I got married. We went down with my wife (then my fiancé), father, sister, and her boyfriend to see a doubleheader that **BOB GIBSON*** dominated. He was a real fast worker. In the ninth inning, Willie Montanez hit a home run and brought the Phillies within two runs. Everyone was cheering. Then, Gibson just reared back—this was in the bottom of the ninth—and it seemed like within a minute the game was over. He just decided this was it and wasn't fooling around anymore. All of a sudden the game was over and the Phillies had lost.

***BOB GIBSON** played basketball with the Harlem Globetrotters several off-seasons....In 1972, Bill Cosby signed a lifetime contract with the Globetrotters for one dollar per year. In 1986, the Globetrotters gave him a nickel raise. Cosby made several appearances with the team and is an honorary member of the Basketball Hall of Fame.

I got a job working for Northwest Airlines in Minneapolis. I never saw the Phillies come through, but I never stopped rooting for them. I listened to the playoffs on the radio in the 70s when they didn't quite make it to the World Series, and then I was transferred to Europe—to Stockholm, Sweden. Northwest Airlines won a route to Scandinavia, and I was named the manager of the sales operation. This was before the Internet, before satellite broadcasts, and Stockholm is far from continental Europe, so there are very few Americans in Sweden. There was an American Embassy and there were a few Americans there. However, there was one American that owned a nightclub in Stockholm, and he was also from Philadelphia. This was in 1980, when the Phillies went on and won the World Series. Of course, I was talking to my father every day through the playoffs with Houston and then the World Series against the Royals so I could find out what happened the day or night before. I read a little bit about it in the *International Herald Tribune*, but just a small synopsis. I was totally distanced from it otherwise. This nightclub owner had one of the early VCR projection systems. It was one of those front projections that had the curved screen—a big floor unit—and he had a viewing room in his nightclub. He told me he had a friend back in Philly who videotaped all the games and that the friend was going to send them to him. He asked if I would want to watch them. I said, "You *bet* I want to watch them!" This is the first time that they ever won a World Series; it might be the last! So in the middle of winter in Stockholm, where it's dark and cold, he gets these videotapes after the World Series. I go to his place about 4:00 in the afternoon, when it's already dark, and put in the tapes. He told me to stay as long as I wanted. I watched each game, 1 through 6, back to back until 4:00 the next morning. I was not bored in the least. I watched every pitch and every minute in the middle of winter and enjoyed it immensely.

I was ultimately transferred back to the states, to Seattle. I've been here since 1986—again an American League city with no National League coming in. So my rooting for the Phillies has always been more in my head and heart than in person. I've often wondered—because I'm here in Seattle and have developed a rooting interest for the Mariners just as I did for the Twins—if I would change allegiance. What if the Phillies and Mariners played each other? Well, finally, interleague play was adopted and I was put to the test. There was an exhibition game in Safeco Field when it was new in 2000. The Phillies played just before the season began. I bought tickets and thought, "Okay, this is going to be the test; who am I going to be cheering for?" But right from the start I began cheering for the Phillies. Now I know to this day that if the Mariners and Phillies meet in the World Series, I'm going to be cheering for the Phillies from the first pitch on.

That's basically the story of my rooting. It's unique that in being an airline family, we were able to indulge ourselves from time to time—even if on a very limited scale—and experience rooting for the Phillies in places where most Phillies fans never would have gone, like St. Louis or Chicago. We went to a game in Pittsburgh once. We went out to San Francisco and saw Rick Wise pitch a three-hitter to win the first game of a double-header, 1–0, in 1971. Then the Phillies lost the nightcap. It was my father, my sister, and me—the only thing that all three of us remember is Willie McCovey hitting the hardest ball we'd ever seen hit, even to this day. It was against Randy Lerch and left the ballpark on a line. In the blink of an eye it was gone. But it was foul, thank goodness. He was pinch-hitting and ended up grounding out.

Our rooting was usually done in opposing ballparks around the country, except for that one game a year we'd fly down to Philadelphia, take the subway, walk to Shibe Park, watch the game—except in 1963 when we couldn't get into that double-header—then catch the train in North Philly to go back to New York and arrive in the middle of the night or early morning. It was worth it, though, because we had that one game a year when we could say we were with the home team.

2008
IT WAS ABOUT PRIDE
IT WAS ABOUT WINS
IT WAS ABOUT TIME

Andy Wheeler

Andy Wheeler, 34, grew up in Aston, PA. His favorite team was the Phillies, so he learned everything he could about them. It paid off, because after graduating Temple University in 1998 he was hired by Fox 29 as a Sports Producer. Since then, he has spend the last 9 years at CBS 3 in Philadelphia where he's been nominated for 13 Emmy Awards, while winning twice.

I had been thinking about a story idea for a long time. I had met Harry before but didn't know how to approach him with my story idea. You know how everybody hears the 'outta here' calls, and everybody hears the NFL Films stuff. It was 2008, when the Phillies got knocked out by the Rockies.

My idea was to have Harry Kalas saying other things. We'd have him do a pick-up line—"Do you come here often?" "Would you like some fries with that?" "Supercalifragilisticexpialidocious." We tried to get all the most ridiculous things you could think of.

I called him and told him who I was. He said, "Hi Andy, how are you." I said, "Good. I was wondering if you would do this story for us." I explained it to him, and he sounded hesitant about it. Then he said, "All right. Sure." Talking to him on the phone was like listening to him when he was doing play-by-play. His voice is the same *all the time.*

I told him we would send over a reporter, Sean Murphy, and he would do the interview there. I called him back and asked for his address where he lived. He said, "Sure," and gave it to me. Well, this is the age of Garmin, where you plug in an address, and it takes you there. But, Harry started giving turn-by-turn directions. I didn't have the heart to tell him we would be able to find it really easy...plus the fact that I enjoyed listening to him giving me directions to his house. It was great, but it was hysterical. I called my boy afterward and excitedly told him that I had just been talking to Harry Kalas and he spent 10 minutes giving me directions to his house. He said to me, "How did it sound? How did it sound?"...

> Talking to him on the phone was like listening to him when he was doing play-by-play.

Harry came in our studio one time, and we did a story where all the Philly announcers would read, *Twas the Night Before Christmas*. It was Merrill Reese, Jim Jackson and Harry. Harry came in and sat in front of the Christmas tree in our studio and read the whole thing through. He's such an amazing guy. He never really told us "no" to any of the requests we made. We didn't have anything to pay him, but he was always such a great guy.

When big stories and big things are happening sports-wise, I'm the one who does damage control. I'm a producer so one of the things I'm good at is getting stories on the air quickly, editing things quickly, turning things around, dealing with craziness and turning it into something that is viewable. You go in and make sure the talent is where they should be and you bring in the guests. I really wanted to get an opportunity to be a field producer for the 2008 World Series.

There were so many media outlets there to give reports and do interviews. We were told that we had to wait until FOX did their thing. We had to wait in a line down a long, long concrete hallway. All of us—60-70 different TV and radio crews were jammed into this hallway, not able to see or hear a thing. I remember thinking, "I'm not even going to get to see the final pitch." It was absolutely painful. You knew you were eventually going to get to go out on the field but not be able to see the final out.

When I was a kid, my parents were at Game 6 of the '80 World Series. They were there when they won it all. I remember the babysitter letting my sister and me watch it on TV. So I was down there at the World Series, thinking, "I've waited all this time to see any Philadelphia team, but in particular the Phillies, win either in person or on television, and I'm in this hallway with 60-70 other stations, and I can't see or hear a thing."

It's the ninth inning...we're all lined up in there...everybody is ready to go. It was dead quiet in the hallway. We are in this concrete hallway so most of us have no cell service. I screamed out, "Does anybody know what is going on?" "One out." We all keep standing there. Waiting. Then you can hear a 'little bit' of a rumble. I thought, "What was that?" Again, I yelled out, "What happened? What happened?" "Two outs, but there's a man on second." It got quiet again. Everybody is waiting. Then you hear another rumble.

At the same time, there were closed doors along the hallway that I hadn't even realized were there. Suddenly, three Phillies employees pop out of these rooms. I yelled, "Yes!" All the media began looking around at them wondering what had happened, "Did we just win? What happened?" All of a sudden, there's a lot of movement. Here come the Philly owners up the hallway going out onto the field. We asked if we could go out and they told us, "No, you can't go."

More people keep coming down—MLB officials, and we were finally told we could go out. We all started jogging down this long, long hallway, which made a sudden left turn. There's still another 20-25 yards ahead of us. We keep running down the hallway and then make a right and go up these steps.

It was like *walking into happiness!* As you walked up the steps, the only thing you could see was the right-field upper deck.

You could see people cheering. People hugging. Then, finally, you are standing on the field. Everyone around you is going completely nuts. I took a picture of the upper right-field area.

I told myself that, at this point, I had to start working. I have a camera crew to my right and have a reporter with me. I looked around the field and could see this mass of people...and a flag! It's Ryan Howard running around left field holding this flag.

I yelled to one of the camera crews to "go-go-go". We had to have one camera crew set up to go live, which would be about a 15-minute wait before the local affiliates could go live from the field. Another camera crew with another reporter was available. There was a weave of 70 or 80 people or more on the field traveling en masse with this flag. We ran out there and the first person I saw was Geoff Jenkins.

The reporter should have been asking the questions, but she was a news reporter so she had no idea what was going on. I grabbed the microphone out of her hand, and we get in on this group interview of Jenkins. I ask the first question, "Does it feel like you thought it would?" He kind of had this glaze in his eyes, "It's amazing. I can't believe it."

I see Greg Dobbs, and he has the trophy. I knew I had to get close to the trophy. We went over, and I had my right hand on the microphone, asking questions. With my left hand, I reached up and touched the trophy. It gave me such a jolt! I was the worst baseball player in the world, and here I was on the field with the Phillies when they won the World Series...I just touched the World Series trophy...I'm absolutely in heaven.

After a couple of interviews had been done, I felt we could go 'live' soon. You know that people from the outside are living and dying with the team—watching the games, talking to friends. But when you're in media *and* you're a fan, it takes up 14-15 hours of your day. You are so invested professionally, and then if you're a fan, which I was, you are invested emotionally as well. When the Phillies went to the World Series, I worked 14 days straight, 15 hour days.

Beasley [Reece] was our sports director so I knew I had to find where he was and make sure he was ready to go live. He had been broadcasting from outside because they wouldn't let us do a live broadcast inside until a certain time. He had to try to work his way inside to the first-base side. We get together... and, we had this emotional burst. I still could not believe I was actually there. We both started to cry and were both thinking, "This is the greatest thing I've ever covered." I thought, "It can't get any better for me no matter what I cover for the rest of my life—I was *on the field* when the Phillies won the World Series."

> "It can't get any better for me no matter what I cover for the rest of my life.

But, we had to get ready to go on the air. I started grabbing guests. Now, my cell phone starts buzzing and going off. I see Ruben Amaro and pulled him over. I see the mayor and pulled him over. Beasley went on live. I got Ryan Howard and started grabbing players.

After things started to calm down, I called my parents. They're crying—they're happy I got to do this because they knew how much it meant to me. I called my sister—she's crying, "You're so lucky. I'm so happy." I called as many people as I could think of calling and sent out mass texts.

It turns out we're in the safest place in Philadelphia. Cops are everywhere. Then...rumors start to come in to the media, "Somebody stole a fire truck and is driving it around town." Craziness was everywhere, and it started to wind down. I decided I wanted to do something crazy.

I walked over to first base. I lay down on my back and started making snow angels in the dirt. I thought to myself, "No one else is going to think to do this, and it might be the most unprofessional thing in the world, but I'm going to actually make snow angels at first base...and enjoy it...and be able to tell people that I did it."

I grabbed a cup from the dugout and started picking up dirt. I put dirt in everything I had and even rolled up dirt in dollar bills. I had a whole thing of dirt I was carrying around. Later I ended up putting this dirt in little tubes, writing "2008 World Champions" on the tubes and gave them to friends and my nephews and nieces for Christmas. Everybody seemed to really like that.

As we left, the parking lot looked like a bomb has hit it. We go to an after-party, which is mostly Phillies employees and announcers—none of the players. It was everybody in the media, collectively blowing off steam with lots of food and drink. I remember it being a chilly night, but there was this sense of calm and peace all over the parking lot. Everything seemed brighter. Everything seemed happier.

I get in the car and turn on the heat and turn the dial to 610 and listen to everybody talking. I had the feeling, "Wow. I was exactly where I was supposed to be. Everything I've done to this point makes complete sense."

I'm sobbing as I'm driving home. You think about all the hours of study, the classes, the tutors, all the holidays you missed working in the media, all the things you miss in real life because of what you do...suddenly *it all became worth it!* Just for that one night. At that point, I realized I still had not seen the final out. I didn't know how it happened. I didn't know how it looked. I didn't know how Kalas's sound was. I get home and turn on the TV. I can't find it on TV. They were doing the news, and I had to wait 15-20 minutes to watch the final out. I finally see the final out. I finally hear Harry's call. Then...I start crying again and thinking, "This is the greatest night ever."

By now, it's five o'clock in the morning, and I have to be back in to work at 9:00. Personally, professionally, there will never be anything ever that tops that for me. A lot of people don't get to work in their home towns, they have to move around to different places, and luckily I've never had to leave Philadelphia. I get to cover the teams I love and to follow them. To have had that wonderful opportunity was unspeakably amazing. Looking back, I know for a fact they won the World Series because I was right there! But I did not get to have that release of watching it as it happened—that's still a little bit of a hole. I know that sounds ridiculous, but to not have that moment stinks. But, at the same time, what I got was something completely *more.* I wouldn't trade that for anything.

Because I had done well getting guests and lining them up in 2008, the plan was to send me to **YANKEE*** Stadium for Game 7 in 2009, if it went seven games. Of course, it didn't, but the day of Game 5, my boss told me they had the credentials and were going to send me there. I said to him, "Why would you do that?" He said, "What?" I said, "It doesn't really make any sense to send me." I reminded him he had told me he was never going to send me anywhere again because of what happened last time. I said, "Why would you send me to New York if I can't get in to the stadium, and we can't go live out of Yankee Stadium until 20 minutes after. I'd just be stuck up there. I'm going to be more useful to you here. You can send someone else who would be not so useful." He said, "Okay." I looked at him and said, "Wait a minute. Did I just talk myself out of going to Game 7 of the World Series with the Phillies and the Yankees in Yankee Stadium?" He said, "Yeah, you did. You did a pretty convincing job, too."

Trust me...I'll never open my mouth like that again. I've learned my lesson. I know I would have just been dying inside if they won at Yankee Stadium in Game 7, and I wasn't there.

*The **YANKEES'** pinstriped uniforms were designed by owner Colonel Jacob Ruppert to make Babe Ruth look skinnier.

IT'S A SMALL WORLD...BUT I WOULDN'T WANT TO PAINT IT

John Nash

John Nash currently serves as a pro personnel scout for the Philadelphia 76ers. Nash has previous held the GM title for the Sixers, Washington Wizards (then known as the Washington Bullets) and Portland Trail Blazers. Through Nash's impressive career, he has held a number of different jobs, including ones with the University of Pennsylvania and as a consultant to the Phillies.

I grew up as a huge Phillies fan. My heroes were Richie Ashburn and Robin Roberts. I even once owned a horse named Richie after Richie Ashburn. However, the **HORSE*** wasn't as talented as Richie Ashburn. The horse won one race.

I remember going to Connie Mack Stadium in the summer of 1955, the year after the Athletics moved. I was eight years old and I went to a game against the Dodgers. My older brother went too. I was a huge Phillies fan and my hero was Robin Roberts. My brother liked the Dodgers and Junior Gilliam. My grandfather was a big baseball fan and he would the two of us to the games. It was a lot of fun.

Years and years later, a lot of us would take the bus from 69th Street to Connie Mack Stadium. The guy who had the job of

---

*In what sport was Chris Evert the leading money winner in 1974? The answer: **HORSE** racing. The owner, Carl Rosen, named his horses after tennis players. The horse named Chris Evert won $551,063 with five wins in eight starts.

selling those tickets at the time was Leo Carlin, who, as you know, works for the Eagles now in a high-profile ticket sales position. Well, I got Leo's job after he left at 69th Street. That was 1964. I sold tickets for people to go on the bus. I saw 76 games in 1964. I missed a couple for high school graduation. I think I saw 76 of the 81. I remember all the big events—Chico Ruiz' steal of home, Bunning's effort on Father's Day. I was a teenager and it was cool. But to see the collapse of the '64 Phillies was devastating. It was emotional. Years later, I was reconnected with the Phillies while I was in between NBA jobs. I got a call from Dave Montgomery, who was an old friend of mine, to see if I was interested in helping them sell off the assets from Veterans Stadium. I helped sell off the assets, including the seats. I worked at that job for six months. You know, it's a small world in sports.

Dave Montgomery graduated from Wharton, walked across the street soon after graduation and interviewed with Bill Giles. He's been working with the Phillies ever since to his role as President now. Ironically, I was working as the group sales director for the Sixers in 1969-70 and 1970-71. I left for the University of Pennsylvania after that. Dave and I crossed paths and he made a great decision, otherwise he might have been trapped in that sales job. Dave and I have remained great friends through the years. Every year, we try to go to lunch at least once before spring training. He asks what I think about the Phillies and he's a huge basketball fan, so he asks me questions about the Sixers.

Years later when I was the GM in Washington, I was asked to play in a celebrity golf outing. I was a celebrity in a five-some with some impressive people, including Jim Bunning. At the time, I believe he was a Congressman in the state of Kentucky. I don't want to say he was upset, but maybe he was a little ruffled by having me in the group because I wasn't really a quote-unquote celebrity. I began asking him questions about Father's Day in 1964 as well as a bunch of questions about the 1964 team. He began to warm up and appreciated my interest. He warmed up quite a bit after that initial meeting.

OUTSIDE OF A DOG, A BOOK IS MAN'S BEST FRIEND. INSIDE OF A DOG, IT'S TOO DARK TO READ

Edward Veit

Ed Veit was born in Philadelphia and raised in nearby North Wales. He retired from teaching high school and college English in 1994 and is a former Washington DC policeman. He published articles on 1950 Whiz Kid outfielder Del Ennis (his favorite player) and former Orioles' player Dave Johnson. Veit, during his retirement, freelances as a sports writer for the York Dispatch and operates the press box elevator at Camden Yards for the Baltimore Orioles. He claims, "My first autograph was from Schoolboy Rowe on a 1947 copy of the Philadelphia Daily News, *but I have no idea what happened to the signature."*

I read a lot of baseball books and get a kick out of them. I read George Vecsey's *Baseball: A History of America's Favorite Game*. He made a comment in there that the last World Series played without an African-American was the 1946 World Series. I said, "Sorry, you're wrong. It was the 1950 World Series when the Phillies played the Yankees." He got back to me and corrected it. If there's anything I know something about, it's the 1950 Phillies.

Pete Golenbock wrote a book called *Bums*. I could never get a hold of Pete, but he had in there that Richie Ashburn was a home-run threat at the Baker Bowl. That's where the Phillies played up until 1938. Ashburn didn't come up until 1948 and played at Shibe Park. I thought that was kind of funny. He also mentioned that if the Dodgers had won their last game in 1950, they would have won the pennant. I had to beg his pardon, but no, they wouldn't have, they would have gotten into a playoff.

I've had some fun with Larry Shenk, the PR guy for the Phillies. Del Ennis was my favorite ballplayer growing up. I lived outside of Philadelphia until I was about 18. I'd always get number 14 when I played soccer and baseball because that was Ennis' number. When Jim Bunning went into the Hall of Fame, they retired his number, which happened to be 14. I got a hold of Shenk online, and there were about five or six exchanges between us. He finally told me that if I'd leave him alone, he'd give me a paper from the 1950 team's 40th reunion when Ennis was still alive.

One of my biggest thrills recently was when I interviewed **CURT SIMMONS***. The '50 Phillies got beat by the Yankees four straight in the World Series. People don't understand what happened to the Phillies that September. Their pitching staff was bothering them. Bubba Church got hit in the face by a ball hit by Ted Kluszewski. Bob Miller, a rookie pitcher, was 11-1 at one time, but his back went south and he was never the same. Russ Meyer and Ken Heintzelman had won 17 games the previous year. Heintzelman won three and I think Russ Meyer won nine in 1950. Simmons was called up to active duty when they activated his National Guard unit because of the Korean War. Simmons had won 17 games. Roberts had won 20 games. Suddenly what the Phillies were left with was Robin Roberts and Jim Konstanty. Konstanty went on to be the MVP. Roberts started four of the last eight games. He went 10 innings to get the last win in Brooklyn. The Phillies played 157 games that year instead of 154. So that even added to how tired they were. Hamner, and Willie Jones played all 157 games. The pitching was so bad that they had

*CURT SIMMONS** was the last Major League pitcher to steal home.

to start Jim Konstanty in the World Series. They had a one-day break before the Series started. Konstanty was a relief pitcher and they lost 1–0. The next game, Roberts came back and went 10 innings and lost on a **JOE DIMAGGIO*** home run, 2–1. And they said it was because he was careless.

The Phillies were such an exciting team in the 50s. They were part of the reason that the Philadelphia A's left town because the Phillies became the darlings of the town, and attendance at the A's games bottomed out.

It was fun to go to Shibe Park. There was always a day game on Saturday and the park was just loaded with kids. Richie Ashburn would lead off, and the kids would holler and scream because Ashburn was the crowd favorite. By the time they got to the third inning the kids were running all over the place, eating hot dogs and not paying any attention to the game. They were in the bleachers and the grandstand. You could get into the bleachers for 75 cents. The box seats were about two or three dollars.

The Phillies won a pennant in 1915 at the Baker Bowl and didn't win again until 1950 at Shibe Park. The next pennant they won was in 1980 at the Vet. Then they won another pennant at the Vet. The next two pennants they won were at Citizens Bank Park. They've won a pennant in four different ballparks, and I don't know any other team that has done that. Atlanta has won a pennant in three different cities.

The first autograph I got was from Schoolboy Rowe and it was on a copy of the *Daily News*. He asked me what the heck I was going to keep that for. That was back in '46 or '48. Dutch Leonard and Schoolboy Rowe were pitching for the Phillies. That was long before they became the Whiz Kids. They'd pitch the

---

*To accentuate a wiggle in her walk, Marilyn Monroe would cut a quarter of an inch off one of her heels.... The combination on Monroe's jewelry box was 5-5-5— **DIMAGGIO**'s uniform number.

Sunday doubleheaders, and the Phillies would usually win those with the two old guys.

The first ballgame I saw was the Philadelphia A's playing the Yankees in '46. But I quickly became a Phillies fan. They had nicer looking uniforms and they were funnier. It was interesting that I was a Philly fan for three years and got a pennant, but they hadn't won since 1915.

I'll never forget the last game of that year. We were up at North Wales High School playing baseball. I had a portable radio that must have weighed half a ton. It had a battery almost the size of a car's. When Sisler hit that home run, everybody up at North Wales went wild. If he had been playing for the Giants or somebody in New York, it would have been called "the shot heard 'round the world." The Dodgers lost two games by home runs on the last pitch of the season—one in '50 and one by **BOBBY THOMSON*** in '51. They never mention Sisler's. The irony is that Sisler was already 3-for-4 off Newcombe when he came to bat in the tenth inning. There's not a manager today who would allow Newcombe to pitch to Sisler.

*When **BOBBY THOMSON** hit "The Shot Heard Around the World" in 1951, Frank Sinatra and Jackie Gleason were at the game. When Thomson homered off Ralph Branca, Dodger fan Gleason did a technicolor yawn (vomited) on Sinatra's shoes...In the movie *The Godfather*, Sonny Corleone died while listening to that game... Dave Winfield was born that day.

IF MY NOSE WAS RUNNIN' MONEY I'D BLOW IT ALL ON THE PHILLIES

Frank Brodsky (right) with Jim Bunning

Frank Brodsky

Brodsky has been in the investment business for 53 years and counting, and has been attending Phillies games for six decades. His son, Chuck, is considered one of the leading baseball songwriters in the country according Tim Wiles, the Director of Research for the Baseball Hall of Fame.

In 2010 I went to my 19th consecutive spring training. I was also down there five times playing at the Phillies' Dream Week Fantasy Camp. Tim Flannery, third-base coach for the Giants, is a friend of ours. He happens to be a professional singer in the off-season and does country, bluegrass, and gospel. He's very, very good. When the Giants come to town, Tim goes out to dinner with us. He's a very close friend of my son, Chuck, because of their singing.

I was at spring training a few years ago and was standing in the first row watching batting practice while Harry Kalas was on the field signing autographs. He was probably five feet away. He had a big crowd, signing everything and talking to everyone. Suddenly, somebody comes out from the Phillies dugout and says, "Harry, the owners are here and they want you to come over and talk to them." Harry said, "I'll be over in a while." He just stood there and continued to sign the autographs for the average fan and let the owners wait in the dugout while he was doing this. My admiration for Harry Kalas zoomed up when I saw that....

My son Chuck wrote the song "Whitey and Harry." I had a couple of baseballs that I asked Harry to sign, and he was so gracious and immediately signed them. He wrote a note to Chuck on his ball with "HOF" and did the same for me. When this song came out that Chuck had written and recorded, Harry didn't know how to get a hold of him, so he wrote a letter to me. He didn't know me, and I don't even know how he got my name, although I've been friendly with Chris Wheeler for 25 years. He wrote the most beautiful note to me saying that he couldn't get a hold of Chuck so he was writing to ask me to please tell Chuck how much he loved the song. He also said how much he loved Chuck's song about Max Patkin, the "Clown Prince of Baseball." It was unbelievable that he took the time to write such a nice note to me out of the blue.

Chuck talks about **MAX PATKIN*** quite often when he introduces the song about him. Max lived outside of Philadelphia and spent his days going into town and hanging out at the courthouse watching murder trials. Max had been on the local talk radio talking about Chuck and the song. When Chuck came up from North Carolina, he met Max at the courthouse. When Max walked in everything stopped. The judge even stopped and asked Max how he was doing. He seemed to be in control of the courthouse, even in a murder trial. In 1999, while Chuck was in Ireland doing a tour, Max called me and said he wanted to be Chuck's agent because he could help him out. I told him he'd be back in about 10 days and to please call him again. About three days later, he called again and said he wanted to talk to Chuck. I told him he wasn't home yet, but would be soon. Two days later, Max Patkin died. I happened to be in the area where the funeral was being held. I went to the funeral home, and it was the funniest thing I ever saw. Max had a huge nose, which he always made fun of. There was his big nose

---

***MAX PATKIN** was part of the entertainment in St. Louis on August 18, 1951, when Bill Veeck, the St. Louis Browns owner, had Eddie Gaedel, a midget, pinch-hit in a major league game. Gaedel wore the number 1/8 on the back of his uniform, which was actually the uniform of the batboy, Bill DeWitt, Jr., who is now the head honcho of the St. Louis Cardinals.

sticking out over the top of the casket. Everybody got a kick out of that. Harry was there and other people from the Phillies. The key people in their organization would remember that.

Chuck and I went to the last game played at the old Connie Mack Stadium. I turned around at one point and I see guys carrying out urinals. Pros came with tools. They were carrying entire rows and urinals right out of the ballpark. I got into it, too, and stood up and started yanking on my seat. These were seats that probably went back to 1910 or whenever. I actually busted the bolts by yanking and pulling on it. That seat is now hanging on my wall with a little note that says "original seat taken from Connie Mack Stadium on October 1, 1970." We ripped our seats out of the ballpark, but I never would have done anything like that if I hadn't seen people carrying the urinals and entire rows out. That was a fascinating experience for me....

There were some hard feelings between Harry and Chris Wheeler. Wheels is a friend of mine and I heard the other side of the story, which I never repeated to anybody and won't repeat now. But I will tell you that I got a note from Wheels that said, "I wish I could talk more about it, but I'm the low guy on the totem pole and can't." I still respect that. When I was down at Dream Week, Wheels was a coach and a couple of the former Phillies used to work on him like you couldn't believe. One of them was Bobby Wine and the other John Vukovich, who was also a very good friend. Whenever they took pictures, Bobby Wine and Vuke always got on opposite sides of Wheels. Just when they were ready to take the picture they would goose him and Wheels would go flying. They'd always have to take the picture over. They did not let up on him and he was a great sport about it.

One day during Dream Week, Greg Luzinski came over to me and said, "I'm playing **GOLF*** today with Del Unser, would you like to join us?" This was unheard of because nobody ever, ever

*While playing **GOLF** in 1567, Mary, Queen of Scots, was informed that her husband, Lord Darnley, had been murdered. She finished the round.

got invited to play golf with the ballplayers. I think he invited me because they all saw how much I was into this thing. I was catching their batting practice. I was out on the field with these guys, and they could tell I loved every second. I told him I would love to but didn't have clubs with me. Just then Chris Wheeler came walking by, heard this, and said, "Frank, I have a set of clubs in my car. I'll loan them to you," which he did. I was the only guy in the history of those dream weeks that went out and played a round of golf with Greg Luzinski and Del Unser. I told Wheels I was indebted to him for life. That was a very special time for me.

Another interesting thing happened at Dream Week that never happened before. One year, I was catching for Larry Bowa, who's known to be a hot head. We're having infield practice one day and Bowa was hitting grounders and I was getting the throw-ins. Bowa says to me, "Frank, after lunch you're going to catch half the game and this other guy is going to catch half the game." I immediately thought to myself that I didn't come down there to catch half games. I came down to play all the time. I went into the clubhouse and got a hold of Richie Hebner. He had a catcher with bad knees. I said to Hebner, "Hey, Rich, why don't you make a trade. Trade this guy Bert Penn to Bowa for me. He can catch half games for Bowa and I'll catch the whole time for you." This never happened before in the history of Dream Week. Nobody ever made trades during Dream Week. But he gets a hold of Bowa, and they had to have it approved by the commissioner of Dream Week, who just happened to be Richie Ashburn. Richie didn't play; he just walked around with his pipe and a bat in his hands. They approved the trade and I ended up catching for Hebner. From that time on, Bowa was really irritated with me. My biggest mistake was that I never went over and talked to him and apologized. I should have told him that I was just like him. I wanted to play every second of every game. I should have done that, but I didn't. For a long time after that, if I was at a ballgame and down by the dugout, Bowa wouldn't say hello, he'd just say, "I'll go get your friend, Vuke, for you." I was the only guy in the history of Dream Week to ever be traded, which I engineered on my own.

WHEN WE CATCH THE GUY WHO STOLE THE PHANATIC'S COSTUME, WE'RE GONNA GIVE HIM A FAIR TRIAL AND THEN WE'RE GONNA HANG HIM.

Robert Watson

Watson was born in Wilmington, Delaware and now lives in Newark, Delaware. A life-long Phillies fan, so are his two children, who are both attend the University of Delaware. He is a self-employed house painter and paper hanger.

One day in 2004, I and some of the fellas from the 4F Club got together down at the local taproom to shake off some of the midwinter doldrums that seem to settle in around this time every year. One thing you can always count on when the fellas from the 4F Club get together is some good, old-fashioned conversation about just about anything under the sun.

On this particular day we happened to be arguing over the differences between concrete and cement when news came over the television that someone had stolen the head of the **PHILLIE PHANATIC***. This may or may not necessarily be news in itself, except for the fact that the event was being covered as if a head of state had died.

*In late 1995, a 68-year-old man won a $128,000 judgment against the **PHILLIE PHANATIC**, who was accused of knocking down the man at a 1991 church carnival.

Theoretically, the Phanatic is naked from the waist down, as his outfit consists of a Phillies shirt, a Phillies hat, and a pair of big red shoes with white laces. He has a big roll-up tongue in his snout, sort of like a Twizzler stick, that he shoots out at people for great comedic effect. A Philadelphia institution for sure—along with cheesesteaks, soft pretzel, and Tastykakes.

The Phillies had held a big, sports-related auction up at the hockey rink sports complex in Philadelphia. They were auctioning off every square inch that ever existed of Veterans Stadium—the multisports complex that the Phillies and **EAGLES*** once called home.

While the auction was taking place, the Phillie Phanatic was running around entertaining the crowd that was assembled at the Wachovia Center. Or, as the locals call it, "Watchoverya Center," which in this case I suppose wouldn't apply. At some point the Phanatic tired himself out enough so that he had to go to the locker room to take a rest. There was no indication as to whether he rested in the home or visitors' locker room.

Once away from the crowd, Mr. Phanatic removed his head to enjoy a soda that team mascots more than likely get on the house. Fringe benefit, I'm sure, for lugging around an 80-pound costume on hot August nights.

After using the bathroom facilities, the Phanatic returned to find that his head was missing. Not just any ordinary head, but a big, green, oversized, sweaty head with a Twizzler stick poking out of its mouth.

A mad search was conducted of the facility, to no avail. Authorities were then properly notified and the investigation was

*Tom Brookshier was a Philadelphia **EAGLES** player and a CBS broadcaster. In 1959, he pitched for Class C Roswell of the Longhorn League and won seven and lost one. After spending two years in the Air Force after that season, he decided to concentrate on football and return to the Eagles.

promptly orchestrated. News teams rushed onto the scene to get a first-hand account of the tragedy that was unfolding. In the barroom, we were given the sickening details of the crime that was committed. Not just a crime against the Phanatic or the sport of baseball, but a crime against humanity, the American way of life, and sports mascoting itself. Newspapers ran with the headline "Have You Seen This Head?"

Rewards were offered for the head of the Phanatic, starting at $1,500, then $5,000, and finally a cool $10,000 for the discovery and return of a big, green, oversized, sweaty head with a Twizzler stick poking out of its mouth. No questions asked, just deliver us the head, authorities pleaded.

Civil action was swift. A team of local mascots, I kid you not, gathered near a minor league stadium for a candlelight vigil in support of the return of the Phanatic's head. Suspects were rounded up and questioned in great detail. Employees of the Wachovia Center faced the greatest scrutiny initially. "Where is the head?" "Did you take the head?" "Empty your pockets and take off your shoes."

Names were bandied about in local circles as to who the culprit might be. The New York Mets smiling baseball head mascot? Didn't he and the Phanatic have a mascot rivalry dating back a few years to the time when they couldn't both fit into the service elevator and nearly came to blows?

Tommy Lasorda? The Dodgers manager that had feuded with the Phanatic for 20 years, ever since the Phanatic ran over a Lasorda ragdoll at the ballpark with his motorized tricycle? Didn't Lasorda also have a Pennsylvania connection and know that the Phanatic would be at the sports auction?

The original Phillie Phanatic? The person that had left the costume of the Phanatic years earlier to start his own team mascot business? Unable to equal the success of the new Phanatic, was the old Phanatic settling an old score?

All of a sudden the Tri-State Area was being inundated with more conjecture about the whereabouts of the Phillie Phanatic than we could process. Now, we had a national manhunt for the safe return of the head. Who in their right mind would steal a big, green mascot's head in the first place, it was asked. That furry head was more identifiable than any painting that hangs in the Louvre. More identifiable than any million-dollar vase from the Ming dynasty.

Was there a black market out there somewhere dealing in sports mascots' heads? Was this the first sports head that had been stolen? Did the **SAN DIEGO CHICKEN'S*** head sit in some abductor's basement somewhere too? Was someone walking around his house with the Phillie Phanatic head on top of his own head, in some sort of twisted case of identity crisis? Was the head of the Phillie Phanatic stolen and cryogenically frozen to sit alongside the head of Ted Williams? To be thawed out one day, each of them to become pioneers in a futuristic baseball league? Or did someone wake up from a drunken stupor, with a big, green mascot head lying next to him and say, "Man, I've got to quit drinking"?

"Not to worry though," the broadcasters informed us, tongues planted firmly in cheek, "the Phanatic has two heads. The replacement head is safe and sound."

---

*The **SAN DIEGO CHICKEN** grosses over two million dollars per year.

TAKE THIS JOB AND LOVE IT

John Brazer

Brazer is the Director of Fun & Games for the Phillies, his 17th season with the organization. Following graduation from the University of Virginia, Brazer spent a year playing professional lacrosse in Manchester, England. He moved back to the United States, and several years later, he joined the Phillies staff.

I never sought out to get a job with the Phillies. It just happened. I was a huge lacrosse fan and following college, I spent a year playing and coaching lacrosse in Manchester, England. It didn't take long to realize I wanted to come back to the United States. So I came back, sold employee benefits in the insurance industry and then worked as a consultant for a couple of years.

At a wedding of one of my good friends in 1993, I met a guy who worked for the Phillies. My friend mentioned the Phillies were looking for a marketing director because someone was leaving after 30 years, a highly respected employee. I began talking to the guy and eventually he asked what I did. I said, "I market lacrosse in England." Then he said, "Come on, really? What do you do?" I said, "I play and coach lacrosse." He said, "You're good at this. Why don't you come in and talk to us?" One thing led to another and I got the job. This is my 17th season with the Phillies. It's a great place to work.

When I officially started, I was wearing a suit, and it was tough because I spent more time explaining my role with the Phillies than actually marketing them and promoting them like I was supposed to do. Finally, one day I decided to ditch the suit, ditch the tie and change my title to a fun and games thing. Now, my official title is Director Fun & Games. It basically stuck.

When I started out with the Phillies, my office was in the Vet. I think one of the coolest things about the job was that Harry Kalas would have a keg up in the box and Freddie ran the keg. After games, we would go up there and Harry would tell stories and sing. For me, at that time, it was the coolest thing. I think one of the greatest things that I get to do, that never gets tiring or old, is listening to stories from Harry Kalas and Larry Andersen and Sarge Matthews. It's just the greatest thing.

In 1997, I took a trip to the Greek Islands with Scott Rolen. It was a tough year for me personally because my dad had died. Scott was pretty new with the Phillies. He had never been to Europe and I was already booked and going. We went and did our own things. I remember Scott had won the **GOLD GLOVE*** Award at third base. This was before cell phones or mostly before cell phones, anyway. The media kept calling and calling him but couldn't get a hold of him. Finally, in Santorini, he checked his messages and he was like, 'I've got a lot of messages here about the Gold Glove. That's cool.' No one could reach him and no one thought of calling his parents because not many people knew where he was.

Wow, I remember this trip in 1998 to Colorado. Did I ever get in big-time trouble. The team had lost something like eight in a row and we were out in Colorado for a day-night doubleheader. They're common now, but I think that was one of the very first day-night doubleheaders. The players weren't too excited about it because they had to get there around 8:00 a.m. and wouldn't leave until after midnight. I went with another team employee and a couple of the team sponsors. After the first game ended with a loss, we had about four hours to kill before

*Ron Darling won the National League pitcher's **GOLD GLOVE** in 1989. Greg Maddux won the next thirteen.

the second game started. I decided to skip the second game and go visit my old buddy Dennis Mannion, who had worked for the Phillies but had had moved and taken a new job with the Nuggets and Avalanche. Dennis decided to have a barbecue. We were at a downtown Denver location and we had heard these women from Wyoming talking about getting tickets. I told them we had four and "why don't you take them?" It sounded like it would be no problem. Well, the tickets turned out to be right next to the dugout. After losing the first game as I said, we also got shutout in the second game. The dugout was getting pretty ticked off because these fans were huge **ROCKIES*** fans and they were yelling and screaming obscenities at the Phillies dugout. It was pretty bad. The Phillies were so mad and then were asking who left the tickets. They went to the Will Call and discovered I had left the tickets because my business card was there. The coaches, most notably John Vukovich, didn't talk to me for a while. It may had been four years before he was completely over it. Oh, he was really ticked off at me. Wow, did it take a long time to smooth things over.

My memory of 2008 is Brad Lidge striking out Eric Hinske and that was it. We were champions. It was amazing. Even more amazing was the parade. I have to say, the parade is one of the greatest things I have ever been a part of in my life. We rode for four or five hours to get through the city and I was lucky enough to ride on one of the player's floats. To see that kind of emotion spilling out from the fans was incredible. You saw people crying, people saying thank you, people throwing flowers and cheering. You had to see it in person. I was telling the players on my float what it would be like. I think for the first time, they saw what it meant to the city and to the fans. You can talk about it. But to see it and be part of it is different.

*At **COORS FIELD** in Denver, in the upper deck, there is one row of purple seats that encircle the stadium designating the "mile high" level.

Yada, Yada, Yada

When **MARK MCGWIRE*** was in the middle of his historic 70-home-run season, we went to see the Cardinals play the Phillies at the Vet. We got there very early so we could get his autograph. With my father-in-law's box seats right beside the third-base dugout it was usually fairly easy to get autographs from opposing players, and my 10-year-old son was especially excited about getting Mark McGwire's. There were more fans than usual along the fence, but we still felt we were in good position to get it when he came out.

As he came out of the dugout many more kids and fans came down to the fence, and as the crowd grew we started getting pushed and squeezed to the back, and before we could do anything about it, we had lost our chance at getting his autograph. McGwire went back into the dugout and, as we took our seats, our son could not stop crying. He was extremely disappointed and no matter what I said, he continued to cry. Just as I told him that crying would get him nowhere, a man and his son came out of the dugout and were let through into the stands. The man's arms were full of magazines, balls, and even a bat. As he was walking up the aisle by us he stopped and asked my son what was the matter. Tearfully my son told him he couldn't get Mark McGwire's autograph. Without hesitating, the man took a ***SPORTS ILLUSTRATED**** magazine out of his hands and gave it to my son and, without saying another word,

*Mark McGwire's brother, Dan McGwire, once a starting quarterback for the Iowa Hawkeyes and a former #1 pick of the Seahawks, is the tallest NFL QB ever at 6 feet 8 inches. Former NBA star and Toronto Blue Jays, Danny Ainge, is the tallest major league second baseman ever.

*In 1955, ***SPORTS ILLUSTRATED*** selected horse owner William Woodward as their Sportsman of the Year. Woodward's wife shot and killed the unfaithful Woodward before the issue went to press. S.I. then selected World Series hero Johnny Podres.

continued up the aisle. As I sat there with my son on my lap I realized he had handed him an autographed copy with Mark McGwire and his son on the cover. I turned around and yelled thanks to the man, who just gave a wave without looking back. The tears turned to astonishment and we sat there stunned for quite a while. I was too stunned to figure out a way to properly thank him, but I don't think he wanted anything other than to make a little boy happy. And he did.

—**Bob McCormick**, Chester, a Phillies fan and proud
father, son Sean threw a perfect game in high school

I hate frontrunners. How seriously do I take this subject? I have a notebook containing the names of everyone I know from Philadelphia. I know exactly where they grew up, and I know exactly which teams they have rooted for. When the next championship comes to a Philadelphia team, and these turn-coat marsupials try to jump on the bandwagon, I shall make a personal effort to cover them contumely and expose them as the front-running lickspittles they are. When they die, I will personally pay for headstones that read:

Pat McGinty
Born: Philadelphia, November 1, 1950
Died: Dallas, May 1, 2008
Rooted for
New York Yankees (1977-78, 1996, 1998, 1999, 2000)
Boston Celtics (1959-66)
Los Angeles Lakers (1972, 1980, 1982, 1985, 1987, 1988, 2000, 2001, 2002)
Montreal Canadiens (1976-80)
San Francisco 49ers (1982, 1985, 1989, 1990, 1995)
Died as he lived: a stinking front-runner

—**Joe Queenan**, Philly native; Critic, humorist, author

It seems we've always been a baseball family. And not just any baseball, really only "Phillies Baseball." I first fell in love with the team in 4th grade, in 1962—just as they were making base-ball exciting with lots of wins. As far as I was concerned, their success came powered by the bat of Johnny Callison, the diving shortstop, Cookie Rojas, and the cool and strategic pitcher Jim Bunning. My passionate interest encouraged my father to take me to my first big league game at the old Connie Mack Stadium. I remember an electricity. I was seeing every player I knew from TV right in front of me. My best friend, Dolores, thought it would be great to collect pictures of our heroes. And we did—from newspapers and magazines and from anyone we knew who went to a game.

Like every fan, I just couldn't believe we could come so close in '64. My interest changed in intensity as I became a teenager. But my love was always intact.

Evidence of that was my heart beating out of my chest when decades later, as a Philadelphia TV news anchor I was invited to participate in a charity event, where former Phillies were headliners. I maneuvered my way through the crowd to shake the hand of my personal hero, **JOHNNY CALLISON***. That was the hand, that held the bat, that connected with so many home runs that had me jumping up in my living room, whooping with joy and then, sitting down with a quiet confidence because I knew—when in a jam—Johnny Callison—could do it.

I've savored my relationship with the Phillies, since becoming a girlhood fan. That made broadcasting the 2008 Championship Parade, among the fans at City Hall more than an assignment. It was a singular honor.

—**Pat Ciarrocchi**, Reporter with CBS 3, Philadelphia

About 20 years ago, Richie Ashburn and Robin Roberts appeared at a card show in Lancaster, PA. I went with my three-year-old daughter Julie and my five-year-old son Jesse. Much to my surprise, the room with the card show was full of people, but only a few people were in the room where Richie and Robin were

*In 1959, the White Sox scored 11 runs against the As in one inning on a single hit. The White Sox had 9 walks, a hit batsman, the As committed three errors, and **JOHNNY CALLISON** got the only hit, a single.

signing. We got in line behind one other man. As we approached Richie, he immediately greeted my kids. He asked them, "Who is that green, fuzzy fellow you are both holding" (Philly Phanatic dolls) Richie carried on a lengthy conversation with the kids, gently teasing them about their Phanatic dolls.

When he asked me if I had anything to sign, I handed him my copy of the 1959 Phillies Yearbook. I had chosen the 1959 issue because it had a nice layout on Richie winning the 1958 National League batting title. Richie immediately said, "Robin, look at this." For the next several minutes the two of them paged through the yearbook, reminiscing over their old teammates. (Chico Fernandez, Puddin' Head Jones, Stan Lopata, Wally Post, Harry Anderson, Curt Simmons, Dick Farrell, Jack Sanford, and others).

Richie made it a great day for us by making my shy kids feel special. Likewise, I was able to add to his and Robin's pleasure through the old yearbook.

—**Dale Gerber**, 66, Manheim, PA, retired educator

I'm pretty much a slacker because in the last 27 years I've missed one Phillies game either in person, on radio, TV or the internet. I had a three-year streak prior to that where I hadn't missed any Phillies games. I do remember my first trip to Connie Mack Stadium. It was 1966 and I was five years old. I don't remember who they played, but I do remember that I just wanted to go home. I didn't get a chance to go back again until 1968, and it was a **BAT*** day. The Phillies gave away bats on a Sunday afternoon against the Dodgers. Rick Wise hit a home run for the only Phillies run of the day, and they ended up losing 2–1. That was back in the days when they were not exactly good.

One of my goals was to see the Phillies play in all the National League ballparks, and I did that. I remember one day we were in Montreal—I was with my future wife—and we saw

*Orlando Cepeda used more **BATS** than any player in history. He felt each bat had exactly one hit in it. When Cepeda hit safely, he would discard the bat. He had 2,364 hits in his career.

Milt Thompson walking around outside the hotel. That was kinda neat.

In 2000, the Phillies had a contest. They wanted to name 10 fans as "the fans of the century" for the 1900s. They picked one fan from each of the decades. In order to enter the contest, you had to write a 500-word essay about why you thought you deserved to be one of the fans of the century. I mentioned this streak, which at the time was only 1,800 games long. I mentioned that I had been to see the Phillies play at all the National League ballparks and that I had one copy of every Topps Phillies card ever made from 1954 on up. I have Phillies media guides dating back to 1971 and yearbooks dating back to 1964. I kept those collections current throughout the years as well. They thought all that was deserving, so they made me one of their fans of the century. As a reward, we got to participate in on-field ceremonies for opening night. There was an 11th fan named for the year 2000. His name was Phil DiRienzo—he was named after the Phillies—and he was born on New Year's Day of that year, so he was this three-month-old kid that was selected as a fan, as well. The 11 of us gathered on the field and all got our names on the back of a Phillies jersey, along with the decade we represented. Mine says "Bogart 60" because I was born in the 1960s. It was so neat meeting the guy who was born in 1908 and went to see the Phillies play in the World Series in 1915. Talking to that guy made my night. He paid 50 cents to get his ticket and sat in the outfield at the World Series when they played against the Red Sox.

They gave us a ball that said "Fan of the Century"—mine said "Bob Bogart, 1960s representative." We got our names on the scoreboard and on the big Phanovision in center field. They read our names over the loudspeaker to introduce us to the fans as they had each of us take a position on the field. Being one of the more mobile people there—I was fairly young, compared to some of them—they had me run out to left field. The girl from the 80s was in center field; the girl from the 90s was in right field. They had the Phillies take the field for the game, so I got to shake Ron Gant's hand that night as he came out onto the field. It was really neat. I was written up in the newspaper and was on the local news. Most of the people were from around Philadelphia, but being from Mid-Central Pennsylvania, I had the Harrisburg and York media there covering me, as well. They did a big story on me when the Phillies went to the World Series in 2008 that got picked up by a number of places. My daughter Googled me, and I actually came up in the *L.A. Times.*

Keeping the streak alive has been challenging. It's gotten easier with the advent of XM Radio. I can travel anywhere in North America and still be able to follow the games. The problem was when I had to go overseas. Last April I had to go to England for a conference. Trying to schedule international flights around the Phillies schedule was quite a challenge. I even have a picture of my daughter holding the phone up to the TV so that I could hear the game.

—**Bob Bogart**, 49, Glen Rock, PA, Mathematician

As an 18-year-old, two other guys and I went to an August 1964 doubleheader with the Giants. We could only get standing room and sat on a girder in left field for the first game. Frank Thomas, who was recently acquired, hit a home run in the bottom of the ninth to win the game 1–0. We were able to move around in the lower deck between home and first for the second game.

It was in that game that I witnessed something I had not seen up to that point in my life nor have I seen since. It was in the late innings and Tony Gonzalez was on second when someone hit a titanic drive to dead center field that Willie Mays caught on the dead run with his back to home plate. Gonzalez then tagged and proceeded to score all the way from second base. I don't believe that occurs very often.

Also in an earlier game that year, I witnessed Wes Covington driving a ball over the Ballantine scoreboard to the left of the clock. I believe it was one of the few balls ever hit there. As a matter of fact, it may have been the only one ever hit there.

In addition, that year I witnessed, on a Tuesday night in September, the first game of the 10-game losing streak against the Reds. Chico Ruiz stole home against Art Mahaffey for the only run of the game.

—**Bob Reischer**

When my uncle, Chuck Klein, started with the Phillies in 1928, he played in a park called Baker Bowl, which had a 280-foot right-field fence. He played right field and still holds the single-season record of 44 assists by an outfielder for throwing out people at second base. The fence was similar to the one that's in Boston, and he'd just play the ball off that fence and throw people out at second.

I was only five years old when he retired, so I mainly know about his career in books and other things that I read. I wasn't old enough to really know what was going on then. He played in the Three-I League and then was called up by Philadelphia is 1928. He had his best years with Philadelphia in 1932 and 1933—he was the MVP in 1932. What I remember is when he was pretty much in a reserve role for the Cubs. It was a lot harder to get to games because we didn't have interstate highways in those days. He owned a couple of bars and restaurants in Philadelphia when he lived there.

We had lots of memorabilia but sent most of it to the Hall of Fame. When he was inducted in the Hall of Fame, we went up to Cooperstown, and I accepted the award for him because I'm the only living member of the family that's left. Uncle Chuck Klein died in 1958, when I was a senior in high school.

—**Bob Klein**, 70, Indianapolis

In 1976, my parents Marc and Roni became season ticket holders for the Phillies. Later that summer they went to the All-Star Game at Veterans Stadium, my mom six months pregnant with me. It was my birthright to be a Philadelphia sports fan.

I was too young to remember 1980, although my parents were at Game 6 to see Tug McGraw strike out Willie Wilson. I don't remember 1983 and Moses Malone's decree of "fo, fo, fo." The first thing I remember is my mom waking me up in 1985 to see Villanova defeat Georgetown for the national championship. I remember the 1985 and 1987 Flyers, and I can still vividly see J.J. Daigneault sending the Finals to Game 7, only to see them lose. I was at the 1993 NLCS and World Series and can now forgive Mitch Williams and Joe Carter. I remember the 1997 Flyers and the disappointment of losing and the 2001 Sixers, who none of us expected to be there but who nevertheless gave us a thrill that spring. Finally, the four straight NFC Championship Games for the Eagles, breaking through in 2004 only to lose in the Super Bowl.

Through the years I have been to hundreds and hundreds of sporting events in Philadelphia, most of them Phillies games. I grew up at Veterans Stadium. I saw Mike Schmidt play, as our seats were in section 244, row 3, right behind the greatest third baseman of all time. I was there the first game after Schmidt retired. I was there for Steve Carlton's retirement ceremony. I was there in 1990 when the 1980 team was honored and Doug Drabek nearly pitched a no-hitter that Sil Campusano broke up in the ninth inning. I was there for Opening Day 1992, when the new uniforms were unveiled. I was there in 1993 for many of the greatest moments in team history. I attended Game 1 of the NLCS, and yes, I was at the 15–14 game with my dad and my brother. I think that night was the first time that I really thought maybe I would never see a championship.

I remember going to Reading to see a guy named Pat Burrell play, because he was the next great Phillies player. In the summer of 2000, immediately after graduating college, I got a job in the organization working for the Reading Phillies and got to meet people like Paul Owens, the Phillie Phanatic (Tom Burgoyne), Larry Andersen, Chris Wheeler, and Harry Kalas. I spent the summer there and will never forget it.

—**Dan Drutz**, 33, native of Washington Township, NJ,
Assistant Director of Athletics, Saint Peter's College

THE SECOND GREATEST STORY EVER TOLD

Joe Queenan

St. Joseph's University grad Joe Queenan is recognized as one of the most talented writers in America. His book Closing Time *is a critically acclaimed account of his growing up in the Schuylkill Falls Project in Philadelphia. Many believe that his* True Believers *(Henry Holt and Company) is the funniest and most insightful book ever written on sports fans. Even though Queenan has lived in Westchester County, New York for many years, he still despises the Yankees and loves Philadelphia teams.*

In August, 1976, I was in France writing a novel, and things were looking peachy dandy. For me, Jimmy Carter's election notwithstanding, 1976 was an astonishing year replete with hope and promise. I had scraped together the money to move to Labecede. I had started my career as a writer. And the Phillies were making their move. Every day I would rush out to get the *International Herald Tribune* and marvel at the Phillies' latest exploits. Dismantling every team they faced, they were seemingly in position to win the most games since the 1954 **INDIANS***. One sweltering morning I received a letter from one of my closest friends announcing that playoff tickets would soon go on sale, and that if I wanted to attend the series against the rampaging Big Red Machine, I should let him know quickly. This put me in a bit of a bind. I had gone to France with the

*In 1916 the Cleveland **INDIANS** experimented with putting player numbers on the uniform sleeves....In 1929 the Indians became the first Major League team to put numbers on the backs of the jerseys... first only because the Yankees were rained out on Opening Day.

specific intention of writing the Great American Novel and was pretty much determined not to return to the United States until I had. The book I was working on dealt with a young college Biology student who, through a series of dangerous skin grafts and appendage transplants involving a frog, succeeded in turning himself into the highest-leaping, greatest basketball player of all time. Needless to say, the novel liberally borrowed from both *The Strange Case of Dr. Jekyll and Mr. Hyde* and *The Fly* and ended with the hero missing a championship-winning dunk because he was diverted by a scrumptious insect that happened to fly past as he was poised to begin a windmill jam. If I was truly serious about remaining in France until the Great American Novel had been written, it was unlikely I would be home in time for the National League playoffs.

> Wherever we decided to settle down, an October detour to the Delaware Valley would be unavoidable.

Further complicating matters was the fact that I had just begun living with an Englishwoman who would soon become my wife. At the time, we were trying to decide whether to remain in the south of France or set up shop in rural England. As neither of us had much money, finding jobs was a pressing concern. In the middle of one of our conversations comparing and contrasting the splendors and of the Dordogne with the delights of the Cotswolds, I happened to recap the entire history of the Philadelphia Phillies, indicating that wherever we decided to settle down, an October detour to the Delaware Valley would be unavoidable.

To this day, I am surprised at how well she took this news. Although she was by no means enthusiastic about this trip to the States, particularly in light of our cash-flow problems, she could understand why I would feel compelled to attend the playoffs because her father and brother had been fervent supporters of the Arsenal football club, the plodding underachievers immortalized by Nick Hornby in *Fever Pitch*. Had my wife not been exposed to delirious fan behavior at an early age, I doubt very much that she would have made the trip. Much less married me.

Unlike Hornby, I was not the kind of fan who needed to take up residence in a house right down the street from my team's stadium, nor was I the kind of fan who would piously abstain from going away for the weekend because it would involve missing a home game. I was a fan, not a fetishist. But was the kind of fan who knew that when his team had a chance to win their first pennant in his entire life, it was time to go home to cheer them on. Even if home was 3,500 miles away.

The *Rocky* movies are set in South Philadelphia, within walking distance of the sprawling sports complex where the Phillies, Eagles, 76ers and Flyers all ply their trades. In the original *Rocky*, a plucky but maladroit underdog from the streets of Philadelphia gives the heavyweight champion of the world the fight of his life. In *Rocky II*, he actually takes the title, as he does in *Rocky III* and *Rocky IV* and, for all I know, *Rocky V*. But movies are not like real life, whereas South Philadelphia is. By the time my wife and I surfaced in the City of Brotherly Love, the Phillies had squandered all but one and a half games of their once massive lead over the **PIRATES**** and barely won the division. Riven by dissension, torn apart by racial animosity, the fatally wounded team crawled into the playoffs, where they were promptly annihilated by the Redlegs, three games to none. Nineteen sixty-four was not avenged; the echoes of the Whiz Kids were not stirred; Dick Allen did not put the team on his back and carry it to victory; the storybook ending did not materialize. In the game I attended with my wife and friends, the Phillies carried a 2-0 lead into the sixth and were then dispatched 6-2. Dick Allen never played another game for the Phillies.

The Pittsburgh **PIRATES was also the name of a National Hockey League team for five seasons in the 1920s.*

In a dark corner of my kitchen, right next to the radio, sits a hideous enamel turtle that has not budged from this position since October 1993. During that memorable year, or so I have come to believe, the turtle's uncanny telekinetic powers contributed in some way to the Philadelphia Phillies winning the National League pennant. Every night that season I would listen to the Phils' barely audible broadcast (I live in suburban New York, 125 miles from Philadelphia, so the signal was rather weak) and adjust the turtle's position according to the game situation. Much as I would like to credit Lenny Dykstra's adroit stick work, Curt Schilling's incendiary fastball and John Kruk's infectious bonhomie for the team's unexpected success that fall, I am now convinced that without the intercession of the enchanted turtle, the Phils would have gotten creamed by the Atlanta Braves.

Though my reptilian talisman was oddly impotent in the face of Toronto's big bats in the ensuing World Series, I have never ceased to be grateful for the yeoman service it provided during the Phils' march through Georgia in the National League Championship Series that year. Moreover, I am firmly convinced that one day the turtle will reemerge from its paranormal slumber and bring the Philadelphia Eagles that long-awaited Super Bowl victory.

In the meantime, I have begun to see a therapist. It was a long overdue decision.

The direction our conversations took provided me with much food for thought. Inevitably, we returned to 1964, the *annus horribilis*. In every other city in the United States, young people first experienced the devastating trauma of JFK's death on November 22, 1963, but then, just when they thought they would never get over it, the Beatles came out of nowhere and literally saved the world. But for Philadelphia fans, the brief emotional uplift provided by the Fab Four quickly gave way to the catastrophe of late September.

At the time of the collapse, I was attending the Maryknoll Junior Seminary in Clarks Summit, Pennsylvania, a nondescript hamlet roughly ten miles outside Scranton, a dying coal town. I was thirteen years old, I had been in the seminary roughly three weeks, and I already knew that I did not want to be a priest. And I certainly didn't want to be a missionary. The first night, after our parents had abandoned us to the clerics' tender mercies, one of the priests showed some of us a wound he had suffered in a Japanese prisoner-of-war camp during World War II. A second discoursed in grisly detail about the sort of treatment we could expect should we fall into the hands of the dreaded Mau Maus, the merciless Red Chinese, the fiendish Soviets. I was thirteen; I had only entered the seminary because of pressure from my father and even greater pressure from Maryknoll recruiters who'd started "scouting" me at age eight after I foolishly set up a mock "altar" in my bedroom; and I had already decided that I did not want to have my fingernails torn out, my ears cut off, or my sautéed liver fed to passing curs just to impress some omnipotent deity whose existence I now questioned. Viewed from the benefit of hindsight, the Maryknolls were a poor choice on my part; I should have sent my application to the Little Sisters of the Poor.

Meanwhile, the Phillies were blowing the pennant.

I do not know if defeat strengthens your character, but I know that it sharpens your memory. Yankee and **LAKER*** fans regularly misremember dates, eras, championships, putting DiMaggio on teams with Maris, putting Bob McAdoo on the 1987 championship team, but not the 1985 one. Less fortunate fans, those in Buffalo, Cleveland, Baltimore, Philadelphia, never forget anything. To this day, I can recall how the Phillies headed down the highway to hell during those last two weeks

*In March 1954 the **LAKERS** and the Hawks played a regulation, regular season NBA game using baskets that were 12 feet high rather than the usual 10 feet...the next night they played each other in a doubleheader.... In 1944 the Chicago White Sox played forty-three doubleheaders. Last year, they played one. True facts, believe them or not!

of September, the whole nightmare starting with a 1-0 loss in a game decided by a Chico Ruiz steal of home with Hall of Famer Frank Robinson at bat. Yes, *that* Chico Ruiz.

Retroactive memory aids were provided by my mother, who would dutifully cut out *Philadelphia Inquirer* accounts of each game and send them off to me, much the way Spaniards living in 1589 Great Tunbridge Wells used to send their relatives in Madrid six-month-old newspaper accounts of the Armada's latest misfortunes. *Thanks, Esteban; we heard.* The neatly clipped articles would arrive two to three days later, by which point the Cardinals would have excised another two games from the Phillies' lead. Of course, I already knew the outcome of the games; I was the only seminarian from Philadelphia, and many of the other ninety-two students enjoyed waking me in the morning with detailed accounts of the Phils' latest tank job. The last clip Mom sent contained a heart-rending quote from backup catcher Gus Triandos, a scrub who had toiled in the wilderness for eleven years since being shipped out of town by the Yankees in the biggest trade in baseball history (seventeen players changed teams). "Some guys want to guzzle the champagne," he told the reporter, "I just wanted a sip."

Me too. What I remember most clearly about that watershed month is that it was my first exposure to the concept of *schadenfreude*. None of the other ninety-two seminarians had any direct stake in the pennant race; none of them were from St. Louis, which eventually won the World Series, or from Cincinnati, which would have taken the flag had the Phils not beaten them the last two games of the season. Most of the students were from obscure burgs with names like Osprey's Redoubt, **WISCONSIN***, or Gideon's Agot, West Virginia, and thus had no stake in the outcome of the pennant race. But they enjoyed taunting me anyway. Those few weeks in the seminary opened

***Arnold Schwarzenegger graduated from the University of WISCONSIN in 1979.**

a rift between God and me that has never closed; while I am grateful to God for giving me my children, my career, and the ability to dance as if no one was watching, sing as if no one was listening, and eat as if no one was paying, I decided at the time that any deity that would let the Phils lose ten games in a row and then hire ninety-two mean-spirited young men to help spread His word was going to have to manage without me. I shuttered my religious career right then and there.

Dick Allen had retired in 1979, so you didn't feel in 1980 that the 1964 team was a completely different era. In 2008, it was a completely different thing. One of the things I loved about that season was that when I would go to Philadelphia, the kids didn't know anything about '64. It didn't matter to them that the Phillies had lost ten thousand games. The kids just knew the Phillies as this very, very, very good team that had a chance to win the World Series...and that's a great thing. It's a great thing when the team starts to get support from young people who are not burdened with all that stuff from the past.

When men are asked to identify the happiest moment in their lives, they always cite their children's birth. But they only say this for the same reason that they pretend to like Joni Mitchell records or Chocolat, because they know it is what women expect to hear. The truth is, the happiest moment in a man's life always involves sports. Yes, I was overjoyed when my daughter was born. But it wasn't like when the Phils beat the **ROYALS*** in 1980. Of course I was beside myself with joy when my son took his first breath in 1986. But do you seriously think that compares with the Sixers sweeping the Lakers in 1983? Saying that the happiest moment in your life was when your kids were born is a knee-jerk, intellectually dishonest reaction to a loaded question. It is the sort of thing people pick up from

---

*In the 1979 baseball draft, the Kansas City **ROYALS** selected Dan Marino in the fourth round and John Elway in the eighteenth round. That same year the Royals hired Rush Limbaugh for their group sales department. Limbaugh left in 1984 for a radio opportunity in California.

watching Billy Crystal movies. The one thing I have garnered from my experiences as a film critic is: You can never learn anything useful from looking at Billy Crystal movies. If you don't believe me, take a gander at My Giant or Forget Paris. Remember Paris. Forget Billy Crystal.

When I worked at *Forbes* magazine some years back, I became friends with a colleague from Chicago named Stuart Flack. Stuart and I would spend days upon days trying to decide whether we loved the Cubs and the Phillies more than we hated the Mets. It was a riveting subject, fraught with Talmudic innuendo. In reviewing the Mets situation, we found it hard to decide what we hated most. We hated their uniforms, we hated their **STADIUM***, we hated their fans, and we even hated Mr. Met, the bobble-headed, maddeningly inoffensive mascot whom we dreamed of luring to his death, ideally in a gangland-style slaying that would point fingers away from us.

In the end what we hated most about the Mets was what everybody else in America hated about the Mets their cultivation of an aura best described as *preemptive hubris*, whereby a team starts strutting around like champions before they have actually won anything. (For further reading, consult the entries under "Ewing, Patrick," "Oakley, Charles," "Mason, Anthony," and "Starks, John" in *The Penguin Book of Choking*.) Say what you will about the arrogant Cowboys, the cocky Yankees, the haughty Celtics, or the imperial Canadiens, these teams had earned the right to swagger by actually winning championships. By comparison, the Mets of the late 1990s were just another dynasty that never happened.

Nineteen sixty-three was the year the Phillies traded the popular Don Demeter for the aging Jim Bunning, who the next

*During a 1979 Patriots game against the New York Jets at Shea **STADIUM**, a remote control model airplane crashed into the stands at halftime, hit a Patriots fan, and killed him.

year would lead the Phillies to within an eyelash of the World Series. Until **JOHN F. KENNEDY*** died in November, 1963 was the happiest year in my life because the Phillies, picked to finish last, unexpectedly finished fourth. The year a team performs well completely out of the blue is always the most enjoyable time for the fan; it is the next season, when the expectations are high, that the nail biting, novenas and heavy drinking start. When teams are on their way up, you can blithely write off their failures as the mistakes of youth. When teams are picked to compete for the title, their failures assume biblical proportions.

At a very early juncture, it became apparent that my father was not going to make a very good role model for me, the budding fan. So I found others. At age nine I went to work for a former U. S. Marine drill instructor and Iwo Jima veteran who ran a bargain-basement, tumble-down clothing store in the starkly proletarian community of East Falls. Len Mohr was the most generous and most interesting man I have ever met. His father was the oldest living fireman in Philadelphia, a retired tiller-man. Though a high school dropout, Len lived in a beautiful house in Bala Cynwyd, a twee suburb on the Main Line. There he would walk his Airedale every night, to this day my symbol of financial success. He had a picket fence, a pool table in the basement, a classy station wagon.

On the side, Len dabbled in the stock market, gobbling up high-flying but ultimately doomed "Nifty Fifty" stocks like National Video Corporation and Ling Electronics. He talked about the stock market all the time, insisting that you couldn't participate in the American dream without participating in the stock market, a view I share. He also was one of the original partners in Cloverlay, a group of well-heeled local business-men that backed Joe Frazier on his way to the heavyweight

***JFK**'s brother, Teddy, once played in the Notre Dame spring football game even though he never attended Notre Dame.

championship of the world. And he refereed amateur fights at a North Philly gym called the Blood Pit.

As if all this was not enough, he also owned three parking lots right down the street from Connie Mack Stadium. On hot summer days when there wasn't much business at the clothing store, he would close up shop early and head over to North Philadelphia, where I would shoo cars onto the lot. Back in those days, there usually weren't many customers. Connie Mack Stadium was in the middle of the North Philadelphia ghetto, and the second year I worked for him the Phillies lost twenty-three straight games, a major-league record that will almost certainly never be broken. Round about the third inning we would wander up to the stadium to watch the rest of the game. It wasn't pretty.

A famous man once said that youth is wasted on the young. No longer young, I now understand that sentiment. When I was a little kid, I thought everyone owned three parking lots right down the street from Connie Mack Stadium. I thought everyone knew Joe Frazier. Because I was young and the world was new, I did not profit from my good fortune as much as I could have. I never attended any of his fights because by the time I was fourteen Muhammad Ali was the idol of every young American and Joe Frazier was the enemy, the white man's champion, the guy your dad rooted for. Thus, even though I worked for a man who had helped a slaughterhouse alumnus from South Carolina rise to the heavyweight championship of the world, I secretly rooted for Muhammad Ali.

My nonchalance about my good fortune did not stop with Smokin' Joe. Even though I got to meet all sorts of baseball players when they parked their cars for free on our lot, I didn't think all that much of that either. The Phillies were horrible, and baseball was not that big a deal back then. It was part of the fabric of life, sure, but in the same way that drinking milk or taking the trackless trolley was. I'd met Joe Frazier and parked cars at Connie Mack Stadium, and one of my classmates at

Cardinal Dougherty High School was the Phillies' visiting team batboy. But it was no big deal. Not to me. Not back then. Back in those days, all I wanted to do was to get out of the housing project and become a famous writer and make a lot of money. Joe Frazier and the Phillies weren't going to help me do that.

My father didn't like Len. He didn't care for the gung-ho Marine Corps attitude. He insisted that the store was a "front," that the reason Len spent so much time on the phone was because he was a bookie. To me, that only made him seem even more exotic. But in truth what I liked most about Len was his passion. He never forgave **JACK NICKLAUS*** for blotting out Arnold Palmer's fleetingly radiant sun, and there were several members of the Phillies squad whom he despised with a venom that surpassed all human understanding. Len hated flashes-in-the-pan like **BO BELINSKY***, the sleek Angels lefty who pitched a no-hitter in his rookie year, dated Mamie Van Doren, and then, once it was apparent that he was a bum, was banished from glamorous Los Angeles to glamorless North Philadelphia. Len had no time for kooks (Bob Uecker), has-beens (Wes Covington), misfits (Dick Stuart), head cases (Dick Allen) or showoffs (Tony Gonzalez, Willie Montanez). But his greatest ire was reserved for guys who couldn't hit. And there was no one, anywhere, ever, who hit worse than Phils' shortstop Bobby Wine.

From 1960 until 1968, or so Len believed, Bobby Wine was always the man at the plate with the bases loaded, two down in the ninth, and the Phillies trailing by a run. A superb fielder with a cannon arm, Wine was one of the worst hitters of that or

*Only three people have ever appeared on Scotland's five-pound note: Queen Elizabeth II, the Queen Mum, and **JACK NICKLAUS.**

*The late **BO BELINSKY** married 1965 *Playboy* Playmate of the Year, Jo Collins, in 1968. They were married for five years...Jimmy Connors married the 1977 Playmate of the Year, Patti McGuire, in 1978.

any other era. He played twelve years and batted .215 with 30 HRs and 268 RBIs. His best year was with the Montreal Expos, when he hit a poky .232 but drove in fifty-one runs. Len hated him. Hated him.

Frequently, he would tell a story illustrating the depths of his animosity. When baseball players turned up, we never charged them to park. One day, he recalled a man with an instantly recognizable crew-cut pulled into the lot, parked and started to walk up the street toward the stadium.

"Hey, buddy, that'll be a buck and a half,"

The man turned around.

"I'm Bobby Wine."

Len didn't miss a beat.

"Hey, buddy, that'll be a buck and a half."

I, too, hate Bobby Wine. I hated his horrible stance. I hated his haircut. I hated his eternal linkage with the 1964 team that pulled the biggest choke job in the history of American sports. Everything I loved about baseball I learned from Len, and everything I hated I learned from him too. Boy, did we hate Bobby Wine.

> So I got an autograph signed by a dud pitcher… His name was Dallas Green.

Ah, but baseball is a game of redemption. When I was a little boy, I once stood outside the locker room at Connie Mack Stadium and tried to get Robin Roberts' autograph. Roberts was not available. Neither were any of the other stars. So I got an autograph signed by a dud pitcher who won only three games that year and won only twenty games in his entire career. He was a loser. He was a bum. Twenty years later, he would lead the Phillies to their one and only championship. His name was Dallas Green.

God knows where the autograph is now.

The summer of 1987, I was given four tickets to see the Astros and Mets play a doubleheader at Shea. The teams had battled each other tooth and nail the previous season in one of the greatest series in the history of the game, but this season was different. The Mets, the defending National League champs, weren't going anywhere fast, and the Astros weren't going anywhere faster. The seats were directly behind home plate, allowing me to chat with the guy who operates the JUGS Gun. One of my guests was a friend from England, who didn't know anything about the sport. I spent much of the first game regaling him with stories about the good old days at Connie Mack Stadium. I tossed in the Bobby Wine story for good effect. The punch line got a nice laugh.

In the second inning of the second game, I looked across the railing separating me from the next box and saw a middle-aged man with an instantly recognizable crew cut. It was Bobby Wine. We got talking. He said he was now a scout for the Atlanta Braves and was here on business. I asked him why he had never been given a shot at the Phillies managing position after spending so many years in the organization. He was philosophical about it; he wrote it off to politics. The Phillies, predictably, had treated one of their own shabbily. It was widely know that when Dallas Green led the Phillies to the championship in 1980, Bobby Wine was a sort of surrogate manager, an *eminence grise*. He was also adjutant to Paul Owens when the Phillies won the pennant in 1983. He had started his major league career as a shortstop who simply could not hit, and had ended it by helping the Phils win two pennants in the space of four years.

I asked him for his autograph. He signed the back of a business card. I sure hope he wasn't sitting there when I told that story about Len Mohr and the parking lot.

I have a few autographs in my office collection. **<u>RED AUERBACH</u>***. Bobby Hull. Billie Jean King. Bobby Nystrom. Jim Palmer. Once, after I rescued Julius Erving from a bunch of gawking rubes ("So, Irving, how tall are you?") at a March of Dimes event in Manhattan, he signed a copy of the *New York Daily News* ("Doc Gets His Ring" was the headline) and handed me a Cabbage Patch Kid Doll for my daughter. But of all the autographs I have collected, the one I value the most is Bobby Wine's. Wine's injury-plagued career illustrates what is best about sports, that there is always tomorrow, that hope springs eternal, that if a determined man can't get in through the door, he'll come in through the window. You just have to keep that window open for about twenty years or so.

*<u>**RED AUERBACH**</u> was Bowie Kuhn's high school basketball coach.

TO BE CONTINUED!

We hope you have enjoyed *For Phillies Fans Only*. Due to space and time considerations over a dozen people with wonderful stories did not make the book. However, you can look for their stories in the author's forthcoming books: *For Penn State Fans Only* and *For Eagles Fans Only*. Next year we'll be putting together *For Phillies Fans Only, Volume 2*. You can be included in any of these books if you have an interesting story involving Penn State, the Eagles, or the Phillies. Email it to printedpage@cox.net (please put PENN STATE FANS, EAGLES FANS, PHILLIES FANS in the subject line and be sure to include a phone number where you can be reached), or call the author directly at (602) 738-5889.

*The Penn State and Eagles books are almost completed, so call **NOW** if you have an interesting story.

OTHER BOOKS BY RICH WOLFE

Remembering Harry Kalas
Da Coach (Mike Ditka)
I Remember Harry Caray
There's No Expiration Date on Dreams (Tom Brady)
He Graduated Life with Honors and No Regrets (Pat Tillman)
Take This Job and Love It (Jon Gruden)
Been There, Shoulda Done That (John Daly)
Oh, What a Knight (Bob Knight)
And the Last Shall Be First (Kurt Warner)
Remembering Jack Buck
Sports Fans Who Made Headlines
Fandemonium
Remembering Dale Earnhardt
I Saw It On the Radio (Vin Scully)
Tim Russert, We Heartily Knew Ye
The Real McCoy (Al McCoy, Phoenix Suns announcer)

For Yankee Fans Only
For Cubs Fans Only
For Red Sox Fans Only
For Cardinals Fans Only
For Packers Fans Only
For Hawkeye Fans Only
For Browns Fans Only
For Mets Fans Only
For Notre Dame Fans Only—
   The New Saturday Bible
For Bronco Fans Only
For Nebraska Fans Only

For Buckeye Fans Only
For Georgia Bulldog Fans Only
For South Carolina Fans Only
For Clemson Fans Only
For Cubs Fans Only—Volume II
For Oklahoma Fans Only
For Yankee Fans Only—Volume II
For Mizzou Fans Only
For Kansas City Chiefs Fans Only
For K-State Fans Only
For KU Fans Only (Kansas)

All books are the same size, format and price.
Questions? Contact the author directly at 602-738-5889.